VOICE-OVER TRANSLATION

D1784442

Eliana Franco, Anna Matamala & Pilar Orero

VOICE-OVER TRANSLATION

An Overview

PETER LANG

Bern · Berlin · Bruxelles · Frankfurt am Main · New York · Oxford · Wien

Bibliographic information published by Die Deutsche Nationalbibliothek
Die Deutsche Nationalbibliothek lists this publication in the Deutsche Nationalbibliografie;
detailed bibliographic data is available on the Internet at ‹http://dnb.d-nb.de›.

British Library Cataloguing-in-Publication Data: A catalogue record for this book is available
from *The British Library,* Great Britain

Library of Congress Cataloging-in-Publication Data

Franco, Eliana.
Voice-over translation : an overview / Eliana Franco, Anna Matamala & Pilar Orero.
p. cm.
Includes bibliographical references.
ISBN 978-3-0343-0393-4
1. Voice in motion pictures. 2. Voice overs. 3. Dubbing of motion pictures. 4. Motion pictures–
Translating and interpreting. I. Matamala, Anna, 1973- II. Orero, Pilar.
PN1995.9.V63F73 2010
791.4302'908–dc22

                                        2010032091

Cover design: Thomas Jaberg, Peter Lang AG

ISBN 978-3-0343-0393-4

© Peter Lang AG, International Academic Publishers, Bern 2010
Hochfeldstrasse 32, CH-3012 Bern, Switzerland
info@peterlang.com, www.peterlang.com, www.peterlang.net

Printed in Germany

To José, Xavi and Marcel

Acknowledgements

This book has been written in and across two different countries. These countries (Brazil and Catalonia) are different in both size and location. However, there is a link between such different realities which can best be described as an entrepreneurial dynamism in the quest for quality in research, teaching and collaboration. The book originates from an old friendship which came into existence through collaboration and from the experience of study, research, travelling, teaching and many years of work translating.

We would like to acknowledge all the 43 people who took the time to reply to our questionnaire (three of them asked to remain anonymous): Rachele Antonini, Morena, Azbel Schmidt, Łukasz Bogucki, Chapman Chen, Delia Chiaro, Chrys Chrystello, Judith Cortés, Jorge Díaz Cintas, Elena Di Giovanni, Jan Emil Iveit, Robert Forloine, Jirina Hradecka, Marta Jorge, Leonardo Kadir Ayarig, Klaus Kaindl, Francine Kaufmann, Irena Kovačič, Daina Krasovska, Jan-Louis Kruger, Martin Landry, Fearchar I MacIllFhinnein, Hedda MacLeod, Mercè López Arnabat, Mario Paolinelli, Robert Paquin, Jan Pedersen, Emlyn Penny Jones, Myriam Peyre, Anetta Radolinska, Paula Alexandra Ramalho de Almeida, Vikki Rangi, Sébastien Reding, Margit Sander, Monica Scheer, Ilias Sifakis, Stravoula Sokoli, Cristina Varga, Pierre Verge, Martin Watier.

We would also like to thank those who made it possible for us to use authentic materials (e.g., scripts, transcripts, translations). A heartfelt thankyou to Vicky Mitchell from the BBC and to the documentary producers Joaquim Pinto and Nuno Leonel, for giving us the permission to reproduce the voice-over script and the original transcript. Thank you also to Alex Holt and Mike Kenna, from Softel, for allowing us to use the picture of the screen on page 103.

We are also very grateful to our friends and colleagues, who sent us their advice, comments and materials: Ricard Sierra, Xènia Martínez, Judith Cortés, Ignasi Olivé, Francine Kaufmann and Jean-Pierre Mailhac.

Thanks are also due to John Milton for his availability, to Jimmy Ureel for his proofreading skills, to Martina Fierz for her enthusiastic reception.

We are also extremely grateful to the Master in Audiovisual Translation at the *Universitat Autònoma de Barcelona* (www.fti.uab.es/audiovisual), offered by the *Departament de Traducció i d'Interpretació* (Department of Translation and Interpreting), for its financial help with the publication of this book. Needless to say, any errors and misinterpretations remain our sole responsibility.

Finally, we would like to thank the many colleagues, friends and family, especially José, Xavi and Marcel, who have supported us while we were preparing this book.

This book is part of the Catalan Government Consolidated Research Group scheme with the reference 2009SGR700.

Contents

Introduction

This book is aimed at providing comprehensive theoretical and practical information about an audiovisual translation mode which has not attracted the attention of many studies up to now: voice-over, or the translation voice that we hear on top of the translated voice. In our fast-moving technological society, multimedia formats have become extremely important and are being used more than paper formats. The three most important features of multimedia in general (and of multimedia formats in particular) are their communication format, which is usually digital, their channels, which are audio and visual, and the simultaneity of presentation, which goes beyond the actual realm of multimedia, since we now have multiscreen and interactive products. The plethora of possibilities offered today by digital audiovisual communication makes writing comprehensively on one of the audiovisual translation modalities a risky exercise, since focus may be lost. Hence, special care has been taken and attention has been paid while preparing this book in an attempt to strike a balance between theory and practice. The book has been drafted from our experience in this field as practitioners, as trainers and as researchers. We have taken into consideration the process of translating for voice-over and its reception, the teaching of voice-over and potential topics for investigation. The book has been drafted to serve as a useful manual to students, but also as a point of departure for further research. While writing the book we never lost sight of the need for a comprehensive study of the modality, although we were aware of the difficulty of describing, studying, analysing and reflecting on something as multifaceted as voice-over. Our aim was to write, in as direct a way as possible, about the complex audiovisual translation modality of voice-over, while at the same time being extremely explicit with examples and exercises related to both practice and analysis, which is the basis of an academic manual. We truly hope that our efforts prove to be worthwhile for students, trainers and those who would like to conduct further research into any aspect of revoicing in audiovisual translation.

Chapter 1, *Voice-over from Film Studies to Translation Studies*, focuses on terminological issues and explains the confusion that has often surrounded a term borrowed from the well-established field of Film Studies and introduced into the more recent field of Translation Studies. After explaining the origins of the term *voice-over*, the chapter clarifies the relationship between voice-over and other audiovisual transfer modes and finally proposes a clear-cut definition.

Chapters 2 and 3, *Voice-over for postproduction (I): Typology and working conditions* and *Voice-over for postproduction (II): The translation process* respectively, deal with voice-over for postproduction, that is, the revoicing of an audiovisual product that has already been edited. After establishing a differentiation between fiction and non-fiction, professional aspects are explained and the characteristics of the source text in terms of speakers and script structure are elucidated. Subsequently, the specific features of the translation process are investigated pointing to the tight relationship between voice-over and the off-screen dubbing of commentaries.

Chapter 4, *Voice-over for production*, explains a completely different approach to voice-over, that is, the revoicing of an audiovisual product that has not yet been finished or completed. In this case, translators generally work without a script and sometimes they even act as journalists, creating totally adapted voice-overs or commentaries.

Chapter 5, *Training in voice-over*, describes two successful courses on voice-over at the MA in Audiovisual Translation at the *Universitat Autònoma de Barcelona*: one course is taught in a Barcelona-based programme (www.fti.uab.es/audiovisual) whilst the other course is taught online (www.fti.uab.es/onptav). The course structures as well as the exercises proposed can be used by trainers to devise courses dealing with this neglected, yet innovative, transfer mode.

Chapter 6, *Giving voice to practitioners and academics: a global survey on voice-over*, presents the results of a global survey on voice-over, in which actual practitioners express their opinions on different issues related to voice-over: this survey highlights the various practices and terminology used worldwide and also the need to systematize terms and concepts.

Finally, the book offers a commented bibliography on voice-over, which includes the most relevant academic contributions to this transfer mode.

The aim of this book is not only to offer an overview of the fascinating transfer mode of voice-over but also to provide some ideas for students and trainers. In some cases, it is important to have first-hand experience in order to understand fully the process of translation and the many issues related to this work practice. Voice-over translation offers wide and enriching opportunities to practise many issues related to other audiovisual translation modalities since it shares features with dubbing, subtitling, audio description, audio subtitling, etc. Since translation exercises are bound to language pairs, we have devised exercises taking some generic documentation as our point of departure. This documentation can then be adapted to any language combination. The book is highly practical and we hope to transmit the enthusiasm that we have for the subject matter to those who have not been captured by it yet.

Barcelona, 4 May 2009

1. Voice-Over from Film Studies to Translation Studies

1.1 The origins of the term *voice-over*

Voice-over is a term which originated in the area of Film Studies and is still used by filmmakers. From the very beginning of cinema in the late 1890s, silent movies relied on 'lecturers' hired by exhibitors to provide running commentaries for the audience of unbroken takes (films) or a string of several films (programmes). The main function of lecturers in fiction films was to fill the gap between "the viewers' inexperience at 'reading' narrative images" and "the filmmakers' lack of skill in conveying temporal, spatial, and narrative relationships" (Kozloff 1988: 23–24). In Japan, for example, the popularity of lecturers (or *benshi*) became enormous to the point of delaying the introduction of sound to cinema.[1] People would go to cinemas mostly to see their favourite *benshis* perform rather than to see the film stars. By 1912, lecturers had lost ground to intertitles and the motives were twofold. Firstly, films had moved from small halls to purpose-built cinemas, which increased the difficulties of voice projection. Secondly, film techniques were developing fast, mainly as a result of the development of editing and new narrative strategies. Despite having lived through an era of glory, intertitles became obtrusive in film and, consequently, efforts were made to avoid them as much as possible. But apart from criticism, the importance of intertitling and lecturing is evidenced in the fact that they have continued to survive in the sound era.

The advent of sound in 1927 represented a sudden leap in the film's narrative pace, which did not exist with intertitles.[2] On the other hand, it also represented a limitation to filmmakers, whose new cameras with sound

---

1   For more on the topic see also Dym 2003, Pujol & Orero 2007 and Standish 2005.
2   However, it is true that films gained visual and aural depth, but these aspects also brought with them additional costs with dialogue specialists and sound engineers (Hayward 1996).

recording systems weighed too much to be carried around, and single
microphones prevented actors to move freely. For these reasons, post-shoot-
ing voice-over narration became one of the most useful devices implemented to deal with the deficiencies of the early sound era. And thus, it
replaced the lecturing of the silent era.

In his glossary of film terms Harrington defines voice-over as "any
spoken language not seeming to come from images on the screen" (1973:
165). In other words, voice-over is defined as a narrative technique in
which the voice of a faceless narrator is heard over different images and
this for different purposes. Compare, for example, the expository voice in
a documentary about the life of animals and the accusing voice of the
narrator towards one of the murder suspects in a thriller film. That is why
it is common in film terminology to talk about *the voice-overs* of a documentary meaning, for example, all the speech sequences whose speakers
cannot be seen. This concept is the one which is also reflected in three of
the most popular reference works. *The Shorter Oxford English Dictionary*
defines voice-over as "narration spoken by an unseen narrator in a film or
a television programme; the unseen person providing the voice" (Brown
1993: 3596), whereas the Merriam Webster's online dictionary provides
the following definition: "1a: the voice of an unseen narrator speaking (as
in a motion picture or television commercial), 1b: the voice of a visible
character (as in a motion picture) expressing unspoken thoughts".[3] The
online encyclopedia Wikipedia defines *voice-over* as follows:

> The term voice-over refers to a production technique where a disembodied voice is
> broadcast live or pre-recorded in radio, television, film, theatre and/or presentation.
> The voice-over may be spoken by someone who also appears on-screen in other seg-
> ments or it may be performed by a specialist voice actor. Voice-over is also commonly
> referred to as 'off camera' commentary.[4]

These definitions of the term voice-over, which originated in the field of
Film Studies, have contributed to the various meanings of voice-over
acquired within the field of Translation Studies. This chapter will attempt
to shed light on the nature of voice-over by discussing both the move
of voice-over from the field of Film Studies to the field of Translation
Studies and the status of voice-over within Audiovisual Translation (AVT)

---

3   <http://www.m-w.com/dictionary/voice-over> [Retrieved on 30 May 2007].
4   <http://en.wikipedia.org/wiki/Voice-over> [Retrieved on 30 May 2007].

Studies in order to come to a definition which is believed to express the characteristics of voice-over as an audiovisual translation mode better and which will be adopted throughout the present book.

1.2 Voice-Over in Audiovisual Translation Studies

Within the field of Translation Studies, the boom of audiovisual translation came about in the 1980s. The term voice-over was then borrowed from Film Studies to become a mode of transfer in the new field, one in which the translating voice is heard on top of the translated voice. The coexistence of the same denomination for two different concepts in two different, yet still related, fields has caused some terminological confusion among audiovisual translation scholars, who have often shown a certain degree of difficulty when attempting to define the new mode and its features (Franco 2000b, 2001b, Orero forthcoming). Maybe because of the lack of understanding about this mode, lack of research interest has also prevailed.

The first article that explicitly mentions voice-over as a mode of transfer and as a form of dubbing, was written by Fawcett and dates from 1983. The second work that refers to voice-over in the translation sense was Daly's article (1985) on simultaneous interpreting. In other words, voice-over is initially found in Translation Studies within the supposedly broader fields of dubbing and interpreting.

Even though the book edited by Luyken *et al.* (1991) is usually quoted in Translation Studies as the seminal work for audiovisual translation, its perspective relies mainly on Media Studies. In fact, it is only recently that voice-over has gained its own status in Translation Studies, but as Gambier and Suomela-Salmi (1994: 243) suggest, this is not a particular case for voice-over since

> Up till now, research has mainly been concerned with the subtitling and dubbing of fictive stories / fiction films. In the light of the huge variety of audio-visual communication, this may seem somewhat surprising; in fact, however, it reflects the prevailing orientation in translation theory, which is still highly dominated by literary translation.

Translation Studies is a new academic discipline and Translation Studies faculties date from the second part of the twentieth century. The discipline of Audiovisual Translation was created at a later stage and initially focused on the main translation transfer modes of dubbing and subtitling. It is only now, as AVT has become firmly established, that other translation transfer modes (other than dubbing and subtitling) that have received little or no attention by scholars so far can be studied in greater detail.

1.2.1 Research on Voice-Over

In the first systematic study of voice-over as a translation mode and of its frequent use in TV documentaries (Franco 2000b) figures were presented to illustrate the little amount of documented research devoted to the factual genre and to the voice-over mode, as opposed to other genres and modes of audiovisual transfer. The data were based on the second edition of the *Language Transfer and Audiovisual Communication Bibliography* gathered by Gambier (1997). By way of summary, the 1,241 entries revealed only 21 entries devoted to programmes regarded as belonging to the non-fictional genre, such as the documentary film (six entries), current affairs (only one entry), news (nine entries), panel discussions and/or political debates (four entries) and commercials (only one entry). Taking into account entries which explicitly mention discourse types and/or other audiovisual modes believed to be related to the factual genre, nine entries could be added to the list (seven entries under the subcategory *commentary* and two entries under the subcategory *narration*). Finally, concerning the voice-over translation mode, explicit reference was made in only eleven entries. Thus, the revised bibliography accounts for a total sum of 41 entries which refer explicitly to non-fiction, including multiple entries of two studies, which dealt with more than one topic.[5]

Six years later, at the MuTra Conference in Copenhagen, Orero (2006b) provided an updated on the amount of research performed on voice-over translation as compared to the publications on subtitling and dubbing. The data come from three different online bibliographies, all of them estab-

---

5   This was the case with Pönniö's *Voice over, narration et commentaire* (1995) and with Luyken's *Overcoming Language Barriers in Television: Dubbing and Subtitling for the European Audience* (1991), which were counted three times each.

General question_ To what extent the extensive work on v-o by filmstudies scholars has been taken into account in this book?

Voice-Over from Film Studies to Translation Studies   21

lished sources of information for audiovisual scholars: the John Benjamins *Translation Studies Bibliography* <http://www.benjamins.com/online/tsb>, the St. Jerome *Translation Studies Abstracts* and *Bibliography of Translation Studies* <http://www.stjerome.co.uk/tsaonline/index.php> and Javier Aixelà's *Bibliografia de Traducció i d'Interpretació* (BITRA), from the University of Alicante <http://cv1.cpd.ua.es/tra_int/usu/buscar.asp?idioma=va>.[6] The survey carried out in February 2006 yielded the following results:

Table 1. Quantitative research data on audiovisual translation modes (February 2006)

translation mode	AVT	Subtitling	Dubbing	Voice-over
John Benjamins	84	206	132	24
St. Jerome	109	175	124	12
BITRA	953	277	239	12

Needless to say, the differences between the numbers of publications on voice-over and on dubbing and subtitling are striking. However, the data provided by the commented bibliography on voice-over in Chapter 7 of this book present a more optimistic landscape, starting already with the number of entries collected (72 in total).[7]

As for the qualitative aspect of the data presented in the bibliography, Table 2 below shows, on the one hand, works published before/until February 2000, in other words before Franco's thesis, and works published after February 2000, in other words in the twenty-first century and, on the other hand, publications that discuss a general audiovisual topic and/ or an audiovisual translation mode other than voice-over but that do make a passing reference or several passing references to voice-over, as opposed to works that focus specifically on voice-over translation.

6   All URLs with no date of retrieval were last retrieved in February 2010.
7   This number excludes publications by scholars of Film Studies which deal with voice-over as a narrative technique and, consequently, do not belong to the literature of audiovisual translation, such as Kozloff (1988). Such publications are found as bibliographical references of this book. On the other hand, the commented bibliography in Chapter 7 includes studies in print as well as in digital form. As far as topics are concerned, the bibliography includes both publications about other transfer modes that make reference to voice over and publications that focus on voice-over as a transfer mode.

Table 2. Qualitative data on voice-over translation works before and after 2000

	Published before/until February 2000	Published after February 2000
Total amount	32	40
Passing reference to voice-over	22	17
Focus on the voice-over mode	10	23

As far as post-thesis works are concerned, the data in Table 2 reveal a decrease in the number of works that refer to voice-over in passing and a significant increase in the number of works that focus specifically on voice-over translation. This means that, whereas before February 2000 works that contained passing references to voice-over ranked first with 22 such works as opposed to 10 works that focused specifically on voice-over translation, from the year 2000 onwards works that refer in passing to voice-over counted 17 item, which indicates a decrease of five works, and works dealing specifically with the voice-over mode reached more than double the amount of works produced before the 2000 (23 items, which is an increase of 13 works).[8]

In terms of the amounts of research developed annually within the 72 items of the bibliography, Table 3 below shows that, on a scale from one to ten, the years 1995, 1996, 1998, 2000 and 2004 were the most prolific. Regarding research done specifically about the voice-over mode, the year 2004 presents the highest number of works (i.e. five, or 50% of specific works during the year) whereas 2006 and 2007 present eight works altogether specifically on voice-over. May of 2008, when the bibliography was last updated, looks promising with one work already published and two forthcoming publications focusing on voice-over and another forthcoming contribution on a more general audiovisual topic.

8   These figures represent items collected until the beginning of June 2007 and updated in May 2008.

Table 3. Volume and focus of AVT research by year

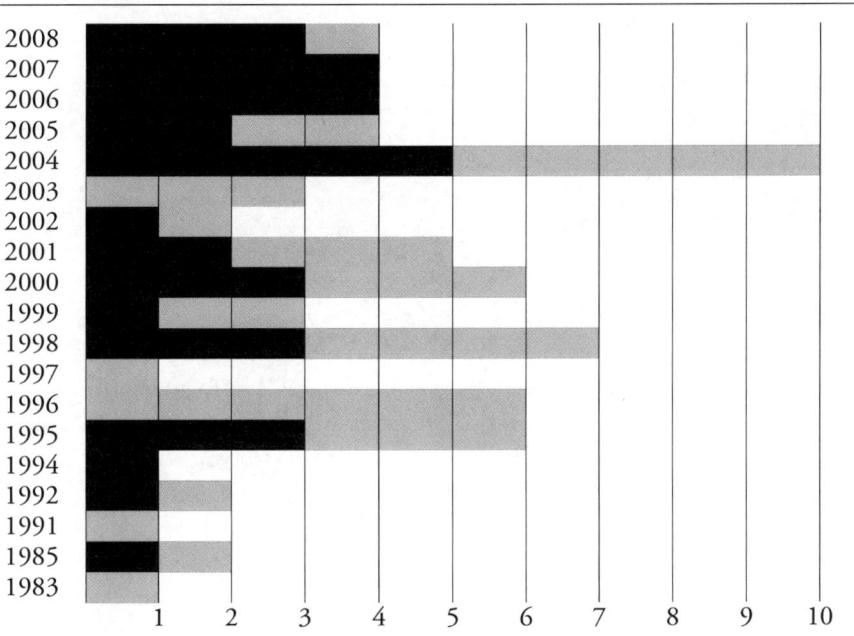

▸ ■ research on voice-over translation
▸ ▨ research on a different AVT mode
▸ 2008 indicates three works that are forthcoming and one work already made public

It may be concluded that the interest in voice-over translation has increased significantly and more rapidly from the year 2000 onwards. However, whether this interest reflects a better understanding, or even, a greater recognition of voice-over as an audiovisual mode of transfer remains to be seen. In the next section, specialized and non-specialized works from all areas of Film Studies, Media Studies and Translation Studies will be discussed focusing on the definitions and the characteristics of voice-over provided and discussed in these works. Contributions from the three fields are required to facilitate a better understanding of the present state of the art and to arrive at a more practical and less blurred definition of voice-over translation.

1.3 Voice-over: definitions and characteristics

> I am listening to the evening news on radio and the newsreader says something about a foreign statesman (say, Mr Yeltsin). The next thing I hear is a (hearably) male voice saying something in a foreign language for a few seconds. This then fades down and over it I hear a (hearably) male English voice speaking that it is not the voice of the newsreader ... Now all this makes perfect sense to me: I *assume* (though I am not told) that the foreign male voice I hear is that of Mr Yeltsin. And I *assume* (though I am not told) that the English voice over that foreign voice is giving me a literal translation of what that foreign voice is saying. (Scannell 1996: 17)

Within the field of Film Studies third-person voice-over was defined as a narrative technique opposed to the so-called 'character narrator', that is, a narrator who coincides with a character from the film who generally tells his story in the first person. Contrary to the character narrator, this third-person voice-over narrator, or commentator, often guides viewers' interpretations of an argument from a certain (authoritative) distance, and was for a long time the preferred narrative technique of films that imitated or claimed to portray reality. This was so because of the multiple responsible functions that the voice performed (the functions of linking scenes, introducing participants, explaining contexts, commenting on events, assessing people and situations) and the authoritarian tone that accompanied these functions, which was immediately acknowledged as expertise by the viewer and thus hardly questioned. The importation of the term voice-over by Audiovisual Translation Studies also resulted in the import of the associations just mentioned as well as the appeal to reality and truth, therefore its regular appearance as the translation mode of factual audiovisual output. As a translation mode, a voice no longer narrated over images, but translation over original speech.

So, apart from most East European countries, where voice-over translation is applied to all genres,[9] voice-over in West European, North and

---

9   It is assumed that the use of voice-over translation first happened in the former Soviet Union under the name of *Gavrilov* translation, which will be discussed later in the book. Russia was followed by Poland, where it still remains the main mode of audiovisual transfer, especially for television documentaries and foreign films (Bogucki 2004). According to recent statistics, voice-over continues to be at the top of the Polish audience's preference, which, together with the low cost it represents if compared to dubbing, may still point to a relatively long future in the country's audiovisual media (Majewski, in Garcarz 2006). Hendrykowski (in Garcarz 2006) even claims voice-over to be "the universal method" in Poland, due to the range of viewers it can reach, meaning the non-literate members of the audience.

Latin American countries has usually been applied to the translation of programmes that belong to the so-called factual genre – be it represented by the news, documentaries, talk shows, political debates, etc. – since its move to the field of Translation Studies. The common ground of all these programmes is that they generally rely, to a greater or lesser extent, on two types of evidence, which they use to support the argument as true or trustworthy. Firstly, they display visual evidence, the strongest argument of all, through images of events, people, documents, archival footage, anything that is able to convince the viewers' visually. Secondly, they display verbal evidence through interviews with generally two types of respondents, experts on the subject being focused on (the voices of expertise) and/or testimonies of the subject being focused on (the voices of experience), or the ordinary people who have been confronted with some kind of experience related to the subject matter.[10]

From a translation perspective, experts and testimonies' words are the material to be voiced-over. As pointed out repeatedly by most studies, voice-over is generally the preferred mode of transfer for the non-fiction genre, along with subtitles, because its defining features contribute to the appeals of reality, truth and authenticity that factual programmes count on in order to prove that their arguments are right or believable.

These features refer, on the one hand, to the contents of voice-over translation, and on the other hand, to the way in which voice-over translation is delivered, that is, the way in which it is realized and received as translation. There is little disagreement among scholars and professionals about these issues.

Let us have a look at some definitions of voice-over translation found in the audiovisual literature and let us try to make the connection between these and the factual genre.[11] Luyken *et al.* define voice-over as follows:

Voice-over is characterized by:
 – the faithful translation of original speech
 – approximately synchronous delivery

10 There is a plethora of Film / Media Studies scholars who discuss the rhetoric of factual programmes and their appeal to truth through visual and verbal evidence (e. g., Corner (1983), Collins (1986), Rosen (1993), Winston (1995), Fairclough (1995) and Scannell (1996)).

11 Most of these definitions have already been discussed in Franco (2001b).

Alternatively, if the translation is recorded as part of the original production, it may follow the original speech exactly. (1991: 80)

Voice-over is used where a sense of authentic presentation is to be combined with an almost full translation of the original text. (1991: 140)

This definition is corroborated by Gambier, who says:

– *le voice over* ou interprétation simultanée, caractérisée par une traduction assez "fidèle" de l'original et émise en quase synchronie. (1996: 8)

and supported by other authors of recent works on the subject, such as Carroll (2004), who emphasizes the fidelity of translation to the screen; and Garcarz (2006), who states that voice-over (or *wersja lektorska*, i. e. the reader's version) has a less arbitrary character than dubbing once it is not meant to naturalize or domesticate foreign items.[12]

In sum, voice-over translation has to be a faithful, literal, authentic and complete version of the original audio. Such definitions give voice-over the status of a trustful transfer mode, because after all, the definitions suggest that original speech will be rendered almost word by word. Not surprising then is Scannell's assumption reproduced in the introductory quote above, that voice-over translation means literal rendering. Interesting is the fact that such an assumption appears in a 1996 study of media intentionality, and that the author claims that the assumption is especially based on "trust of the institutions of broadcast news" (1996: 17). This immediately confirms the role of voice-over translations as authenticating the underlying appeal to truth of media factual output, and of the institutions that broadcast media factual output. It is not surprising then that voice-over is mostly applied, at least in the Western world, to non-fiction, along with subtitling. Conversely, modes that hide original speech, such as dubbing, tend to be applied to fiction.

In terms of voice-over delivery, let us look at some relevant comments:

The delivery of the voice-over translation cannot take account of the speaker's regional accent in his own language or any characteristic feature of his voice. The most that can be done is to try to provide a translator or reader of the same gender as the speaker. Fluffs, hesitations, grammatical errors made during the interview must be

12   The author, however, adds that because in Poland voice-over translations are applied to fiction, an average level of manipulation (e.g., the linking and restructuring of facts as well as the summary of the story) can also take place in these versions.

ignored; and the same applies probably to expletives and to idiosyncratic language or behaviour. (Luyken *et al.* 1991: 141)

La voix de l'original n'est préservée que dans les amorces de début et de fin. Le reste du temps, elle est maintenue en fond sonore, couverte par la voix d'un acteur qui lit la traduction de la réplique en respectant les intonations et les mimiques du personnage qu'il voit à l'écran. (Kaufmann 1995: 438)

[Translation from French]

L'important est ici d'obtenir un produit fini équilibré, fluide, cohérent et "confortable" à l'écoute. [...] L'interprète à l'antenne, doué d'empathie, cédera donc à un certain mimétisme [...] (Moreau 1998: 227–8)

In voice-over, the translator should basically look for text-image coordination, select the proper register (if voice-over is used in a documentary, the register need not be the same as in a book on the same topic) and pay attention to the time component (it should be possible to deliver the translation in the same time interval as the original or else the reader is forced into accelerated speech, difficult to follow; therefore there is no room for overtranslations or descriptive explications of e. g. culture-specific terms, unless at the expense of some other part of the text). (Kovačič 1998: 127–8)

Delivery is then characterized by the recording of the translating voice on top of the still audible original voice. Following her 1995 definition, Kaufmann adds in a later publication (2004) that the actor's voice super-imposed on the on-screen speaker's voice is mainly used in dialogue and monologue sequences. Important for authenticity is also the few seconds left at the beginning and at the end of the recording of the translation. This illusory device provides viewers with the impression that what is being told in the translation is what is being said in the original. That is why translation recording is usually delayed until the original speaker has uttered a few syllables.[13] With regard to synchrony, definitions point to the need of faithful or literal rendering being delivered in total synchronous recording with the original version, whose volume is kept low but still audible to the target viewer, who can sometimes spot inadequacies.[14]

13 It otherwise does not justify the fact that finishing recording a few seconds earlier than the end of original speech, as happens in some language versions, may actually destroy any claim to authenticity. *[inaccurate explanation]*

14 Contradicting Mayoral (2001), who says that the authenticity effect achieved through the co-presence of translation and original has no sense in Spain since viewers rarely understand the foreign original. The case is different in Brazil when it comes to English-spoken programmes. This is so because Brazilian viewers often enjoy comparing the original and the translation in voiced-over and subtitled audiovisual products, and they also tend to complain when they do not find some degree of literality in translated versions.

The authenticity effect has for too long been an issue for filmmakers. It is believed to result primarily from the synchrony between sound and image, which proves essential for the validation of the words spoken. In an article on the technology and aesthetics of film sound, Belton (1985) explains that, as opposed to the authenticity of the reproduction guaranteed by the photographic image, sound belongs to the invisible, non-concrete world that is recorded by the microphone and consequently

> Sound achieves authenticity only as a consequence of its submission to tests imposed upon it by other senses – primarily by sight. One of the conventions of sound editing confirms this. In order to assure an audience that the dialogue and/or sound effects are genuine, the editor must, as soon as possible in a scene, establish synchronization between sound and image, usually through lip-sync. Once that has been done, the editor is free to do almost anything with the picture and sound, confident that the audience now trust what they hear, since it corresponds to (or is not overtly violated by) what they see. (Belton, 1985: 64)

What the Film Studies scholar calls 'lip-sync synchronization' is in fact the mixing of film original soundtrack and images, or the actor's lip movements that are seen on screen with his own voice that is heard and that has been recorded in a separate track. So, it is not dubbing in a translation sense. Nevertheless, when the idea of authenticity is analysed from a translation perspective, dubbing as a transfer mode is commonly rejected by non-fiction film scholars, who believe that is causes the opposite effect to sound authenticity because of the clear disparity between the language heard and the lips that utter it, as Belton argues:

> By the same token, dubbing, and especially the dubbing of foreign films in which one language is seen spoken but another heard, is "read" by audiences as false. [...] The rather obvious intervention of technology involved with dubbing severely circumscribes our faith in both sound and image, provoking a crisis in their credibility. (Belton, 1985: 65)

In line with Belton, Jean-Marie Straub says in an interview about direct sound in films (in Weis & Belton, 1985: 150) that dubbing (as a translation mode) is an ideology and the dubbed film is the cinema of lies, for it gives no space to the viewer nor does it provide him/her with any relationship between what it is seen and what is heard. In this sense, translation modes that are not used to fake the image are preferred by film scholars and filmmakers to achieve a positive impact on the audience's trust. This impact is mostly achieved by the availability of original and translated sound in parallel, both at the viewers' disposal, and voice-over is one of the modes that make such simultaneous availability possible.

Therefore, it seems that the field of Translation Studies has imported not only the term voice-over from Film Studies, but also many associations made by scholars in that field, such as the importance of synchrony for the "making believe" effect in voice-over as well as the idea that this is a more suitable mode for audiovisual genres that are meant to portray reality, such as documentaries. So, corroborating with Film Studies scholars' distrust on dubbing as a potential mode to achieve authenticity is the observed practice of AVT in many Western countries to make use of the voice-over mode, alongside with subtitling, in the so-called factual output, with both original and translation being audible at the moment of delivery and reception.[15]

Although there is no lip synchronization, synchrony with image is rather important, and invariably achieved if the translation follows original speech length. Orero (2006a) calls our attention to kinetic synchrony, which requires body movements to match the visuals (for example, when speakers are pointing to an object or parts of it), and action synchrony, which imposes a certain order in speech, thus limiting syntactic inversions that might occur for the sake of target language fluency. In turn, markers typical of oral discourse are better eliminated for the sake of voice synchrony and content relevance. And this again has to do with the factual genre, where content has precedence over form so that information becomes the *skopos* and focus of voice-over translations, and objectivity, the aim of such translations.

Suggested earlier by Fawcett (1983, 1996), the rather new topic in the discussion about the orality of voice-over translation delivery concerns the mimetic reproduction of the original speaker's accent (Zinik 2006). Despite Luyken's *et al.* view on the impossibility or inadequacy of reproducing original accent in the target language, such reproduction has been practised in the UK. This somehow points to a change in viewers' habits

---

15   The issue of authenticity promoted in nonfiction by voice-over translations somehow
      proved true by the answers respondents gave to our questionnaire, which are reported
      in detail in Chapter 6. In short, according to the respondents, voice-over is used
      mostly in factual programmes such as documentaries, news reports, commercials,
      etc. for generally three main reasons: tradition, authenticity and as a money-saving
      measure. In addition, the great majority of respondents agreed that translators tend to
      be literal at the beginning of utterances, when the original is left audible for some
      seconds, which contributes to the credibility of the voice-over translation.

stated in the second part of a survey conducted by the BBC in 1985, in which viewers manifested a preference for standard British accent in spoken versions of documentaries. However, the reproduction of original accents in voice-over versions can be tricky because it may, on the one hand, be positively assessed as even more authentic and, on the other hand, be attacked as a form of caricature or a fake.

So far, the relationship between voice-over translation and audiovisual factual output – a relationship that is reflected in accounts by scholars and/or practitioners on how content is rendered and delivered – is hardly controversial but rather greatly influenced by accounts from Film Studies. Nevertheless, this does not imply that the supposed faithful, literal or full translation actually takes place in voice-over versions, as Franco (2000b), Krasovska (2004), Kaufmann (2004), and Darwish and Orero (forthcoming) demonstrate. Controversy really occurs when terminology used to describe and compare voice-over with other modes of audiovisual transfer is studied. This is also the case when the impact of borrowed terms from Film Studies is observed, as will be shown in the following section.

1.4 Terminological issues and the impact of Film Studies

Terminological issues related to voice-over translation have already been the topic of Franco's 2001b publication. Because so little investigation has taken place, some scholars and practitioners appear to find it difficult to describe voice-over as a translation mode *per se*. Moreover, the fact that the term voice-over was borrowed from Film Studies allowed for equivocal comparisons and the subsequent borrowing of terms such as *narration* and *commentary*, whose meanings, having been reformulated within the field of Translation Studies, simply added to the terminological fuzziness. To give a general idea of terms that have been already associated with voice-over, some of them have been listed below. The literature commented on in Chapter 7 defines *voice-over* as and/or compares voice-over to:

(a) a category of *revoicing*, along with lip-synchronization dubbing, narration and free commentary (Luyken *et al.* 1991, Baker 1998, Chaves 1999, Russo 1995);

(b) a type of *dubbing* (Fawcet 1983, Gavrilov Translation 2007), either "non-synchronized or non-lip sync dubbing" (Dries 1995); or (surprisingly) its opposite "doublage synchrone" (Kaufmann 1995), followed by *doublage voix off* (Kaufmann 2004); or just "half dubbing" / *demi-doublage* / *semidoppiata* (Gambier 2004, Mayoral 2001, Perego 2005);

(c) *subtitling* (Espasa 2004) or *oral subtitling* (Gambier 1996);

(d) a type of *interpreting* (Pönniö 1995, Gambier 1996, 2000, Chaves 1999, Díaz Cintas 2001b, Elias 2006, Espasa 2004, Gavrilov Translation 2007);

(e) *traducción en sincronía* (Del Águila & Rodero Antón 2005);

(f) *spoken translation* (BBC Broadcasting Research 1985);

(g) *live translation* (Elias 2006);

(h) *simultaneous translation* (Ávila 1997, Russo 1995, Del Águila & Rodero Antón 2005);

(i) *wersja lektorska* or *the reader's version* (Garcarz 2006);

(j) a type of *narration* (Karamitroglou 2000);

(k) *l'adaptation en aval* (Kaufmann 1995);

(l) *recorded commentary* (Mailhac 1998, Russo 1995).

Even more items may be added to the list above if we take into account the 43 answers collected in the questionnaire designed to map voice-over translation worldwide (see Chapter 6). These were answered by 22 practitioners of voice-over translation, 9 scholars and 12 practitioners/scholars of the voice-over translation mode. Among the 43 respondents, the vast majority (35 respondents) affirmed that they did not refer to the voice-over mode using others names. Nonetheless, the remaining eight respondents identified the voice-over mode using:

(a) *cteny komentar* or *read commentary* (Prague);

(b) *speakning* from the verb *speaka* and the noun *speakertext*, when the original is never heard, so that voice-over is compared to narration or commentary (Sweden);

(c) *sinkronizacija* or *synchronization* (Croatia and Slovenia), meaning "any non-subtitling process of translation";

(d) *dubbing* (Venezuela and Catalonia), like some audiovisual translation scholars;

(e) *off-camera speech* (Canada);

(f) *off-screen narrative* or *interviewee's speech* (Catalonia).

There are quite a few terms that refer to the same transfer mode (voice-over), or the comparisons of voice-over to different modes. Moreover, voice-over translation is often presented as subordinate to other modes, not to mention the competing meaning of terms that cannot even be considered as audiovisual transfer modes. If interlingual voice-over translation is supposed to be a category of *revoicing*, so are other types of oral translation, such as *dubbing* and *simultaneous interpreting/translation*, where a different voice is given to the original, or revoices it, either with or without lip-synch. The same goes for the name *spoken translations*, the Polish *wersja lektorska* (the reader's version), or the Swedish *speakning*, which may be said to include all renderings that are delivered orally, so not typical of voice-over translation only.

Still focusing on oral reproduction is the Film Studies related-term *sinkronizacija* (synchronization), used by respondents from Croatia and Slovenia to identify "any non-subtitling [meaning 'written'] process of translation."[16] Here, original and translated speeches have to synchronize or coincide as far as delivery duration is concerned. The same idea is expressed in *traducción en sincronía* (synchronous translation), which is delivered orally and in relatively the same pace of the original. But if the terms synchronization/synchronous translation help to identify any audiovisual translation process different from subtitling, one may ask what the comparison of *voice-over* to *subtitling* accounts for.

1.4.1 Voice-over/subtitling

Firstly, according to Espasa (2004), the comparison of voice-over translations with subtitles refers to the co-presence of two linguistic codes – the foreign original and its translation. Secondly, Gambier's comparison (1996) of voice-over to oral subtitles has to do with the fact that voice-over versions tend to be more reduced than originals due to their need to synchronize with the duration of original speech and image. A study by Grigaravičiūtė and Gottlieb (2000) has actually demonstrated that voice-over versions can be even more reduced than subtitled ones.

The need for synchronization also takes place in subtitling as well as in any other mode of audiovisual transfer, although for different reasons. In subtitling, synchronization is realized by the condensation of content, which

16 Authors' observation.

is usually constrained by the number of characters available on-screen. And, the fact that Gambier even compares voice-over to *live*, instead of pre-prepared subtitles, refers back to the immediacy of interpreting. Thus, the comparison allows for the definition of voice-over versions as condensed texts (subtitle sense) produced on the spot and delivered simultaneously with the original (interpreting sense). This latter comparison, however, was abandoned in his later discussion (2004) of audiovisual translated modes.

1.4.2 Voice-over/interpreting

With regard to the comparison of voice-over translation with *interpreting* and what is called by some authors *traducción en sincronía (simultaneous translation)* or *live translation*, most accounts emphasize only the delivery dimension of voice-over versions (that is, simultaneity with the original) and the performance of actors and journalists/commentators when recording voice-over translations. In this respect, the *Gavrilov translation* refers to first-hand, unprepared recordings, which may result in defective versions either in terms of content or in terms of delivery performance. But this comparison with interpreting may also imply that voice-over is used in live performance, as has actually been the argument of few accounts on the topic (cf. Elias, 2006). Kaufmann's many years of experience as an interpreter[17] made it possible to distinguish between live transfer modes, or those used in live broadcasting or *in situ*, such as the simultaneous or consecutive interpreting of live debates and interviews (1995: 436), and recorded transfer modes, or those recorded prior to broadcasting or *en aval*, such as the dubbing and voice-over of a *finished* product in its original version into a foreign language (1995: 438).[18]

This finished product may or may not be edited, which leads us to the concepts of production voice-over and postproduction voice-over proposed by Orero (2004a). In the former, the voice-over translation is done from rough unedited material, which is generally an uncut video that is passed on to the editor after being translated. In the latter, the voice-over translation is done from edited material, which coincides fully with the text of the

---

17 See also Russo (1995) and Kurz and Bros-Brann (1996).

18 We can also find a similar distinction between *las voces superpuestas* (superimposed voices) and *la interpretación simultánea* (simultaneous interpreting) in Agost (1999: 18–19).

finished programme. The difference between production voice-over and post-production voice-over is that the translator will invariably work harder in the unedited text to realize that his/her one-day labour has turned into a one-hour documentary. But in both cases, the shooting of the originals is already finished and the voice-over versions are recorded prior to broadcasting.

It is not suggested that voice-over and simultaneous interpreting do not share any characteristics. The facts that when translating for production no transcript is available and that translators work from screen make the relationship between the two modes tighter. The difference, however, is that interpreters have temporal limitations, which forces them to deal with fast decision-making whereas voice-over translators are able to work 'at leisure' as it were. Though one of the features of the working conditions of the voice-over translator is the rapid turnover of translations, compared with the simultaneous delivery of a translation provided by an interpreter. The truth is that voice-over translators do enjoy some time – albeit extremely short – to perform some documentation and checking procedures.

Badly written

1.4.3 Voice-over/dubbing

Going back to the discussion of terms that are used to characterize the voice-over mode, it is now interesting to observe the perspective from which voice-over is also compared with dubbing. Despite focusing on the delivery aspect of voice-over translations, the distinction between Dries's *non-synchronized* or *non-lip sync dubbing* (1995), which is somehow what Gambier means by *demi-doublage* or *half-dubbing* (2004), and Kaufmann's *doublage synchrone* (synchronous dubbing) (1995), is that the former talks refers to the absence of lip-synchronization between translating and translated voice while the latter refers to timing, or rather, the audio synchronization of the translation voice with the on-screen speaker's voice. Audio parallelism, as Kaufmann explains in her later article (2004), is necessary not only for the sake of speech duration, but also for the sake of speech credibility. That is, the translation of terms such as proper nouns and foreign terms that can be recognized by the audience is kept parallel with the original.

This coincidence between the duration of original and translated speech eventually leads to audiovisual synchronization, where normally no voice-over translation will be heard after programme participants are seen to have closed their mouths.

1.4.4 Voice-over/voice-off

Doublage voix off was also recently put forward by Kaufmann in her 2004 article, as the alternative French term for voice-over. Because it is not labial, but simply read by an unseen voice talent, the *doublage* is characterized as *voix off*. This, in turn, refers to the Film Studies literature,[19] or the position from which the translating voice comes, that is, somewhere outside the screen frame. In this case, the French *doublage voix off* does refer to voice-over translation, but as Kaufmann herself puts it:[20]

> And when dubbing: not "labial" dubbing (the "real one" in French, when you say only "doublage") but the "doublage voix-off", you have always a "voice over" which is in "voix off", because the translating voice is "off" the screen … So the original person may be on or off screen but the voice over is only off (if it is not simultaneous translation by an interpreter on screen) …

The insistence on the term *dubbing* to define another audiovisual transfer mode certainly does not help, especially since voice-over is not the "*real* dubbing*" in Kaufmann's terms. Apparently, the author tries to stick to the terminology adopted by professional translators, which is most of the time influenced by Film Studies. In Singleton's *Filmmaker's Dictionary*, the verb *dub* means, among other things, "to combine the different SOUND TRACKS by MIXING to produce a master recording from which the final sound track is then made"[21] (1990: 53); the term *off-screen* refers to "a sound or action that comes from, or happens in an area OFF-CAMERA, so it is not seen on the screen when the film is PROJECTED" (1990: 114, original emphasis).

The impact of Film Studies on the concept of voice-over as a translation mode and on the French use of the term *dubbing voice-off* may be observed above. Thus, *doublage voix off* denotes the mixing of the original and translation soundtracks, which are recorded separately, on different dates and in different languages, by a on-screen speaker who is generally onscreen (e.g., a real interviewee) and an invisible voice talent actor, the off-screen source of the voice-over version.

19 Sometimes the absence of the speakers, mainly in dialogues or interviews, can be temporary, when the camera pans around different directions and then goes back to them. In this case, viewers are already familiar with the faces of the voices heard and cinematographic terminology refers to this phenomenon as *voice off*.

20 In a personal e-mail of January 2006.

21 All forms of emphasis can be found in the original.

A good illustration of the French use of the term voice-over to refer to dubbing voice-off is an online advertisement offering a course on *voix off*.[22] Part of the advertisement is reproduced below:[23]

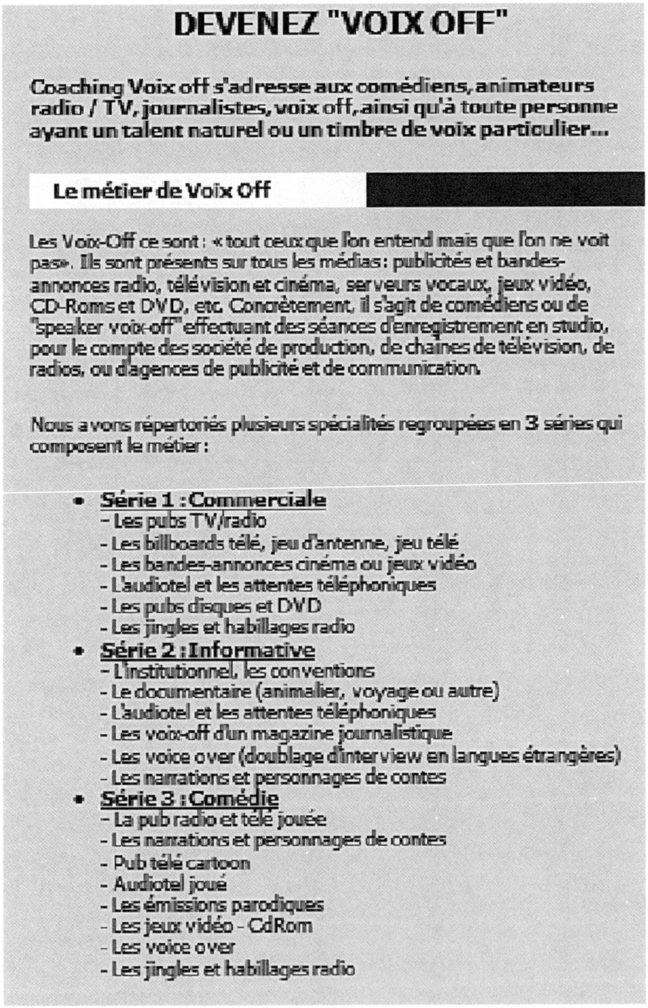

DEVENEZ "VOIX OFF"

Coaching Voix off s'adresse aux comédiens, animateurs radio / TV, journalistes, voix off, ainsi qu'à toute personne ayant un talent naturel ou un timbre de voix particulier...

Le métier de Voix Off

Les Voix-Off ce sont : « tout ceux que l'on entend mais que l'on ne voit pas». Ils sont présents sur tous les médias: publicités et bandes-annonces radio, télévision et cinéma, serveurs vocaux, jeux vidéo, CD-Roms et DVD, etc. Concrètement, il s'agit de comédiens ou de "speaker voix-off" effectuant des séances d'enregistrement en studio, pour le compte des société de production, de chaines de télévision, de radios, ou d'agences de publicité et de communication.

Nous avons répertoriés plusieurs spécialités regroupées en 3 séries qui composent le métier :

- **Série 1 : Commerciale**
  - Les pubs TV/radio
  - Les billboards télé, jeu d'antenne, jeu télé
  - Les bandes-annonces cinéma ou jeux vidéo
  - L'audiotel et les attentes téléphoniques
  - Les pubs disques et DVD
  - Les jingles et habillages radio
- **Série 2 : Informative**
  - L'institutionnel, les conventions
  - Le documentaire (animalier, voyage ou autre)
  - L'audiotel et les attentes téléphoniques
  - Les voix-off d'un magazine journalistique
  - Les voice over (doublage d'interview en langues étrangères)
  - Les narrations et personnages de contes
- **Série 3 : Comédie**
  - La pub radio et télé jouée
  - Les narrations et personnages de contes
  - Pub télé cartoon
  - Audiotel joué
  - Les émissions parodiques
  - Les jeux vidéo - CdRom
  - Les voice over
  - Les jingles et habillages radio

Figure 1. Advertisement voice-over course.

---

22 Kindly sent to us by Francine Kaufmann in January 2007.
23 <www.coaching-voix-off.com> [Retrieved on 31 January 2007].

hear

As can be read above, *voix-off* is everything we can understand but not see (*"tout ceux que l'on entend mais que l'on ne voit pas"*). It can be applied to three media genres that are divided into the commercial, the informative and the entertaining genres. Within the informative genre, *voix-off* is applied, among others, to the voice-overs or dubbing of interviews in foreign languages.

The idea that voice-over translations are instances of voice-off speech may be disputable in film theory if we take into account that most film scholars do not view *voice-off* as a 'permanently' disembodied cinematic device. Quite the contrary, Doane argues that "the voice-off is always "submitted to the destiny of the body" because it *belongs* to a character" (1985: 167).[24] In this sense, she affirms that "its [the voice-off] efficacy rests on the knowledge that the character can easily be made visible by a slight reframing which would reunite the voice and its source" (1985: 167–168). In contrast, *voice-over* belongs to a disembodied voice outside of the diegetic space. When talking about the voice-over commentary in the documentary, Doane explains:

> As a form of direct address, it speaks without mediation to the audience, bypassing the "characters" and establishing a complicity between itself and the spectator-together they understand and thus *place* the image. It is precisely because the voice is not localizable, because it cannot be yoked to a body, that it is capable of interpreting the image, producing its truth. Disembodied, lacking any specification in space or time, the voice-over is, as Bonitzer points out, beyond criticism-it censors the questions "Who is speaking?," "Where?," "In what time?," and "For whom?" (1985: 168)

Thus, despite being justifiable when the source of sound is put into perspective, viewing voice-over as an instance of voice-off speech does not seem useful in a translational sense when the realization of sound and its authenticating function are the priority. In other words, when looked from the perspective of voice-over translation strategies, when the speaker/interviewee/talking head is there, on the screen frame, most of the time, the voice-over version works as an echo of the speaker's talk on the screen, reproducing what he/she is saying. One of the devices is the frequent use of the personal pronoun *I* in voice-over versions, which somehow neutralizes the presence of the translation reader, although it is obvious, and

bad English

good

---

24   *Voice-off* is also called *voice-under* by Handzo (1985).

it needs to be, for the sake of argument credibility. For the target viewer's understanding of the text, however, the echo is what matters, because
it is in the viewer's native language. The amount of acting that the voice
talent will put into the reading (for example, by means of stress and intonation) is another strategy of voice-speaker identification. Voice identification is so important for voice-over versions that, as already mentioned, the reproduction of the speaker's accent has been a hot item of
discussion lately.

1.4.5 Voice-over/narration and commentary

Moving away from sound source into sound realization, Singleton's *Filmmaker's Dictionary* defines *voice-over* as "DIALOGUE or NARRATION
which comes from OFF SCREEN" (1990: 182). According to this definition and to the definition found in the *voix off* advertisement, it is possible
to understand why, in cinematographic terminology, filmmakers talk about
the *voice-overs* of films, referring to all speech sequences (dialogues and
narration or commentary) realized audibly by speakers that are not visually available for the viewer at the moment of film projection. It also becomes possible to understand the remaining definitions/descriptions of
voice-over translation – 'a type of narration', 'recorded commentary', '*cteny
komentar* or read commentary', 'off-camera speech', and 'off-screen narrative or interviewee's speech' – provided by our questionnaire respondents,
and 'off-camera commentary', provided by Wikipedia and mentioned at
the very beginning of this chapter. All of these definitions/descriptions
derive from the concept of voice-over that is found in the Film Studies
literature and they focus on mainly delivery. By way of illustration, the
English advertisement below offers voice-overs for narrations, but in effect, what is being referred to are voice-talents.[25]

---

25   <www.mktmania.com> [Retrieved in May 2007].

Worth asking if it is useful to differentiate terminology from that of film studies. Yes, useful for the establishment of a new discipline, but why distance from market and work experience?

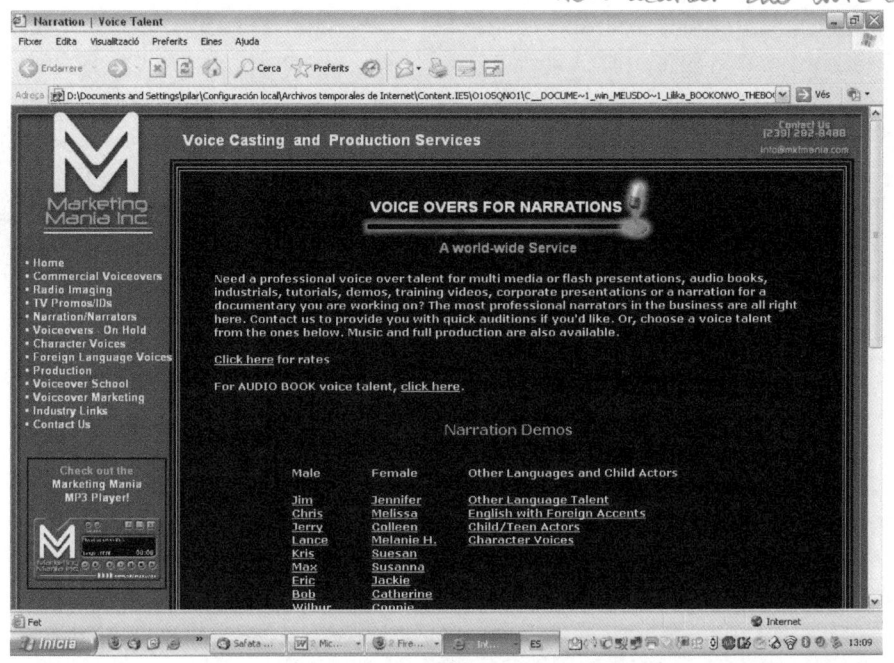

Figure 2. Advertisement voice-over for narration.

One of the negative consequences for Translation Studies of the association between voice-over and narration/commentary established in Film Studies is the fact that we end up with the idea that translated commentaries/narration are instances of voice-over translation. If we assume, as the authors of this book insistently do, that voice-over versions are realized through the recording of the translation voice on top of the original voice, which remains audible, there is no way that commentaries can be accepted as instances of voice-over translation. The reason is simply because one of the defining features voice-over translation is the co-presence of the original, which does not exist in commentaries, neither translated nor untranslated. The result is that viewers are hardly ever aware that commentaries are translated, because there is nothing there that is indicative of a translation. And, in practice, commentaries of translated programmes may be generated in three different forms: (a) translated commentaries closer to the original, (b) an adapted/domesticated commentaries and (c) created commentaries. The created commentary may be said to be a case of inter-semiotic translation, once its original verbal text is non-existent and the

→ "where"

invented commentary inserted into the translated version originates from the film's uncommented images. There is no way, however, that the viewer can tell if the commentary has been translated or has been originally created in the target language.

But, as already suggested, some audiovisual translation scholars and practitioners have also decided to adopt the film-related terms *narration* and *commentary* as transfer modes. One of the definitions of narration in the Film Studies literature is "voice-over commentary that advances the story line" (Singleton, 1990: 110). Commentary, in turn, is said to include voice-over narrators (Nichols, 1991). Thus, narration and commentary are both used by film scholars to refer to speech sequences by invisible speakers over programme images.[26] However, terminology differs mainly according to genre and to the functions that narration and commentary have within each genre, with *narration* being the preferred term for fiction, and *commentary* the preferred term for non-fiction in Film Studies. As audiovisual translation modes, narration is defined by Luyken *et al.* as an "extended voice-over" (1991: 80) that should be applied to documentary monologues. In addition, the authors affirm that the difference between voice-over and its extended form is linguistic. Pönniö puts that in detail:

> L'emploi de ce mode de transfert linguistique diffère du voice over en ce sens qu'il permet de s'éloigner davantage du texte de départ. Celui-ci se trouve, pour ainsi dire, *rapporté* et aussi *distancé* stylistiquement. La narration se trouve en général effectuée par une seule voix. Le langage qui pour le voice over a pu être du langage parlé, se trouve maintenant sous une forme plus soignée, sinon parfois plus littéraire. Les dialogues sont en général transposés en discours indirect. La narration permet également de légères interventions d'édition, pour alléger, compléter ou éclaircir le contenu. En fait il s'agit plus ou moins d'un compte-rendu de ce qui est dit ou dialogué. Le ton sépare pourtant la narration du style "commentaire". (Pönniö 1995: 304)

The most interesting part of Pönniö's statement is the suggestion that, as a mode of transfer, narration makes use of reported speech. For the rest, it seems useless to differentiate the voice-over mode of transfer from the extended voice-over modes of transfer because both refer to the translated version of an interview being read on top of its original version, with the number of voices and register as the only distinguishing features between

---

26 See, for example, Rabiger's account on how to write narrations in *Directing the Documentary* (1998).

the monologue and the dialogue interview types. Following this line of thought, reported utterances should be viewed merely as translation strategies typical of voice-over versions.

When dealing with commentary as a transfer mode, the following accounts sum up its characteristics:

> Par son caractère, le commentaire se trouve être le plus souple, le plus libre des modes de transfert linguistique audiovisuels. Il permet le mieux de prendre en considération le style, le ton et même la capacité de réception intellectuelle et le niveau culturel de l'audience visée. La culture de la langue source peut des fois différer considérablement de celle de la langue cible. [...] Ces différences trop marquées peuvent être évitées en éditant le texte de sorte qu'il corresponde au goût et aux normes habituels de la culture du pays de la langue cible. (Pönniö 1995: 305)

> Or nombre de programmes sont rendus par des commentaire [*sic*] libres, libres dans la mesure où ils ne suivent pas littéralement l'original, où ils permettent une certaine créativité, où ils sont synchronisés avec l'image plutôt qu'avec le texte de départ: ils exigent un traitement original, différent des contraintes du sous-titrage et du doublage, aussi bien au niveau textuel que technique. (Laine 1996: 198)

As already discussed, commentaries are speech sequences that do not always imply the translating activity; and even if they *do*, the fact that there is no conflict of discourse types between the original version and the translated version (both are presented as commentaries) makes it difficult for the viewer to recognize commentaries as *assumed* translations. Besides, translated or not, commentaries are viewed as original texts in their own right. In a personal correspondence, Mailhac remarked: "'Commentary' refers to the material to be translated, not to the actual process of linguistic transfer applied to it. I am not aware of any label equivalent to 'subtitling' and 'dubbing' for it, but that does not excuse loose terminology."[27]

Accepting that commentaries are not modes of audiovisual transfer, and knowing that original commentaries sometimes go through adaptations to reach a new audience, how could one name the transfer that takes place from original commentaries into translated ones? Due to the absence of the original track and of on-screen speakers, and therefore, of any visual evidence of lip synchronization, we have decided to call it *off-screen*

27 This was part of an e-mail sent on 7 December 1998. Not all scholars agree with Mailhac's view on commentary and they insist on defining *commentary* as a transfer mode. As explained by Remael (2007), local use seems to play a decisive role in the way in which people perceive the term. *why?*

dubbing. In a translated documentary we may have a narration / commentary that undergoes off-screen dubbing, that is, an adaptation process that defines a certain degree of closeness to the original (from extremely close to a created narration/commentary) and that is delivered exclusively in the target language, and, at the same time, a series of interviews that undergo voicing-over, or the revoicing of the translated voice by the translating voice with the original soundtrack remaining slightly audible and the degree of closeness to the original also varying.

1.4.6 Voice-over/reported and direct

In relation to direct/reported speech in voice-over versions, Grigaravičiūté & Gottlieb (2000) provided us with a helpful hint that led to a refined classification of voice-over. That is, in the same way that film narrators can be divided into first (character-narrators) and third (invisible narrators) persons, so can voice-over translations. This means that translations either incorporate the original talking head through the use of the personal pronoun *I*, or report what the talking head says through the use of the singular and plural third person personal pronouns. The former process is more often applied whereas the latter process appears in rare moments where a certain degree of content manipulation is verified.

Reported and direct voice-overs do have consequences for the translator's invisibility and ethics. That is, in direct voice-over the translator personifies the original speaker, which results in greater invisibility. In reported voice-over, on the other hand, the translator as mediator becomes more visible and avoids taking too much responsibility for what the original speaker says. This is more likely to occur in programmes that deal with ethical issues such as political affairs.[28]

Having sorted out the good and bad influence of Film Studies in accounts of voice-over translation, it is now time to come to terms with the concept of voice-over translation.

---

28 In interpreting, the same situation may take place. A study on court (consecutive) interpreting in Brazil by Neto (2002) demonstrated that interpreters, when rendering questions posed by the judge, generally adopted the first person personal pronoun, whereas when interpreting the accused they often resorted to indirect speech.

1.5 Coming to terms with the concept of voice-over translation

In sum, we can say that voice-over translation

- is mainly applied to non-fictional audiovisual programmes, although in certain East European countries it is also used in fictional programmes;
- renders the words of interviewers/interviewees (dialogues)/talking heads (monologues);
- is the revoicing of a text in another language, or a translating voice superimposed on a translated voice;
- is oral or spoken rendering that is delivered simultaneously and in synchrony with original speech length, recognizable words and images (kinetic/action synchrony);
- does not account for lip synchronization;
- usually starts a few seconds after the original;
- is prepared and recorded before programme broadcasting, so never produced live;
- is derived from unedited material (production voice-over) or from edited material (postproduction voice-over);
- can render content more closely to the original (voice-over translation) or less closely to the original (what the authors have decided to call free voice-over translation);
- can personify the original speaker (first person voice-over) or report his/her words (third person voice-over);
- reproduces mimetic features to a certain extent (accent, age, emotion, gender, intonation, orality markers, stress);
- keeps its performer (voice talent) invisible.

1.6 Suggested exercises

1. Table 3 illustrates research on voice-over translation and on different AVT modes up to May 2008. Try to update this table using research found in national on-line and printed bibliographies.

2. Taking into account the discussion regarding the definitions and characteristics of voice-over in 1.3, comment on the quote by Scannel (1996: 17) below as regards synchronism, mimesis and literality:

    > I am listening to the evening news on radio and the newsreader says something about a foreign statesman (say, Mr Yeltsin). The next thing I hear is a (hearably) male voice saying something in a foreign language for a few seconds. This then fades down and over it I hear a (hearably) male English voice speaking that it is not the voice of the newsreader ... Now all this makes perfect sense to me: I *assume* (though I am not told) that the foreign male voice I hear is that of Mr Yeltsin. And I *assume* (though I am not told) that the English voice over that foreign voice is giving me a literal translation of what that foreign voice is saying.

3. Have a look at your country's TV programming that make use of voice-over and try to answer the following questions:

    a) Is voice-over used for fictional and/or non-fictional programmes?
    b) Is voice-over delivered mostly as direct or reported speech?
    c) What are the characteristics of voice-over translation in your country in terms of synchronism, mimesis and content reproduction?

4. Using a search engine look for advertisements that offer voice-over services in your country. Do these advertisements talk about voice-over in the translation sense or in the narration/commentary sense?

5. Comment on each point of the concept of voice-over translation offered by this book in 1.5 as related to the way it is practised in your country.

2. Voice-over for postproduction (I): Typology and working conditions

Voice-over, as we have seen in the previous chapter, is an elusive audiovisual translation mode. It has defied classification – hence a possible explanation for the lack of studies – and it is by nature a complex process which requires detailed analysis in order to provide a possible description with some level of reliability and accuracy. It can be described and classified from the field of Translation Studies, taking into consideration many of its characteristic features. It has been traditionally classified by the genre, relating it to non-fictional genres, see for example Kilborn (1993), Franco (2000a, 2000b), Matamala (forthcoming) and Díaz Cintas and Orero (2005), by its feature of being an easy transfer mode for translation (Orero 2004a), and even by its lack of synchronicity (Luyken *et al.* (1991), Delabastita & Lambert 1996, Chaume 2004, Orero 2006a). It could also be classified taking into account the various media in which it is used. It has, for example, been popularly classified as a screen translation modality because it is more patent in motion pictures or on television, but it is also still used quite frequently in radio programmes, as can be heard, for instance, on the BBC World Service.

No extensive study up to date has looked at voice-over by the number of occurrences, that is, the number of times the audiovisual translation on a screen or on the radio is voice-over versus subtitling or dubbing. Given the fact that in most countries films and TV are either subtitled or dubbed, it seems that these two modes are those used most commonly. But looking at TV, at least in Spain and UK, France, Francophone Belgium and Germany, it can safely be said that voice-over is used more than subtitling and if we take the instances rather than the time, voice-over is probably used more than dubbing both in open and closed channels. It is used, for instance, in most news bulletins, sometimes it is only a matter of seconds for a politician or the person who is in the news, in documentaries, in interviews, even in sports programmes – we all like to hear David Beckham or Bin Laden's voice.

In the next three chapters voice-over will be studied following a bottom-up approach: from the practitioner's point of view, looking at the many cases and trying to draft a wider picture close to a taxonomic classification. Looking at the process of translation voice-over can be divided into two large categories: translation for postproduction and production. Chapters 2 and 3 will focus on the first modality, whereas Chapter 4 will be devoted to the second. Since the aim behind this book is to offer a comprehensive overview of voice-over from both academic and practical experience, and to provide a realistic approach, we have decided to describe the many and varied situations that a voice-over translator may be confronted with. Since voice-over is often combined in the same product with the off-screen dubbing of commentaries – which can be either closer to the original, adapted or even created, as was discussed in Chapter 1 –, references will also be made to this transfer mode in the following chapters.

When working for postproduction, the translator is given a finished product – either fictional or non-fictional – which has to be rendered in the target language. Due to the fact that real-life and authentic materials taken from the authors' own professional experiences will be used, and given the relationship between factual programmes and voice-over in Western Europe discussed in the previous chapter, the focus in this book will be on non-fictional products, mainly documentaries (see both Section 2 in this chapter and Chapter 3), although general comments will be made about the voice-over of fictional products (see Section 1). Further information on the situation of voice-over around the world can be found in both the questionnaires and the commented bibliography in Chapters 6 and 7 respectively.

2.1 Translating fictional products

From the 1980s and 1990s, most bibliographies on Audiovisual Translation defined voice-over as used in some countries – mainly in Eastern Europe – as the preferred translational mode for fictional and non-fictional products. This may be the case for the comparatively few postproduction requirements which represent reductions in costs (time and/or money). Though at one time this translational mode, for fictional products, seemed to be doomed, giving rise to either subtitling or dubbing as was the case in Denmark:

In the infancy of television, voice-over techniques were used in some of the countries that later turned to subtitling, for instance Denmark. Before introducing subtitling in 1955 [...], DR, Danish national TV, had its (few) foreign films translated by a film professor who read all the lines off-screen to the small, but enthusiastic Danish audience (Grigaravičiūtė & Gottlieb, 2000: 88)

It seems, though, that nowadays voice-over continues to be the translational mode preferred in many Eastern European countries as Bogucki (2004: 12) describes:

Voice-over, where the target text is read out by a *lektor* and superimposed on the original, which is also audible, originated in the former Soviet Union and was brought to Poland, where it still enjoys popularity. According to recent research (a poll by Inst. SMG KRC Poland, 2002) 50.2% of Poles prefer voice-over and 43.4% opt for dubbing; subtitling has only 8.1% supporters. A staggering 72.1% of Poles, when asked which type of AVT was the worst, chose subtitling. The latter is a standard in Polish cinemas (intralingual subtitles seem to be gaining ground on Polish television in documentaries with authentic utterances played back from a low-quality recording, e.g. telephone conversations), and dubbed cartoons as well as certain commercials are gaining popularity, but documentaries and foreign films for television are voiced-over. This technique may be beneficial for foreign language learners, – although subtitling is undoubtedly a better choice in this respect (Brett, unpubl.) – and less costly than dubbing in that only one reader is hired, but its imperfections are many. Notwithstanding these, it remains the main mode of transferring foreign programmes onto the Polish television market, because of target audience expectations.

However, dubbing is welcoming new adepts in countries (such as Poland) where voice-over was generalized,[29] where high-quality dubbed versions of new releases such as *Shrek* are accepted by an audience who was keen on the traditional audiovisual translation offer.[30]

As explained on the Internet and mentioned in Chapter 1,[31] this modality originated in the former Soviet Union, when simultaneous in-

---

29 This was highlighted by Chmiel in the unpublished paper "Translating postmodern networks of cultural associations in the Polish dubbed version of *Shrek*", delivered at the MuTra Conference in Copenhagen, in May 2006.

30 Conversely, factual programmes that were traditionally voiced-over, such as the travel show *Lonely Planet* or *Jamie Oliver's Kitchen* are beginning to be dubbed in countries such as Brazil. This is so because the protagonists are so funny and special that they are more like characters in a series than travel guides or cooks. Thus, for being almost fiction-like, they started to be dubbed.

31 <http://en.wikipedia.org/wiki/Gavrilov_translation> and <http://en.wikipedia.org/wiki/Dubbing_(filmmaking)>.

terpreters were hired to translate many Western films in closed-door screenings organized by the USSR State Committee for Cinematography and
also in film festivals opened to the general public. One of the most famous
interpreters was Andrey Gavrilov – next to Alexey Mikhalev and Leonid
Volodarskiy –, and this is why "Gavrilov translation" was the term used to
refer to this modality. Later on, with the introduction of VCRs, the interpreters' voices were recorded on tapes. Whereas sometimes they had time
to watch the film and prepare the translation, which was then revoiced by
themselves, it was also often the case that time constraints forced them to
interpret the film without any previous preparation, which resulted in
their making various mistakes as result of time pressure. Sometimes, in
complicated films with intense speech, as explained by a voice-over translator from Belarus (Baranitch 1995: 309), the translator could work from
an editing list with time codes, sitting in front of the screen and reading
simultaneously into the microphone while listening, a hybrid modality
similar to the one used in non-fiction programmes broadcast by the television network *Arte*, as will be explained in Chapter 4. Some of the translators even specialized in film genres, such as Gavrilov in action films
(*Total Recall* and *Die Hard*) and Mikhalev in comedies and dramas
(*A Streetcar named Desire* and *The Silence of the Lambs*).

After the collapse of the Soviet Union, Gravrilov translations were
maintained on cable television and in the pirate video industry and were
later included in additional audio tracks on DVDs. New names entered
the market, such as the famous Dmitry "Goblin" Puchkov,[32] well-known
for his use of profanity when translating. This is a controversial issue in
Russia because previous Gavrilov translators did not use obscenities except when it was absolutely essential, whereas Puchkov advocates quality
translations that reproduce the tone of the original. As a hobby, Puchkov
has translated films such as *Pulp Fiction, Snatch* or *Platoon* and cartoons
such as *Chicken Run,* but has also been commissioned for commercial
translations of, for example, *The Sopranos* or *South Park.* Moreover, he is
also known for his funny translations, in other words, translations in which
references not included in the original are added, producing a comical
effect.

---

32 Information retrieved from the Internet: http://en.wikipedia.org/wiki/Dmitry_
    Puchkov.

The main characteristic of a Gavrilov translation of a fiction film – be it a series or a feature film, for example – is that, although the original might contain various characters, male and female, the voice-over is generally performed by a single voice talent, usually male, who depicts a extremely fast-paced discourse, usually overlapping the original dialogue – which can be partially heard – and expressing no emotions. Very often, as pointed out by Grigaravičiūtė and Gottlieb (1999), the original dialogue is not left uncovered at the beginning and at the end as it seems to be the theoretical norm in non-fictional products (see Chapters 1 and 3) and, due to the strategies implemented to condense speech, the target version is less emotional. This view is shared by Krasovska (2004), who analyses the Latvian voice-over of the film *The City of Ghosts* and concludes that some reductions – in the form of ellipsis, omissions or deletions – take place in voice-over although apparently being free of time and space constraints.

Despite being considered by many inferior to lip-synch dubbing, Gavrilov translations have many fans who even post voice-over versions of their favourite films online. It seems therefore that new technologies and the availability of simple video processing software will give a new boost to voice-over: in a similar way as fansubs (subtitles provided by fans) are available on the Internet, voice-over translations provided by non-professional translators will also be available.

Apart from the traditional use of voice-over to revoice fictional products in Eastern Europe, voice-over also seems to be enjoying a healthy growth in new areas and in new complex media formats, such as subtitles and voice-over or audio subtitling. This popularity is due to two new situations. On the one hand, thanks to the latest technical advances, globalization, which in some areas may have a negative impact, allows for smaller languages to be present in media communication. That is two language transfers will take place simultaneously, one of them being voice-over. As Krasovska (2004) explains in Latvia, it is now possible to receive Latvian voice-overs and Russian subtitles combined in the Latvian commercial TV channels, in an attempt to satisfy the needs of a bilingual audience.

On the other hand, we find audio subtitling or spoken subtitling (Theunisz 2002, de Jong 2006, Orero 2007a) in the realm of media accessibility. This mode is one of the many transfers which make voice-over a complex transfer modality, since audio subtitling has the effect of voice-over, though its production is completely different from the voice-over that we have presented up to now. We find a written text on the screen –

surtitles in opera (Matamala 2005a, Matamala & Orero 2007) or subtitles in films – which needs to be read aloud for those who have difficulty reading texts. For films we can find many examples in, for example, *Hero* (2004) directed by Zhang Yimou. In the DVD format we find that the film is originally in Mandarin with English subtitles. When we make the choice of watching the film with "English" or "English Audio Descriptive", we are able to hear original soundtrack of the film in Mandarin, and a voice which reads the subtitles. The overall effect is one of English voice-over on Mandarin. This case is one more example of the many and diverse factors present when attempting a taxonomy for voice-over. Another example is the film *The Passion of Christ* (2004) directed by Mel Gibson, in which Jesus speaks Aramaic. In this film we find audio subtitling read by a female voice. The overall effect, as in the previous example – is one of English voice-over on Aramaic. The audio subtitling of recent film releases such as Pedro Almodovar's *Volver* (2007), in which one female voice reads all the subtitles, puts into question the practice since a film in which some scenes have up to five women having a conversation, makes identifying characters with voices an impossible task (Braun & Orero forthcoming).

All in all, with the proliferation of TV channels, the production of audiovisual products, and the broadcast versatility offered by digital technology it is not difficult to predict an increase in the translation of audiovisual products with voice-over, since it offers both financial and time-saving benefits.

2.2 Translating non-fictional products

We shall consider non-fictional products all sorts of documentaries (history, science, nature, archaeology, etc.), current affairs programmes, investigative journalism, docu-dramas, reality shows, talk shows, etc. There is also a growing market of corporate videos, instruction manuals and infomercials, which abandon the realm of written language to offer attractive audiovisual products to the audience. Voice-overs and translated commentaries can also be used in interactive displays in museums, corporate websites, bonus materials, advertising, etc.

In the following sections we will delve into the general professional working conditions of translators that deal with these products (2.2.1) and focus on the source text (2.2.2), analysing both the transcripts and scripts that translators are given (2.2.2.1) as well as the general structure of non-fictional products such as documentaries with regard to the type of speakers included (2.2.2.2). In Chapter 3, we will describe the main challenges posed by the two main transfer modes used in the translation of non-fiction, i.e. voice-over and off-screen dubbing, and show the different layouts used by translators. These layouts reflect the various tasks that professionals may be commissioned to take on. These tasks depend on the clients and their specific requests.

2.2.1 *Working conditions* *this applies to the Spanish audience, not the UK, for instance*

The translation of a wide range of audiovisual products is usually outsourced to a dubbing studio, which generally outsources the translation to a freelance translator.[33] The translation is later recorded by a voice artist or voice talent. The freelance translator usually receives a call from the studio with the offer to translate, for example, a documentary. A video plus a script – on paper or by e-mail, if available – is sent to the translator, who after working on text sends back the translation by e-mail. The translator usually works to a tight deadline (48 hours) or might be lucky enough to receive a bulk of documentaries to be translated during a certain period of time, for example a month, but the pace is generally frenetic. Some five years ago, audiovisual translators received a VHS tape; afterwards, DVDs were sent, and it is now standard practice to receive video files through file exchange systems such as DigiDelivery <http://www.asperasoft.com/en/products/digidelivery_11/digidelivery_11>.Translators then work with a software program such as VLC <http://www.videolan.org/>, Zoom Player <http://www.inmatrix.com/files/zoomplayer_download.shtml> or Media Player Classic <http://sourceforge.net/projects/guliverkli/>, which allows to go forward and "rewind" frame by frame, something which is not possible with a regular DVD player.

33 Some TV networks, such as TVC (Catalan television), select audiovisual translators by means of a public examination and dubbing studios can outsource translations to only those professionals who are in touch with a group of linguists who are permanent members of the staff and who offer advice on translation norms.

Sometimes, when the translation is needed urgently, or when dealing with certain products, the television network or the client outsources the translation directly to a translator, who works at home on a translation draft (with a script and no image) and goes to the television office to make the final adjustments with the recorded material. This work practice is a hybrid in between production and postproduction voice-over translation. We can see how we find ourselves describing mixed scenarios, practices, genres, which highlight the complexity of describing voice-over as a neat language transfer.

There is still a further possibility that is the situation in which the translator is given a written text with a standard layout with nothing to distinguish it as an audiovisual product and is not even told that the translation is to be recorded. Cues such as "look at this!" might help the translator discover the product is an audiovisual text,[34] but it is obvious that many features of voice-over related to synchronization cannot be kept if the image is not available.

Apart from the two last exceptional cases, the working process in which the translator is given a script and a video does not differ much from translating other types of audiovisual products by means of other types of transfer modes: the videos are usually of acceptable quality – although sometimes a defective version can be sent forcing the translator to ask for a new one, if there is enough time – and the script or transcription may often reveal some surprises, such as erroneous transcriptions, not unique to his transfer mode but so common that they merit further description/analyses.

Once the translator has watched the product and has solved all the comprehension problems, the audiovisual items – sound and written text on the screen – are translated, bearing in mind the transfer mode chosen by the client and generally delivered in a pre-established layout.

2.2.2 The source text

When talking about the source text in audiovisual translation, there is no doubt that we are referring to the audiovisual product, which can give voice to different speakers and which is the product that the translator will

---

34   This was explained by Mary Carroll in the MuTra Conference held in 2005 in Saarbrücken, Germany <http://www.euroconferences.info/2005.php?konferenz=2005>.

have to render in the target language. Its written version, in the form of a script or transcript, is nothing but a supplemental aid whose quality varies, as will be demonstrated below.

2.2.2.1 Scripts and transcripts

The spectrum of postproduction scripts is extremely wide: it varies from the loose transcription to the highly detailed script, in which the transcription is accurate. Some of scripts have been created specifically for translators and include a note explicitly stating "for dubbing purposes". The scripts contain the name of the speaker on the left-hand side plus the transcription of what is said on the right-hand side. Other postproduction scripts contain notes related to the image and time codes. The translator does not have to translate all those indications – a common error made by new translators who are used to translating written language – but they can be used to follow the text. A quite rare but wonderful situation is when the script also includes a list of all the specific terminology used in the programme, for example, animals and plants plus their scientific names in documentaries.

[not unusual ?]

　　The first pages of three documentary scripts have been reproduced below. The first transcript is from the Portuguese production *Surfavela*, directed by Nuno Leonel and Joaquim Pinto (1996). The original version is in European Portuguese, voiced-over into French and German and broadcast by the bilingual channel *Arte*. In this transcript, no indications about visuals, speakers or their positions in relation to the screen frame can be seen.[35] The second example – from a documentary on Venice – includes the simple transcription of the text spoken, with time codes and a few scarce indications included, whereas the last example, which has been taken from the documentary *Europe: a Natural History*, reproduces the complete transcription of both audio and visuals found in the documentary, and it even includes a list of scientific terms.[36]

35　We would like to thank both producers, Nuno Leonel and Joaquim Pinto, for responding to our request for permission to reproduce the original transcript.

36　We would like to acknowledge the BBC for kindly granting us permission to reproduce the scripts included in examples 1 and 2.

Example 1. Surfavela

Surfavela:

Oh KUNKA!
Foi quando num dia que
.eu estava pegando na onda lá no pontão ai todo o mundo estava pegando onda.ai eu falei: "só
eu é que não estou pegando onda Ai não tinha ninguém perto de mim. Todos tinham descido
das ondas. Ai subiu a maior onda do dia. eu remei, remei igual a um condenado.
Quando eu desci a galera vibrou. Amandei um batidão. A galera foi ao delírio.
Muito bom, não tive medo de nada. Fui com Deus e tchau!
Quando aprendi a remar, quando comecei a apanhar onda lá nos picos. onde os surfistas
ficam. Eu comecei a entrar pela correnteza.
onde a gente tem que ter o braço mais forte para entrar. sen ão...
Aí. o meu irmão me jogava. quando estava na correnteza, ele me jogava na correnteza para eu
aprender a nadar mais rápido
para caso quando se eu estiver no Hawaii assim na vida. se o estrepe arrebentar vou ter que
saber nadar

O KUNKA tá pegando bem para caramba. Deste tamanho se ele continuar eu não sei. Do meu
tamanho vai estar um batedor cruel. Cheio de patrocinio na prancha.

O meu nome é Leonardo. tenho 13 anos. Moro no Morro do Cantagalo, conhecido mais como
Galo. Surfo há mais ou menos 2 anos, sou pico de origem Arpoador, como vocês vêem.
Quê mais, o que posso dizer mais sobre mim?
Gosto muito de desporto que eu faço
É, gosto muito, eu amo ele, adoro.
E se não fosse por esse projeto "Surfavela", eu não ia estar aqui.
este dia surfando, com essa prancha que eu tenho . É isso

Essa aqui é a Maria Gorda... sacanagem...
Esse é o Rodrigo, representa lá o pavão. é competidor. Categoria Júnior.
Esse aqui é o Jaime,.turma de apoio.
Esse aqui é o Kunka, vai ser um competidor também brevemente.
Esse aqui é o Adalto.\/O Gótico   ~'   ~'
Gótico é o nome de competidor dele

Isto são os poucos que temos no momento. não é....
Mas no todo são 120. Cento e porrada de moleque chato que me ficam perturbando o dia
inteiro
se concentram mais em dia de campionato e de excursão.
Aí, até aparece nego que eu não conheço na terra, no Surfavela.
Eu estou tentando cercá-los de todas as formas.
Então cada um dels vendo participando até informalmente.
sem a formalidade de escolhinha de capacitação, mas involvido com o projecto involvido
comigo, de ver como a coisa acontece, aprender.   do lado
E, mais tarde ter essa perspectiva de não precisar partir de errado, como eu parti na hora do
meu desespero, e sim partir para esse lado do meio alternativo de sustento.
O projecto "Surfavela" foi uma cura até para mim.
Eu já fui viciado em droga.
Já usei cocaina, ja fumei maconha, já fiz um monte de merda nessa vida.
Ja passei necessidade, e roubei.
E hoje em dia o projecto "Surfavela" foi uma continuidade da cura.
A cura mesmo foi Deus.

Eu vou lá sempre, ele dá orientações para gente, como a gente faz as coisas lá, quando a gente
tiver uma certa idade, trabalhar com o Rogério,com os outros que concertam pranchas.

Example 2. Venice

10:00:00 – 10:00:30 – Titles sequence and music

10:00:30 – 10:00:45 – Graphic of Map
Situated just off the tip of northern Italy

10:00:30 – 10:01:00 V/O 1
Hello and welcome to Style World which today comes from the romantic city of Venice. We'll dropping in on a craftsman who make the masks for city's famous carnivals … and be travelling Venetian style, in a gondola, along the city's famous canals. And with interior design in mind, Style World, checks into Venice's finest hotels and restaurants, and we'll also be visiting some of the best Venetian homes to see what's classical and what's vogue.

10:01:16 – 10:02:17 V/O 2 GVs
The beautiful city of Venice was built on mud flats over a thousand years ago, and boasts some of the most breathtaking landmarks in the world. From the exquisite Basilica building to the famous Piazza San Marco, the landscape of Venice radiates a romantic elegance. What makes Venice so unique is that it is a city linked by canals instead of roads, cars being replaced by boats and Gondolas. The Venetians' taste for the finer things in life is evident in the art and architecture. Everything is bathed in enticing and sensual colours, and the narrow canals and secret doorways give Venice a romantic intimate feel. The beauty of the city's canals are matched by the design of some of it's bridges, from the impressive Rialto Bridge over the Grand Canal, to the Bridge of Sighs, traditionally a walk way for condemned prisoners. (2:12) The city is renowned for traditional mask making; the famous carnivals are based on the allure of anonymity – hidden identities behind exotic masks. Despite being built in the water all those years ago, the ingenuity of the design has kept the city standing, despite a the constant threat of subsidence – which has claimed a few victims over the years, such as the Bell tower in San Marco Square that had to be rebuilt, after collapsing 1902. Next to the Bell Tower is one of Venice's most impressive buildings, the Basilica. Away from the public attractions, the classical architecture is brought to life by the local Venetians who live a traditional life.

10:03:00 Traditional House V/O 3
The buildings are of the city's greatest heritage. One woman whose life's passion is Venetian architecture is Matilde Marcello Terzuol who has lectured in restoration. Her beautiful home captures the opulent grandeur of Venice. Matilde is a trompe l'oeuil artiste and she has personally restored and decorated her apartment in a traditional Venetian style. The rooms have been painted in light pastel colours and decorated with traditional paintings and antiques. The classic mix of tapestries and wood help to evoke a rich sense of history. Matilde carefully researched the period characteristics to accurately recreate her traditional flat.

Example 3. Europe: A Natural History

BBC POST PRODUCTION SCRIPT

EUROPE: A NATURAL HISTORY

Programme 3: Taming The Wild

BBC WORLDWIDE VERSION (50')

Narrated by
SEAN PERTWEE

In the last 10,000 years Europe has been transformed from a largely forested, virgin landscape in to the manicured continent we know today, and at an ever-accelerating rate. As culture spread its influence across the land with monumental symbols of ownership, animals were tamed, seeds were sown, forests decimated and minerals excavated. How did wildlife cope with these drastic changes, and what impact did they have on ourselves?

Producer:	Klaus Feichtenberger
Series Producers:	Patrick Morris/Klaus Feichtenberger
Executive Producers:	Walter Köhler/Michael Gunton/Reinhard Radke
Duration:	**49'00"**
Spools:	BKD 12897
Prog. No:	50/NBR Y598A
Prog. Ident:	50/NBR Y598A/71
Music Copyright:	Specially composed by **BARNABY TAYLOR** (See attached pages and P4A)
Film Copyright:	See attached and P4A
Stills Copyright:	See P4A for stills information

STEREO
A BBC/ORF/ZDF Co-production
4:3 Aspect ratio

MUSIC COPYRIGHT:

Incidental music sequences specially composed by **BARNABY TAYLOR**
(see P4A for contract details), as follows:-

No.	Description	T/code in	T/code out
1	Pre-title & Title	00:00	01.50
2	Hunt	03:58	05.22
3	Taming	05:51	06.15
4	The Med	06:22	06.56
5	First fields	08:55	09.38
6	Monuments	09:48	12.06
7	Marching Romans	13:42	14.35
8	Cornish Tin	15:39	16.33
9	Rome's End & Legacy	19:01	20.55
10	Spanish Desert	20:55	21.40
11	Alhambra	23:26	24.20
12	Norway	24:33	26.00
13	Forests	26:40	27.04
14	Monks	27:22	28.12
15	Plague	29:20	31.34
16	Nature Recovers	33:43	35.06
17	Ireland	37:33	37.56
18	Growth & Blight	38:57	39.47
19	Exodus	40:27	41.08
20	City sprawl	42:44	43.49
21	Train	44:24	45.26
22	End montage	46:20	48.22
23	Credits	48:22	49.00

Programme narrated by **SEAN PERTWEE** (See P4A for contract details)

FILM COPYRIGHT:

BBC specially shot on Super 16mm and transferred to digi-beta, except for some sequences
(see P4A for details of other footage used in this programme). See P4A for details of B/W archive
footage and stills used in this programme.

<u>BBC Post Production Script: Europe: A Natural History – 3: Taming the Wild</u> 3
<u>- UK TX</u>

SHOT   T/CODE   COMMENTARY
MUSIC

SPECIES LIST/LATIN NAMES

Common Name	Species Name
Musk ox	
Wild boar	
Ibis	
Moose	
Wolf	*Canis lupus*
horse	
goat	
Red Squirrel	*Sciurus vulgaris*
Wild Boar	*Sus scrofa*
Red Deer	*Cervus elaphus*
Pine marten	
Domestic Cow	*Bos Taurus*
Whooper swan	
herring	
White-tailed sea eagle	
Cod	
Grey heron	
carp	
Otter	
dragonfly	
terrapin	
Barn Owl	*Tyto alba*
Brown Bear	*Ursus arctos*
Fox	*Vulpes vulpes*
Stoat	*Mustela erminea*
Rat	*Rattus sp.*
Great crested grebe	*Podiceps cristatus*

VT CLOCK/IDENT				
Europe: A Natural History **Programme 3** **'Taming the Wild'** **50 NBR Y598A** BBC tx version 4:3 full height	by	Preceded **10: -**		by Preceded **10: -**
Aerial LA GV glacier, track fwd (TF), mts. b/g		00.00		00.00
Aerial GV glacier		00.04		**SEQ. 1**
		00.06	Europe ... For 2 million years ice has swept the continent. Not just once, but many times ... (00.16)	
GV windblown ice cornices and snow		00.07		
MCU musk ox in snow		00.09		
		00.10		
LS musk oxen, walking L				
		00.12		
MS rocky gorges and ice frozen waterfall				
Mix to a/b, waterfall flowing		00.15		
CU sun above skyline		00.19		
CU icicles, water flowing b/g		00.20		
		00.21	Then, some 20,000 years ago, the bitter climate begins to ease its grip. (00.28)	
MCU same		00.22		
MS ice cave interior at glacier toe, river flowing out		00.24		
CU ice melt and water falling down		00.26		
CU water falling down		00.29		
MCU waterfall, tilt down to rough, flowing water (slo-mo)		00.31		

However, as Matamala (forthcoming) points out, quite often scripts or transcripts contain inaccuracies and can lead to errors if the translator is not an expert on the subject matter and is not fully aware of the fact that everything that is heard and seen on the screen must be translated, regardless of what is written in the script or transcript. Some examples of erroneous transcriptions are the following:

Transcription	Correct audio
We were just discussing the name for a while at what we should call our little collective. I really had a fascination with the name *Medullamagada*, which is the brain stem. (Source: *Hackers*, by Russell Barnes, 2001.)	*Medulla oblongata*
Grant listens with interest to Professor Didier Raoult, director of the *French National Defence Centre* for rickettsial disease. (Source: *Red Storm*, by Matthew Flanagan, 2000)	*French National Reference Centre*
The work we're standing on is called Ancient Language. It was the first of three geoglyphs. It's a double headed llama and *Señor Bekalos* is a figure of power which is a recreation of an eight thousand year old picture-glyph. (Source: *Monumental Vision*, by Laura Zusters, 2006.)	*Señor de los Báculos*

In a few cases, though, the transcriber indicates that the text might be wrong by including notes or adding an interrogation mark after the "suspicious" word. This can be found, for example, on the postproduction scripts of the series *Philosophy: A Guide to Happiness* (presented by Alain de Botton and directed by Celia Lowenstein, 2000). In the episode *Nietzsche on Hardship*, three names are followed by a question mark (Pitzkorwatsch, Sils Maria, Monica Perego) and in the episode *Schopenhauer in Love* there are four of them (Joachim Stolberg, Elizabeth Neigh, Atma, Bramines).

It is not uncommon to find a script like the following one from the TV series *Style World*, in which many mistakes, poor composition ("Venice is a city dominated by classical architecture and homes") plus three different ways to spell *avant-garde* can be found in a few lines:

> 23:02 V/O 19 *Modern Flat*
> Although Venice is a city dominated by classical architecture and homes, behind this traditional exterior is a very modern apartment belonging to designer Cleto Munari. His flat is one of the only modern homes in Venice decorated in an *avante garde* style. Cleto asked his friend, renowned designer Ettore Sottsass to create the contemporary look of his home. The spacious interior is adorned with bright colours and bold shapes in pronounced contrast to other homes round Venice. The *avant-garde* style of the flat reflects Cleto's own designs which include innovative silver ware and jewellery.
>
> 10:23:45 – 10:34:21 Sync Cleto
> I think that my style is *avant guarde*. I've always lived in old houses and all the furniture was is at least two to four hundred years old. *So to work on and design an old house in a modern style was very different from what I would do normally and my style of life which had always been the same.* However I felt that I should something different with this house.

Bad transcription can also be one of the obstacles for the reproduction of colloquial language. When speakers are mainly children and adolescents who come from social groups with lower incomes, documentary participants in general tend to speak the language of the young and the underprivileged, that is, language marked by vocabulary (swear words), slang terms and colloquial/idiomatic expressions which are common to all of them. The two script fragments below (our emphasis) come from a documentary entitled *Gosses de Rio*, directed by Thierry Michel (1990). The documentary is about a group of street children in the city of Rio de Janeiro. The scene begins with a close-up on China and one of the street boys who says:

> O carnaval é a época mais fácil que tem para se roubar, é a melhor que tem, não tem época melhor do que o Carnaval, todo o mundo da *molhe*, todo o mundo bebe fica todo o mundo doidão …
> (p. 21 of script)

> […] saio por ai, roubo um, vendo relógio, vou la, comprar comida, *arrumando* para os colegas […]
> (p. 22 of script)

According to Franco (2000b), the two fragments provide evidence of what Thierry Michel referred to in an interview (14 July 1998), that is, the difficulty felt by transcribers (probably Portuguese) in coping with the Brazilian speakers' colloquial language. When China says in the first fragment (p. 21) that everybody *dá "mole"* during carnival, he means that in this period of the year everybody relaxes and drinks and does not pay much attention to anything around them, so that stealing is easier for the pickpockets. Its transcription *molhe*, on the other hand, comes from the verb *molhar* [to water or to get wet] in Brazilian Portuguese. In the second fragment, the problem originates from the slang word *rango*, derived from the English *hungry*, which, in Brazilian Portuguese, means *meal* (i.e. when you are hungry you have a *rango*). So, instead of saying *"arrumando" para os colegas*, which does not make much sense, China actually says *"pag'um rango" para os colegas* [(I) *"pay a rango"/"meal" for my mates*],[37] which is what he usually does after having stolen some money. Although the videotape version *pag'um rango* and the transcribed version *arrumando* sound similar, the latter ends up nonsensical in that context.

Even working for postproduction, the translator can receive a pre-production script, that is, a script which does not correspond to the final edited product. In this type of script, scenes are often missing and the translator has to work from the screen. For a non-native speaker, understanding a narrator is generally easy but it gets more difficult with interviewees, and it becomes an absolute nightmare trying to understand spontaneous speech (scenes in which people talk without any previous preparation, probably unaware that their words will be broadcast), especially when slang or even marked local accents appear.

For instance, in the episode *Gator Raid* from the popular series *Croc Hunter Diaries*, with Steve Irwin, the translator was given a script with time codes, the name of the speaker plus a transcription of what is said. This series features real-life scenes from the Australian Zoo and in this particular episode the audience gets to see how Steve risks his life to save an injured koala, how eggs are taken away from a cranky mother alligator and other exciting adventures. However, in the script that was provided there was no transcription of some scenes, such as the scene in which Bruno the koala has an arm operation, or the scene in which a python is wedged under a car and no one can get it out. Understanding the contextual information provided by the narrator was easy, but understanding the technical language used during surgery with poor sound quality and understanding what was being said under a car with a strong Australian ac-

---

37   From now on, translations of examples in languages other than English will be provided between brackets.

many authentic examples

cent was definitely a challenge for a non-native translator working with English and even for a native speaker of English.

Sometimes the translator may receive a partial script, or there are times that a few pages may be lost if paper copies are used. For example, when translating the documentary *Hackers*, the translator was first sent a script with all the narrator transcriptions but no interviews and, after asking for a complete transcription, a postproduction script was sent. Luckily, there was enough time to wait for the correct transcription because otherwise the translator would have had to work from the screen and the task would have been much more daunting due to the computer jargon hackers use in this documentary, the marked local accents and the speed of some of the interviewees. It is when scripts or transcripts of postproduction products are not available that this modality edges closer to voice-over for production since one of the main features of this last type of translation is the systematic absence of a script or transcript.

A different type of situation arises when the translator works with an international script translated into English but the video is in another language, that is, when the translator works from a pivot translation. The series *City Folk*, for example, a European co-production, was translated into Catalan from an English script, although in the original videos other language were used (for example, Slovenian in *City Folk Ljubljana*). And in *The Russian Newspaper Murders (Les cimitières de la Glasnost)* (Jenkins, 2004), for instance, the translator was given an international written version with English translations of both commentaries and interviews, a French written version with commentaries in French and interviews in Russian, and a VHS with English commentaries and Russian interviews, a melting pot, which ended in a product revoiced in Catalan.

A last possibility is when the original product – for example, a French production – has been translated and revoiced in English and the translator is given both the transcript and the video in English. Although no problems should arise from this situation, the reality of the situation is diverse and whilst some international versions in English can be regarded as originals because of the high quality of the translation, others contain translation mistakes – either wrong translations, incomprehensible sentences or wrong transliterations –, making the translator's job even harder. For instance, the French production *World Discoveries / Découverte du monde* (Lafargue 2001) is available in French and English. When translating it into Catalan, the professional sometimes had a French version (both script and image) and sometimes an English version (both script and image), which suspiciously looked like a translation – an issue which sadly we have not been able to confirm. Various problems arose when only the English version was available: it was commonplace to find French transcriptions of many names such as "Boukhara" instead of "Bukhara" and a documentation process to avoid these interferences was of the essence. But the worst nightmare for the translator was detecting wrong information probably due to erroneous translations, as in the following example:

> Most of Samarkand's palaces date from this period, the most prominent in the city being the Reghistan. Known as "The Place of Sands", it has become world famous. Like many monuments, the Reghistan is surrounded by gardens, which have mythic connotations in the Muslim imagination, symbolising an inaccessible haven.

According to many sources, the Reghistan is a famous square in Samarkand – known as *la place des sables* –, not a palace. Therefore, writing that the most prominent palace of Samarkand is the Reghistan is undoubtedly a mistake which have arisen – and this our hypothesis – due to confusion between *un palace* (a palace) and *une place* (a square).

2.2.2.2 Speakers and script structure

The non-fictional product which the translator receives can be of a diverse nature and can vary from a linear structure to a complex composite of different audiovisual texts: interviews, previously broadcast programmes, films, etc. Translators may find ourselves coping with the translation of an excerpt of a film plus various interviews in the same documentary. Or a situation which arises a lot is the following: a chapter from a wildlife documentary such as the long running television series *Natural World* (also called *Wildlife on One)*, narrated by David Attenborough, in which animals are the leading characters of the actual programme and are accompanied by an off-screen narrator, who describes their actions and features. The language is fairly formal, although some puns might be used now and then. Here is an excerpt from an episode entitled *Piranhas.*

> *Wildlife on One: Piranhas. Narrated by David Attenborough. 1997*
> Red-bellied piranhas ... and they are hungry! Above them, young great white egrets –
> unable to fly but strong enough to leave the safety of their nests. This is a dangerous
> time for the chicks. One slip could be disastrous. Piranhas have been called the most
> ferocious freshwater fish in the world. It's time to take a closer look. Piranhas, of which
> there are some 30 different species, live in South American, where rivers like the Orinoco
> in Venezuela and the Amazon in Brazil wind through open grassland and dense tropi-
> cal forest. Over millions of years, fruit from the jungle trees has influenced the evolu-
> tion of monkeys as we know them today. In the Amazon, where fruit is both abundant
> and nutritious, it has also shaped the evolution of certain kinds of fish. However con-
> tradictory it may seem, these piranhas are vegetarians. They're no threat to living ani-
> mals. Blunt faces house teeth best suited for crushing and grinding seeds.
>   Another kind of piranhas lives a more solitary life. Its jaws are long and they house
> teeth like needles. It hunts by stealth and a lightning attack on other fish, nipping out
> chunks of their fins and tails. It's a parasitic piranha.

A variation of this type of documentary can be found when there is an off-
screen narrator plus other off-screen speakers. For example, in the episode
The Coast of Loneliness from the *Skeleton Coast Safari*, directed by Jen and
Des Bartlett, a narrator explains what the Bartletts discover on the Skeleton Coast showing images of breathtaking scenery and of their life on
this desolate coast in Namibia. Although most of the documentary is narrated by a third-person narrator, Des and Jen Barlett's voices are heard
from time to time in off-screen commentaries.

> *Narrator:* For some plants, the safest place is at ground level, with much of the swollen
> leaf underground, to conserve moisture and avoid being eaten. Stone plants are peren-
> nials, storing water in their rounded leaves, virtually indistinguishable from the sur-
> rounding pebbles. Jen found the vastness around them especially inspiring, as she gazed
> across the empty plain.
>
> *Jen:* One feels humble and insignificant in the midst of this immense nothingness. But
> scanning with binoculars it's surprising what one can see on these seemingly barren
> plains, especially in the early morning, when the air is clear. This is the best time of all
> for spotting suricats or meerkats, those delightful little creature that live in groups,
> sleep in burrows, and emerge to warm themselves in the sun's first rays.
>
> *Narrator:* Meerkats find their food by digging through the dusty surface, looking for
> any of the multitude of insects and spiders that burrow to escape the dry heat of the
> day. Their ceaseless energy, and their almost comical alertness have endeared them to
> television audiences all over the world.

Sometimes narrators can also appear on-screen, especially when opening or closing a programme. In fact, the reader probably has in mind the typical travel documentaries in which the narrator is a known person and appears at the beginning and at the end of the programme. As Attenborough explains in León (1999), the presence of the narrator on-screen can also accomplish other functions, such as providing more information about the weather conditions or helping the audience imagine the actual size of a certain animal by comparing it to the narrator.

In spite of the fact that documentaries in which only a narrator appears are quite common, there is also a whole range of products in which different elements are combined so let us take a look at a few examples. The documentary *Mysteries of Easter Island* (Scheinfeld & Steen 2002) is a typical combination of off-screen narrator and excerpts of interviews or talking heads and in the documentary speakers appear on-screen. The documentary deals with the mystery that surrounds the enormous monoliths on Easter Island, and it tries to explain who made them and why and what the significance of these statues is. The narrator is never seen and the documentary is interspersed with excerpts of interviews with experts. These fragments of interviews are carefully selected and edited in order to recreate a story line, and questions are not heard, as is shown in the following transcription.

01:06:45 Narrator: The bulk of the known history of Easter Island is based on legends and myths passed along in the form of oral tradition. How the island was settled is no exception.

01:06:55 Patricia Vargas: *Oral traditions refer to a priest that had a dream and his spirit went to search for the new land that his people need. And he arrived to Rapa Nui, and he walked and his spirit all around the island, and he find out that, that it was the right island the king need.*

01:07:21 Narrator: The oral tradition of Easter Island tells of King Hotu' Matua, said to have been the original monarch of Rapa Nui and father of its unique culture.

01:07:31 Claudio Christino: *Legend says that Hotu Matua that was in trouble in his land, fled with, uh, all his retainers and, in 29 days, they discovered and settled in Easter Island.*

01:07:47 Narrator: The original settlers of Rapa Nui found the island very different from the way it appears today. It possessed all the natural resources to make it an attractive new home for the seafaring wanderers.

The series *Pathfinders: Exotic Journeys* (1996) resorts to the use of an off-screen narrator (Cheryl Tiegs), who appears on-screen at the beginning of the programme to introduce each episode. In every episode famous people are taken to different interesting locations in the world to experience true adventures.

Pathfinders: Exotic Journeys. Episode 13: Costa Rica

Tiegs ON CAMERA: Welcome to Pathfinders. When a Hollywood director wants a jungle scene an entire set is built so that nature doesn't interfere with the movie making. But, what happens when the same director goes into a real jungle? Well, that's what we'll find out on today's adventure as we take some of Hollywood's hottest film makers into the middle of the Costa Rican rainforest.

Tiegs OFF CAMERA: Costa Rica is a land bridge between North and South America. As a result the Central American country is as rich in wildlife variety as anyplace in the world. Here a patient explorer can spot over a half a million different plants and animals in a country smaller than West Virginia.

So what?

In Episode 13, the guests are Danny Elfman and the Hughes Brothers, the directors of *Menace II Society*, and they are taken into the middle of the Costa Rican rainforest. The narration is combined with excerpts of interviews with the guests, both on-screen and off-screen, and spontaneous dialogues in which the guests know that they are being filmed although they do not address the camera directly.

Another example is the documentary *Little Women: A Day in the Life of a Tweenager*, directed by Kate Townsend (2001). It portrays the life of a group of teenagers combining excerpts of interviews with psychologists, parents, marketing agents, clothes designers, etc., with pop songs, music and shots from the life of a group of girls. There is no narration and the story builds up interweaving all the previous elements. Let us take a look at a transcription of a fragment with excerpts of two interviews at the beginning (with Becky McBride, from the magazine *Cosmo Girl*, and Judith Edwards, child and adolescent psychotherapist), followed by a dialogue between a father and his daughter, who is coming out of a dressing room in Harrods in different outfits, and a dialogue between two young students and their science teacher, whom they meet by chance in the street.

> (10:21:22)
> McBRIDE: This group of girls has emerged, this group of girls that have been dubbed tweenagers, as a result of changes in society so of the increase in divorce, the increase in standards of living and the increase in the number of households where both parents work, so they're very cash rich but time poor and they compensate for that by spending more on their children.
>
> EDWARDS: You know it is something that everybody in society has to take responsibility for. I don't think one can just make it the commercial world's responsibility but I also think that they actually do need to take some responsibility for thinking about where there needs to be boundaries drawn and where one needs to say 'enough is enough, this is, this is too much'.
>
> LEIGH'S DAD: That one I don't mind. The other one was nicer
> GEORGIA: Do you like it?
> LEIGH'S DAD: No not really. […]
>
> (10:24:32) ALEX: This is our science teacher.
> SCIENCE TEACHER: Good morning.
> JADE: He's gone all red.
> SCIENCE TEACHER: I have, yes, it's very early.
> ALEX: Okay, we're going to go now. Bye.
> SCIENCE TEACHER: Bye.

Another type of non-fictional product are making-of documentaries or programmes related to the film industry in which narration, talking heads, spontaneous dialogues coexist with clips from famous films. This is the case with the series *Hollywood Inc.* (Day, 2002) as can be seen in this transcription of the first episode (minute 21:51), *Shut it Down,* which features different elements, as is shown in the following table.

Off-screen narrator *Visuals:* 8mm footage of the sun setting/ Music IN	*Narrator:* But the final decision rested with the Director who was on location in Toronto.
On-screen interview *Visuals*: interview with Bryan Singer (talking head)/ Music-out	*Bryan Singer:* Hugh Jackman flew into Toronto and when he walked in the room I was like – that's Hugh Jackman – mmm. And we sat down and did a screen test with him and Anna Paquin.

There examples need to be discussed no point in just quoting them here.

Clip from a film *Visuals:* Clip from *X-Men* showing Hugh Jackman talking to Anna Paquin	*Wolverine:* Get up. *Girl:* Where am I supposed to go. *Wolverine:* I don't know. *Girl:* You don't know and you don't care. *Wolverine:* Pick one.
On-screen interview *Visuals:* interview with Bryan Singer (talking head)	*Bryan Singer:* We were shooting in this – this building that we were using for one of the locations and some security guard – some young security guard comes up to me – and I don't think he even knew I was the director. I think he – as most people – thought I was a production assistant and he asked me – he – he kind of comes up next to me and quietly says, is that the guy they got to play Wolverine. And I though for a moment. Then I turned to him and I said yeah. And he said, cool. And then – then – as soon as the screen test was done I walked up to Hugh and offered it to him.
Off-screen narrator *Visuals:* Clip from X-Men showing Hugh Jackman fighting in cage.	*Narrator:* He looked good but nothing like the comic book hero. Everyone was nervous. What would the fans say?

Variations of this last type are, for instance, historical documentaries, in which narration and interviews are often combined with archive footage. In the documentary *Trial at Nuremberg*, by David L. Wolper (1964), for example, images from the trials are included in additon to the voice of an off-screen narrator. In *Voix Indiennes*, a TV documentary directed by Mari Corréia & Henri Raillard and broadcast by *Arte* in 1997, cinematic narration alternates among indigenous people talking to the camera, explicit interviews, internal/spontaneous dialogues among indigenous participants, and archive fragments about the colonization period, showing the first encounters between indians and missionaries. Or *Kurt and Courtney*, by Nick Broomfield (1998), in which interviews with potential murder suspects of the singer, the director's off-screen narration and archival films of Kurt Cobain as a child and adolescent were presented side by side.

bad English

After this elaborate discussion in which we have explained the types of speakers that documentaries can contain and hence their structure in terms of the agents that are given voices, we now return to the translator who has received one of these documentaries – hopefully with a good postproduction script – and starts translating it. Let us investigate how this task is carried out in the following chapter.

2.3 Suggested exercises

1. Watch an excerpt of a fictional product with voice-over. You can find
   several examples on satellite television (for example, Polsat or Polsat 2)
   or online. You simply need to search on YouTube using the keywords
   Poland / Polish and *voice-over* and different examples such as the trailer
   for *The Courage d'Aimer* <http://www.youtube.com/watch?v=dw
   Heu8LXTcg> will appear. Now read the following statement:

   > According to recent research (a poll by Inst. SMG KRC Poland, 2002) 50.2% of
   > Poles prefer voice-over and 43.4% opt for dubbing; subtitling has only 8.1%
   > supporters. (Bogucki 2004: 12)

   Answer the following questions:
   a) Why do you think Poles prefer voice-over?
   b) What are the advantages of using voice-over in fictional films?
   c) Are there any disadvantages?
   d) Do you think the situation will change in the near future?
   e) Is voice-over used in your country to revoice fictional products?
      And what about non-fictional products?
   f) What do you think about voice-over? Do you feel differently if it
      is used in non-fiction or fiction?
   g) Do you think it can be a useful practice tool to learn foreign lan-
      guages?

2. Puchkov, known as *Goblin*, has created many voice-overs which do
   not conform to the established norms, especially as far as expletives are
   concerned. More information can be found here: <http://en.wikipedia.
   org/wiki/Dmitry_Puchkov>.
   If you can understand Russian, identify the main differences of any of
   Puchkov's voice-overs compared to officially released voice-overs.
   If voice-over is not used in your country to revoice fictional products,
   try to find amateur translations either in dubbing or subtitling (called
   fandubs and fansubs) and compare them to officially released versions.

3. Select a ten-minute excerpt from a movie which contains both subtitles and voice-overs and compare the amount of information that is omitted in the subtitles and in the voice-over. In a research paper by Aleksonyte (1999), 14% of information is omitted in subtitles whilst in voice-over only 10% is lost. After analysing your data, do you agree with this statement? Why do you think voice-over reproduces the content more fully than subtitles?

4. Look for five different scripts on any of the numerous websites where they can be freely downloaded (for example, the Internet Movie Script Database, <www.imsdb.com>, Drew's Script O'Rama, <www.scriptorama.com>, Movie Scripts and Transcripts <www.moviescriptsandscreenplays.com> or the Panorama Archive, <http://news.bbc.co.uk/2/hi/programmes/panorama/current_archive/default.stm>. Compare the structure of the scripts and answer the following questions:
   a) Are they preproduction scripts, postproduction scripts or transcripts? How do you know it?
   b) Do they contain any extra information that can help the translator?
   c) How many speakers are there? Is there only a narrator? Are there various interviewees?
   d) Just by reading the script, what challenges can you predict?

5. Read the following two excerpts and try to identify the wrong transcriptions. Even without listening to the original soundtrack, you might be able to identify the problem.

(a)	While looking at a group of trees, a woman says: "These are Camiffera trees this is the mare of the Bible." Can you imagine what she is referring to?
(b)	Disaster can be avoided. In 1994, in Papua, New Guinea, fifty thousand people heated warnings and got away just one day, before the robaled volcano erupted. Even at Mount St. Helens, twenty thousand were evacuated, thanks to watchful scientists.

the odds of meeting a woman like this.

That this book refers primarily to a continental
reality is shown by the fact that the globalized
market of voice overs is not discussed, for instance
multilingual projects, centrally managed.
Also, voice-over for the Internet and for
commercial projects is not discussed either.
corporate products

Also, ftps>

3. Voice-over for postproduction (II):
The translation process

In the previous chapter we established a dichotomy between fictional and non-fictional products as far as voice-over is concerned and, after giving a few general ideas on each genre, we focused on the latter. We presented the variety of scripts and transcripts that a translator can receive when working for postproduction and we described the characteristics of the source text in terms of structure. In this chapter, we would like to focus on the translator who has received a documentary and is eager to start translating it. Non-fictional products such as the ones described in Chapter 2 can be transferred using various modes such as voice-over, subtitling or dubbing, to name the best known, but it will be the client – influenced by the country's traditions – who will decide which one to choose. For example, on Catalan television *(Televisió de Catalunya)* the narration soundtrack is usually substituted with the target language version, using the transfer mode called *off-screen dubbing* in this book. Interviewees, dialogues and other interventions are voiced-over, except for those dialogues delivered in a language different from the language of the programme. These dialogues are subtitled. Finally, when archive footage or scenes from a film are included, subtitling is also used. This is the case with documentaries on the French-speaking channels *Arte, RTBF, TF1* and *France3*, where interviews are often voiced-over in French and archive footage may be subtitled in the same language or in other languages. This combination of transfer modes implies that the audiovisual translator must be versatile and must adapt to the client's requirements.

In this chapter, we will tackle the main challenges that translators are confronted with when translating a non-fictional product for postproduction and we will focus on specific difficulties associated with the process of translating for voice-over and off-screen dubbing, the two commonest transfer modes in these types of products. Specific and shared features of both modalities will be differentiated, disregarding the peculiarities of other transfer modes which can be used in documentary translation but which are not the object of study of this book.

3.1 Voice-over in non-fictional products: specific features

Voice-over in non-fictional products can be used to revoice a wide variety of speeches. Sometimes, commentaries or narrations are voiced-over, that is, the original soundtrack is heard underneath the target language version, as a result of the client's wishes or of technical constraints which might prevent technicians to substitute the narrator's track with a commentary in the target language. However, as already mentioned, voice-over is most commonly used to revoice interviews and spontaneous excerpts and we will focus on these using different examples which illustrate the main features of voice-over.

3.1.1 Voice-over isochrony and oral features

The key element when translating an interview for voice-over is the need to create a fluent translation that is going to be read aloud and which fits in the space available, that is, which keeps "voice-over isochrony", in the words of Orero (2006a: 259). When people are interviewed or excerpts of spontaneous conversations are recorded, language is generally not planned and there is no previous script – although in some interviews there might be some preparation. This implies that language is generally full of hesitations, false starts, syntactic anomalies and other oral features which have to be changed into precise discourse so that the final audience understands it. Whereas in dubbing some of these oral features are maintained to recreate the illusion of true dialogues, in voice-over these elements are sacrificed, unless they are especially meaningful, in order to achieve voice-over isochrony and for the sake of clarity and intelligibility that is required by the genre. In the examples below, taken from two interviews included in the documentary *Hollywood Inc. Shut it down* (2002), translated from English into Catalan, repetitions are eliminated. In the first excerpt the speaker appears as a talking head, with an on-screen caption that reads "Bryan Singer. Director – X-Men, The Usual Suspects", whereas in the second excerpt it is Bill Mechanic, the then Fox Studio chief, who is speaking as a talking head.

Original	Translation	Back-translation
Bryan Singer You are trying to get things done – you, you've got multiple units going and, and, and you, you're running out of money – you are running out of time and the studio is breathing down your neck and you, you're just er – you just get real tense.	*Bryan Singer* Vols enllestir la feina, tens moltes coses en marxa al mateix temps, se t'estan acabant els diners, el temps i l'estudi t'està a sobre. Et poses molt tens.	*Bryan Singer* You are trying to get things done, you've got many things going, you are running out of money and time, and the studio is breathing down your neck. You get real tense.

In this case, repetitions such as "you, you've got" or "you, you're, er, you just get" become "you've got" and "you get", and a structure such as "and, and, and you, you're running out of money, you are running out of time" is translated as "you are running out of money and time".

Original	Translation	Back-translation
Bill Mechanic The first thing that happens is we find out that er – Eddie is afraid of animals so as soon as he reads the script we have this movie where he is seen with animals in virtually every scene and what are we going to and so a lot of the animals that he interacts with aren't real and there's a lot of cut aways and you know, that was one problem.	El primer que va passar és que vam descobrir que tenia por dels animals. Es llegeix el guió i veu que a la pel·lícula surt amb animals a gairebé totes les escenes. Què havíem de fer? Doncs molts animals que es relacionen amb ell no són de debò i hi ha molts plans de recurs. Això va ser un problema.	The first thing that happened is we found out that he was afraid of animals. He reads the script and he sees that in this movie he is seen with animals in nearly every scene. What should we do? A lot of animals that he interacts with aren't real and there's a lot of cut aways. That was one problem.

As for the second example, hesitations such as "er" disappear, as well as discourse markers such as "you know". Moreover, in this example one can notice that a single sentence in the original script with many linking words ("and") is reformulated in five sentences, in order to facilitate the comprehension of the original.

In the French documentary production *Carlinhos Brown*, directed by Claude Santiago and broadcast by *Arte* in 1996, the famous (and quite

prolix) Brazilian musician talks about his need to make music. Note that
the verbose expressions in his discourse are almost completely eliminated
in the translation.[38]

Original	Translation	Back-translation
Por que ... er ... as pessoas falam que eu crio muito? Eu nem considero que eu ... crio que eu realmente necessito né? Mas também ... o que sai de mim me ... me mantém ... do lado de fora. Ou seja, eu tanto poderia estar na cadeia como no hospício. [Why ... er ... do people say that I create a lot? I don't even think that I ... create that I really need it you know? But also ... what comes out of me ... keeps me ... outside. That is, I could be either in jail or in a mental institution]	Pourquoi dit-on que je fais beaucoup de choses? Pour moi, ce n'est pas la creation, c'est un besoin! Ce qui sort de moi me preserve de la prison ou de l'hôpital psychiatrique.	Why do people say that I do many things? For me, it's not the creation, it's a need! What comes out of me prevents me from prison or from the mental institution.

There are times, however, that original repetitions should be maintained
in voice-over versions, not so much because of content, but because of the
fact that body language, lip movements and tone of voice clearly emphasize such repititions. A good example is the French and German voice-
over versions of the emotional testimony by Berzó – the leader of the
project *Surfavela* – and also the title of the aforementioned Portuguese
production. The documentary is about Berzó and his ideal of driving kids
from Brazilian slums away from drugs and into sports such as surfing.
This testimony sequence (in Franco 2000b: 239–241) tells us how hard
the people from the slums work to build their own brick houses.

---

38 This example appears in Franco (2000b: 226) as an illustration of French voice-over
    tendencies to eliminate redundancy, as opposed to German voice-over tendencies to
    reinforce explicitation of content.

Original	French translation	German translation
Então o pessoal vai e já faz um barraquinho ali, aí passa um tempo, *rala rala rala, trabalha trabalha trabalha*, e monta a sua casa de alvenaria. [Then the people go and build a little wooden hut there, then time passes, (they) *work work work their ass off, work work work*, and build their brick house]	Quand ils l'ont trouvé ils construisent une bicoque, ils se mettent à *bosser bosser bosser comme des fous! Ils galèrent* et um jour ils *arrivent à se construire une maison en brique.*	Dann geht er und baut da eine kleine Hütte. Die Zeit vergeht. Er *plagt sich und plagt sich ab, schuftet und schuftet*, und baut sein *Ziegelsteinhaus.*

One does not need to understand the translated versions in order to see that the Brazilian Portuguese slang *rala* and its synonym *trabalha* repeated three times each are reproduced in French as *bosser bosser bosser comme des fous! Ils galèrent* and in German as *plagt sich und plagt sich ab, schuftet und schuftet*. The French translation even ended up being a little longer than its original, but the pace of Berzó's emotional testimony allowed for it to be so.

On the other hand, when not emphatic, the elimination of oral discourse markers does not mean that informal language or even strong language has to be eliminated. On the contrary, the final product has to maintain the tone or degree of formality of the original. However, the final product has to be intelligible and easily readable by the voice talent. In the same documentary mentioned above, Berzó talks about his previous drug addiction and does so in a wide shot, in which he appears with the boys who are participating in his project (Franco, 2000b: 251).

Original	French translation	German translation
Eu já usei cocaína, já fumei maconha, já fiz um monte de merda nessa vida. [I've already used cocaine, already smoked pot, already done a lot of shit in this life]	Avant je prenais de la coke, je fumais de l'herbe, j'ai vraiment *déconne.* [Before I took coke, I smoked pot, I went completely crazy]	Ich *hab'* Kokain genommen, Gras geraucht … ich *hab' schon* eine Menge *Scheisse* in diesem Leben gemacht! [I have taken cocaine, smoked grass … I have already done a lot of shit in this life]

Compared to French, the German voice-over makes a harder effort to represent colloquial style through the shortened pronunciation of the first person singular of the verb *haben* (*hab'*), the use of the informal adverb *schon* and the presence of the swear word *Scheisse*.

3.1.2 Accents in voice-over

Another situation arises when an interviewee does not have a good command of English or whatever the original language is and makes many grammatical mistakes. Whereas in dubbing, the translation would have to render this peculiarity for the sake of characterization, in voice-over these features generally disappear in order to facilitate the comprehension of the final audiovisual product.[39] This may, however, produce a clash between the image and the language version, even if content is the priority in voiced-over factual programmes. This is the case with Gordian Troeller's documentary *Rechtlos im Rechtsstaat* (1996), in which a poor old woman, her face full of wrinkles and no teeth whatsoever in her mouth, talks about her suffering because of the situation of landless people who are being forced to leave the land that they have occupied for some time. This simple and uneducated woman speaks poor Portuguese and with an accent typical of the countryside. Nevertheless, the German voice-over version leaves no trace of any of these markers despite the clues that her on-screen face provides to viewers.

Original	Translation	English translation
Qué dizê que nói num aceitemo saí de dentro de Camocim, com todo sofrimento, mai num dia será que a gente num lute, e num ganhe um um um tempo, a gente será que num vê que Jesus no poder da gente e a gente num fique situado no setor da gente né?!	Wir aber wollen Camocim nicht verlassen. Trotz aller Leiden, denn wenn wir aufgeben, und Christus uns nicht hilft, werden wir bald gar nichts mehr haben.	We don't want to leave Camocim. Against all odds, but if we give up and Christ does not help us, we will have almost nothing else.

39   Franco (2000b) has already pointed to the fact that in voice-over versions of documentaries, individual voices tend to be neutralized, so that interviewees end up talking similarly to commentators.

The Portuguese text is characterized by incorrect pronoun-verb concordance *(nói aceitemo)*, repetitions *(um um um)*, odd construction *(a gente será que num vê que Jesus no poder da gente)*, and a countryside accent (*nói* [nós-we], *mai* [mas-but], *num* [não-no]) that do not exist in the German voice-over.[40]

Regarding the accent of the original speaker in relation to voice-over delivery, one must take into account that accents are not generally kept in the voiced-over version. However, this convention is not universal since, in the UK for example, the voice-artist usually originates from the same geographical location as the person who is revoicing (Fawcett 1983), probably to enhance the authenticity of the voiced-over version.[41] Nevertheless, according to the special report published by the BBC (1985) and already mentioned in Chapter 1,[42] 60% of the audience prefer a British voice, as opposed to 14% who would rather listen to a slight foreign accent and 26% who answered "it depends / no preference".[43]

Paquin (1998), a professional translator working in Canada, confirms what has been explained so far.

> When a voice-over technique is used, the length of your text has to correspond to the length of the speaker's text, and even be shorter. That's when you see the speaker on the screen and a translation is supplied so that you hear the person speaking a foreign language in the background and an actor's voice is "voiced over" that, drowning it and

40 An interesting point also discussed by Franco (2000b:184) and related to this example, but not at issue here, is that original and translation present quite different perspectives. In Portuguese, we hear an old woman full of hope, determination, who foresees a better future while, in German, this woman becomes a discouraged lady who seems to be expecting the worst from life. Such a negative perspective was conveyed in the translated version by using translations of the original information with negative connotations: e. g. *wenn wir aufgeben* [*if we give up*] / *a gente lute* [*we fight*]; *Christus uns nicht hilft* [*Christ does not help us*] / *Jesus no poder da gente* [*Jesus on our side*]; *werden wir bald gar nichts mehr haben* [*we will have almost nothing left*] / *a gente fique situado no setor da gente* [*we are situated in our place*].

41 The BBC has gone even further in the voice-overs of the documentary *US troops target Sadr City*, broadcast on Tuesday, 15 May 2007, in the programme *Newsnight*. In this documentary, the voice talent not only mimics the accent of the original but also shouts and cries, imitating the original speakers' emotional states. (see <news.bbc.co.uk/player/nol/newsid_6650000/newsid_6658900/6658981.stm?bw=nb&mp=rm>).

42 We would like to acknowledge the help that we received from the BBC Written Archives Centre, which kindly provided us with a copy of this report.

43 This survey also detects that a 56% of the audience prefer what they call "spoken translation" (i. e. voice-over), rather than subtitles (34%).

taking its place, though the audience always hears the foreign language in the back. This provides the illusion that an interpreter has stepped in and is simultaneously translating what that person is saying. The studio actor / interpreter does not play a role with emotions as if it were acted out. He or she is merely an interpreter who repeats what the person is saying. Here the difference between a translator and an adapter is that the adapter must make this speech – which is often improvised – sound as if it were a well thought out discourse. No hesitations, no ungrammatical sentences, no interrupted utterances, no mistakes – unless they contribute to the scenario. The studio actor must have a flawless text, even if the character on the screen is hesitant or speaks English as a second language, not mastered very well. With documentaries, the constraints that require adaptation are thus mostly timing and grammatical soundness. Most documentaries have both narration *and* voice-over, but in all cases the main objective is to give the audience the illusion that they are watching an original production. (Paquin 1998)

3.1.3 Literal synchrony

When fitting the text, the translator must take into account that a few seconds might be left at the beginning and even at the end. This issue is quite controversial since there is no agreement on the number of seconds that should be left or even if it is necessary to leave them to simulate a simultaneous interpretation. Sometimes, a few seconds are left both at the beginning and at the end and, sometimes, no seconds are left anywhere, but the general practice seems to be to leave a few seconds at the beginning. Instead of talking about seconds, some professionals prefer to talk about "speech units" and this is what can be heard before the translation version begins. Each professional context is different and there are even translators who have never been asked to adapt their translation to the time available. If software is used in the future to translate for voice-over, it may be that the software programs take care of the start and finish automatically, as is the case for audio description software, which ensures that the audio fades at the beginning and at the end of the recording.

In order to make sure that the translation fits into the available space and can be easily read by the voice talent, reading it aloud is recommended. This technique cannot be substituted with an inner reading because of the fact that reading speeds vary and may affect synchronization. In fact, synchronizing the text can be a problem when there are many spontaneous dialogues and overlapping sentences. The translator then has to erase the irrelevant information and keep only the most important pieces of infor-

The future of voice-over?

mation. This was the case with the *Croc Hunter Diaries*, a series of documentaries in which scenes from everyday life in a zoo where shot. A whole series of overlapping interjections, such as *right* andor *OK*, had to be eliminated so that the meaningful text would fit.

Some authors have pointed out that literality is needed in those seconds that can be heard:

> The first and last words will not only be heard by the audience but very often be understood by some of them. Because of this, the translator, while struggling to render the message contained in the statement, will also have to give a much more exact translation of the two to four words at the beginning and the end. Sometimes even a well-considered semantic translation will not suffice and a literal translation will have to be given. (Luyken *et al.* 1991: 141)

This is the case especially for proper nouns, which, even if not understood by the audience in the foreign language, can nevertheless be spotted. The delivery of the proper noun in the voiced-over version must coincide with the proper noun in the original soundtrack. Although it is obvious that voice-over is a type of a partially "vulnerable translation" (Díaz Cintas 2003a: 46–47) and that people with a vague knowledge of languages might tend to mistrust non-literal translations of the few seconds in which the original soundtrack is heard, professionals consider that maintaining a genuine language structure is their top priority, rather than rendering a literal translation or reaching "literal synchrony" (Orero 2006: 261).[44]

3.1.4 Kinetic synchrony

Another aspect that the translator has to take into account is body language, which has to be synchronized with the text in order to reach what Orero calls "kinetic synchrony" (2006a: 258). In the documentary *The great pharaoh and his lost children* (De Vries 2001), of the series *Egypt: Beyond the Pyramids*, the narrator appears on-screen next to the fallen colossus of Ramesses the Great and says:

> This jumbled pile of huge stones was once a statue of Ramesses the Second, ruler of Egypt over twelve hundred years before the Christian era. His face gazes towards the

44   This and other facts are confirmed by the respondents of our questionnaire which was designed to map voice-over worldwide (check dossier in Chapter 6).

sky, and here's a shoulder. This was one of the greatest statues ever carved ant it was erected here at the Ramesseum, Ramesses' mortuary temple close to present day Luxor.

When saying "his face gazes towards the sky" and "here's a shoulder", the narrator points to both the face and the shoulder, and hence a translation that follows this order has to be created. As a matter of fact, the translator can indicate that gesture and text have to be synchronized by including a note or a time code. However, the inclusion of notes and time codes, and even of a list of characters, depends on the client, and translators can be asked to take care of different tasks resulting in different layouts. At the end of this section, after describing common challenges, authentic materials and different layouts used by professionals will be presented.

3.1.5 Action synchrony

Finally, as in all audiovisual products, the translator must be aware of the relationship between image and text in order to keep what Orero calls "action synchrony" (2006a: 259). This means that if the interview refers to an element on-screen, the translation must keep the synchrony and refer to this element as it is shown. A good example is found in the series *Monumental Vision.* In one specific episode shot in Sri Lanka, international sculptor Andrew Rogers explains where he will construct his geoglyphs: "We have three sites, two on one rock, one is here, Rhythms of Life here. We're going to build Pride over here, the Lion. And over here we're going to build the more vertical structure". As he utters this sentence, different sites where his three sculptures (*Rhythms of Life*, *Pride or the Lion* and *Ratio*, which is described as a "vertical structure") will be built are shown on a map, compelling the translator to keep the same order to achieve synchrony.

3.1.6 First-person vs third-person voice-over

All the previous elements apply to what has been called first-person voice-over, in which the translating voice keeps the same person of the translated voice instead of reporting the person's words. This means that if the speaker says "I think", the voice-over version will read exactly the same in the target language, instead of a reported sentence such as "The speaker thinks".

Visibility, Ethics?

However, sometimes third-person voice-over can be used and the information provided by the speakers is included in a reported voice-over, as already explained in Chapter 1.

For instance, in an excerpt from a documentary about the landless people from the south of Brazil entitled *Hundert Morgen Paradies*, directed by Lourdes Picareta & Philip Siegel (1995), we see the team shooting the documentary following the landless people in their march to the capital Porto Alegre, where they will camp and wait to talk to the authorities. The march is hard, people sleep in tents and barely eat. It is raining. The cameraman follows one of the men, Mr Oliveira, more closely. Mr Oliveira is walking and turning back to the camera to answer the cameraman's questions. Despite all the adversities that the landless people experience during the march, the cameraman asks if the man is enjoying it, if he thinks the march is worthwhile, to which the man replies "Yes, I think it's good" in Brazilian Portuguese. This interaction is put to the WDR German viewer as part of the off-screen commentary, whose narrator reports *"Er findet den Marsch gut"* [He thinks the march is good]. In the French voice-over provided by *Arte*, however, Mr Oliveira speaks for himself: "J'approuve la marche des sans terre" [I approve of the landless people's march], in first-person voice-over (Franco 2000b: 234–235).

As pointed out in the first chapter, when used deliberately first-person and third-person voice-over can lead to questions of visibility and ethics.

3.2 Off-screen dubbing of commentaries: specific features

Voice-overs generally coexist with the off-screen dubbing of commentaries, which, despite being apparently the easiest type of transfer mode, also present some peculiarities. Even though there is a general feeling that the professional *only* translates without paying attention to synchronicity constraints, the translator must take into account the recorded visuals and be aware of the relationship between image and text, as is the case with all audiovisual products, and maintain what has been called *action synchrony*.

Paquin explains his first experience as an audiovisual translator, and Aaltonen highlights the same constraints:

At first, I was given documentaries to 'adapt' into French. Well, there wasn't much adaptation to be done here. It was mostly straightforward translation. Except you had to take into account certain elements you would not necessarily pay attention to in a written translation. For instance, time and tempo. In the case of a narration, the translation has to follow the image and refer to its various elements as they appear on the screen. So, even if an inversion would be more appropriate in the target language, it may not be indicated if it does not suit the picture. The illusion to be maintained always is that the audience is watching an original production. (Paquin 1998)

When there is a narrator reading the text, the narration has to follow the appropriate scenes and the rhythm of the speech has to stay the same, in other words, the translator cannot squeeze in extra words when needed. (Aaltonen 2002)

Taking into account that the original is not heard, one could think that the translator has absolute freedom to alter the text. However, coherence with the images has to be maintained, as pointed out in the previous quotes. For instance, in the documentary *Hippo Beach* (2003), dealing with the life of hippos in Africa, the narrator says: "This mother and baby are caught between predatory crocs on the bank and belligerent bulls in the water". In a written translation, the translator could maintain the order "between predatory crocs on the bank and belligerent bulls in the water" or could change it to "between belligerent bulls in the water and predatory crocs on the bank", but in this specific context the image shows a group of crocodiles and, subsequently, a belligerent hippo bull in a lagoon, thus forcing the translator to keep the same order. In this case, when the language allows us to maintain the same structure, there is no problem, but for some language combinations such order constraints might pose a challenge to the translator, who has to juggle with words in order to create a translation which sounds natural in the target language and which conforms to the image.

As far as the language is concerned, the translator recreates the degree of formality of the original – generally (but not always) formal language in commentaries – taking into account that the written text will become an audiovisual product. In fact, an audiovisual product (created from a written script or not) is generally rendered in a postproduction written form so that the translator can create a new written version in the target language, which will be revoiced and received as the original product, that is, audiovisually.

Although no lip-synch and no voice-over synch are needed, the three main constraints when translating commentaries for off-screen dubbing

This term is being introduced here what does it mean? Is the statement correct?

are (a) that the translated text has to fit into the space available, that is, isochrony has to be retained, although there is more flexibility than in lip-synch dubbing, (b) that the translated text has to follow the image (action synchrony) and (c) that the translation has to be written, keeping the degree of formality and tone of the original but at the same time bearing in mind a speaker who will read it aloud. The audience will receive the translation as an audiovisual product, not a written one.

3.3 Voice-over and off-screen dubbing: common features

As for the common challenges encountered in the translation of both interviews for voice-over and commentaries for off-screen dubbing, there are a few remarkable challenges which are not unique to these transfer modes but which are nonetheless quite common and will therefore be highlighted below.

3.3.1 The quality of the original: form and content

Problems sometimes occur with regard to the quality of the original (problems relating to both the form and the content). The language in the original may be so poor and difficult to follow that the translator becomes an editor and has to rewrite the whole text. This demonstrates that the degree of faithfulness to the original can vary not only because of the country's traditions or the client's requirements, but also because of the features of the original, which can force the translator to act as a writer or a journalist.

> Translating a documentary differs from ordinary (fictive) film translation in what the audience would automatically expect of it: the 'facts' presented in the program being indeed true. Making sure that this is the case is the responsibility of the translator who is, in this sense, an editor. This means that the translator has to familiarize her/himself with the topic by reading about it, for example, or sometimes contacting a specialist in the area (doctors, dog-breeders, teachers, etc.). (Aaltonen 2002)

As for the content, this is quite a controversial issue. Why should the translator be held responsible for any errors in the original? Is it the translator's job to check that the content of the original is truthful? In our experience, the quality of the documentary will define the role of the translators. When detecting a low quality documentary, they usually try to find 'suspicious' information, check it and inform the client of any changes.

For example, in the documentary *Old Masters* a talking head comments on synaesthesia and the ability by some people to hear colours. After giving some examples of famous people (for example, the writer Nabokov), the talking head continues and provides examples such as listening to the colours of Van Gogh's picture *Sunflowers*, which can be seen in the National Gallery in London. Subsequently, the picture on the left appears on the screen.

Figure 3. Van Gogh's *Sunflowers*.

However, *Sunflowers* is not a single picture but a series of paintings. There are three similar paintings with fifteen sunflowers in a vase, and two similar paintings with twelve sunflowers in a vase. The picture which was shown is the one in the Sampo Japan Museum of Art, not the picture painted in 1889, which can be seen at the National Gallery in London (see picture on the right).

so what? Explain better

3.3.2 Terminology

Another item that translators highlight as a challenge in the translation of non-fictional products (Matamala forthcoming), especially in the translation of wildlife and scientific documentaries, is terminology and since voice-over is mainly used in this genre –at least in Western Europe–, it seems fair to say that terminology can be a challenge when translating for voice-over. This challenge is closely linked to another challenge, namely understanding the original, in the sense of grasping the concepts behind the speaker's words. In order to solve terminological problems and understand the original, the translator has to undertake a documentation process, which, once again, is not unique to voice-over or non-fictional products but which is extremely common. Let us have a look at a few examples.

A translator is asked to translate into Spanish *Reef Encounter*, a thirty-minute documentary from the series *Wildlife on One*, narrated by David Attenborough. The translator is given a complete postproduction script with four columns: vision (a short description of what is seen), T/Code (time codes), Sound (transcription) and Music (Time codes (TCs) where the music starts to play and stops). There is only a narrator and the style is formal, as can be seen from the following ten-minute excerpt. The main problem in this case is the vast number of fish species that appear.

Narrator (01:21): The coral island of Sipadan lies off the coast of Borneo in warm South-east Asian seas. The island is tiny, but it has masses of treasure lying just offshore. *Sea turtles* come here in great numbers to plunder it. For these seas contain the richest variety of life in the oceans. Turtles can make the most of a diverse menu. Crammed around the coral growths there are a few thousand varieties of animals and plants to choose from. […] There are many techniques to catch the drift, but the *porcelain crab* is particularly adept at fielding any morsel the ocean pitches at it. Underwater life has had time to specialize here. These waters are home to the oldest reef communities in the world, the birthplace of coral families. Millions of year of evolutionary refinement, together with the pressure of limited space, have spawned a natural paradise which is elaborate and finely tuned. Even voracious predators such as *big-eyed jacks* are part of a delicately balanced whole. Compared with the ancient founders of the reef society, turtles are gate-crashers. […] Other turtles compete for food, so more effort is required to find it. The *hawksbill*'s beak may be an ideal instrument with which to winkle out sponges, but it's a messy eater. Hawksbills seem to wreak havoc as they feed, but they're a great help to little fish, always on standby for the scraps which the turtles stir up. Areas of dead and broken coral are where a turtle likes to rummage. Their tool-like jaws are well adapted to picking out the worms, molluscs and crustaceans sheltering among the broken coral shards. Hundreds of fish benefit in the turtle's disruptive wake. The scavenging *sandperch* sits on the sidelines, waiting for something edible to emerge from a *goatfish* scrummage. But the *wrasse* defends its right to the scraps. With so much food just under the rubble surface, reef fish do not need to be long-distance swimmers. They've put their muscles where their mouths are, to uncover their prey. *Rock-mover wrasses* work like a pair of hands, using teamwork to capture tiny animals from under bits of dead coral. No stone is left unturned, the brute strength of a *Titan triggerfish* sees to that. Once the rubble rousers have moved on, the mantis shrimp must repair its burrow. Then it checks that the coast is clear … before venturing out for dinner. It collects a tiny snail before scuttling for cover. Sharks constantly patrol the reef wall, but some of the strongest jaws on Sipadan belong to the *bumphead parrotfish.*

As would be the case with any other type of translation, the first step in the translation process is finding the scientific names in Latin and, subsequently, finding the equivalents in the target language. A hindrance is that, when working with certain languages, an equivalent might not exist and the translator might have to act as a terminologist creating a new name for this animal (helped by a specialist, if possible), use a more general denomination or simply use the Latin name, depending on the type of product and the audience.

In the previous example, even though there are terms that the translator has to look up in specialized works, the text is easy to understand. The concepts in the text have not elaborated on in too much detail, even for someone who does not know anything about marine life, and the concepts are reinforced by means of images. However, sometimes documentaries might address specialists or university students (for example, *Open University*) and concepts may be more elaborate and difficult to follow for a lay audience and for the translator. The main problems then are understanding the text, grasping the main concepts and the relationships behind these concepts and, identifying the terms and their equivalents. This was the case with the documentary *Crater of Death* (Belderson 1998), in which the mass extinction of dinosaurs as a result of the impact of a comet is explained using the testimonials of scientists, who talk about different scientific topics (astronomy, botany, geology, etc.) in a fairly elaborate way.

As we can see, audiovisual translators in general and voice-over translators in particular have to deal with a wide range of topics which embrace all areas of knowledge (from tropical reefs to dinosaurs; from computer sciences to Chinese art; from the art of embroidery to cutting-edge technology), meaning that they are not specialists in a specific field but they must be able to obtain all the information needed about a specific area to understand the documentary and translate it in a extremely short period of time. This is undoubtedly one of the main characteristics of audiovisual translation.

In order to solve the terminological problems, audiovisual translators follow the same steps that they would if they were working with written texts and so they consult all kinds of resources, but have one additional element at their disposal: images. In fact, the audiovisual context can provide invaluable information such as the image of the animal whose target language name is required. Such an image allows the translator to capture the animal digitally and send it to an expert in the field along with the information provided by the text.

Although many documentaries – though not all of them – contain a great amount of terms, their degree of specialization is different, as well as the final intended audience, and this implies different types of translation strategies. Espasa illustrates this point with information provided by two translators:

> In the translation of a documentary for four- to ten-year-old children, the Catalan translator Jordi Mir decided to avoid the Latin scientific names of animals so as to foster comprehension, whereas in most documentaries he painstakingly researches the most appropriate scientific name (Mir 1999: 53). Likewise, in a documentary on Chernobyl and the effects of radioactivity on children, the translator Ramon Burgos considered using a specific term for the expression 'anti-sick serum' in the source-language text, but when he found out that the Catalan medical term was 'antiemètic', he deliberately avoided it as unintelligible to most lay spectators. It is worth noting that, generally speaking, some terms might be regarded as more specialized in English than in Romance languages. Besides, popular scientific English texts, both audiovisual and written, tend to paraphrase specialized terms, especially from Greek or Latin origins, such as 'hypertension', which might be glossed as 'raised blood pressure', or 'neuron', as 'nerve cell'; terms which in Spanish or Catalan may be used without further explanation. Similarly, in the Catalan translation of a documentary on Antarctica, the translator substituted well-known scientific terms for general terms in the original: 'the face of Antarctica is changing' was translated as 'l'ecosistema de l'Antàrtida està canviant' [the ecosytem of Antarctica is changing]; 'people doing plant research' was rendered as 'botànics' [botanists], and 'this place' as 'paisatge' [landscape]. These examples are offered, therefore, not as prototypical translation solutions, but as samples of how translation solutions try to fit the conventions of a specific genre in the target culture, taking into account its potential audiences. (Espasa 2004: 193)

The previous cases correspond to technical or scientific documentaries, but human science documentaries also pose challenges, even if terms can somehow be more hidden and difficult to identify. It is easier to identify as a term an *ornated horned frog* or *tschermigite* than identifying *transition*

what is this

home (according to Termcat[45] *llar de pas* in Catalan or *residencia temporal* in Spanish and according to the Google database *lar de transição* in Brazilian Portuguese) or *student portfolio* (*dossier d'aprenentatge* in Catalan or *portafolio de aprendizaje o del alumno* in Spanish or *dossiê do aluno* in Brazilian Portuguese) as units which have fixed translations.

c) Proper nouns

Other types of documentaries contain no terms but a great amount of proper names (for example, travel documentaries). Again, this is not unique to voice-over or even to audiovisual translation, but the problem is that even working for postproduction the transcription can be erroneous and the translator has to 'discover' what the speaker is saying, which can be quite easy when confronted with well-known names but rather difficult when confronted with more specific anthroponomy or toponymy (Matamala forthcoming). In fact, if we have a look at the previous examples of wrong transcriptions in Chapter 2, we can see that these are mainly transcriptions related of proper names.

A curious example concerning proper nouns occurs in the German voice-over of *Carlinhos Brown* (CB) (in Franco 2000b: 195–196) which could also occur in any off-screen dubbed commentary. The part of the transcription to watch out for is the final sequence of the documentary where the musician speaks off-screen while the viewer watches boys who are sitting on the pavement and playing different musical instruments; followed by the image of the same boys making a circle around CB, who is playing and running around the circle. We hear Brown's voice:

---

então … viva Luis Caldas! *viva* Sara Jane! *viva* Bel! *viva* Chiclete com Banana! *viva* Bel Machado *né?! viva* Jerônimo! *viva* Tony Mola! *viva* Ivan Huoi! *viva* Vovô! *viva* os Candomblés! *viva o* Olodum! *viva o* Ilê Aiê! *viva o* Apache *né?! viva* Muzenza! Arakêto! *viva os blocos de carnaval, os alternativos, e os da praça! viva os foliões! viva Cuba né?! viva tudo! essa é a grande celebração!*

[so … viva Luis Caldas! viva Sara Jane! viva Bel! viva Chiclete com Banana! viva Bel Machado right?! viva Jerônimo! viva Tony Mola! viva Ivan Huoi! viva Vovô! viva **the Candomblés**! viva the Olodum! viva the Ilê Aiê! Viva the Apache right?! viva Muzenza! Arakêto! viva the carnival groups, the alternatives, and those from the street! viva the fun-makers! viva Cuba right?! viva everything! this is the great celebration!]

---

45   Termcat can be found at www.termcat.cat

> *alors ... vive* Luis Caldas! Sara Jane! Bel! Chiclete com Banana! Bel Machado! *vive*
> Jerônimo! Tony Mola! Ivan Huoi! Vovô! *vive* **les Candomblés!** *vive* Olodum! Ilê Aiê!
> *vive* Apache, Muzenza, Arakêto! *les groupes de carnaval! les alternatifs! les gens de la rue!*
> *les fêtards! vive* Cuba! *vive le grand tout! c'est ça la grande célébration!*
>
> *es lebe* Luix Caldax! Sara Djein! Bel! *es lebe* Gilete com Banana *und* Bel Machado! *es lebe*
> Jerônimo! Tony Mola! Ivan Huau! Vovô, *und* **les Candômbles!** *es lebe* Olodum! Ilai!
> Apache, Musenza, Araguêto! *es leben die Trommeln des Karnevalls! die Leute der Straße!*
> *und diejenigen, die gerne Feste feiern! es lebe Kuba! es lebe das Leben! laßt uns gemeinsam*
> *ein großes Fest feiern!*

All proper names that appear in the original refer to either Brazilian solo singers or musical groups. Apart from considerations regarding the French and German pronunciations performed by the voice talents, there is a clear hint that the German text made use of the French version as a translation model. This is indicated by the fact that <u>os</u> *Candomblés* [*the Candomblés*], the name of a Brazilian musical group which is preceded by the plural masculine article *os* [*the*], was rendered in German as <u>les</u> *Candômbles*, as if the Brazilian noun was preceded by the French article *les*. Being a French production, it is very likely that the French voice-over came first, becoming then one of the translation models for the German voice-over.

again, so what? Is this a characteristic feature of proper noun translation

d) Captions and written information

Another element which cannot be neglected in translating non-fictional products are captions or written information on-screen. How is this information integrated into the final product? Audiovisual products do not generally take into account that they might be revoiced in other languages and be used to address an audience that does not understand written captions on-screen. In such cases, the translator has to translate all written signs and captions so that they can be introduced into the new version, either by means of another caption or by means of an off-screen voice. However, it is also true that lately some production teams have begun bearing in mind that the product might be sold to other countries and, instead of creating a version in which captions are integrated, an international version with no written captions is produced. Written captions are then included in the script delivered to the translator, who, exceptionally, will have to render into the target language something which is not seen on-screen but only on paper. A prototypical case is that of the name of the person speaking together with the person's affiliation.

e) *Cultural transfer*

Finally, an issue which is especially relevant when translating is adaptation in the sense of cultural transfer. Let us take a look at an example from the documentary *Pathfinders*.

> Cheryl Tiegs: Costa Rica is a land bridge between North and South America. As a result the Central American country is as rich in wildlife variety as anyplace in the world. Here a patient explorer can spot over a half a million different plants and animals in a country smaller than West Virginia.

The target audience might not know how big West Virginia is and, therefore, this reference might have to be adapted for a shared reference which occupies approximately the same area as West Virginia.

It could be said this is not unique to non-fictional films or the transfer modes analysed, and it would definitely be true. However, in documentaries the client might even give explicit instructions with regard to the adaptation of surfaces, etc. For example, the Catalan programme *60 minuts* broadcasts current affairs stories with a journalistic approach, rather than a more literary style so to speak. This is why translators are specifically asked to update texts (changing verbal tenses, if necessary), convert foreign currencies into euros in the commentary in addition to mentioning the original currency, and adapt comparisons concerning areas or places unknown to the target audience. The result can be an adapted or domesticated commentary, halfway between a so-called faithful commentary and a created commentary, as defined in Chapter 1.

Another view of cultural transfer is when the content is somehow adapted in the new language version in order to fit the perspective that the institutional channel advocates. The example (Franco, 2000b: 173–174) comes from the German documentary *Hundert Morgen Paradies* (already cited earlier on), whose German version was broadcast by *WDR* and later translated into French as *100 arpents de terre de paradis* and broadcast by *Arte*. Throughout the French voice-over, an explicit sympathy for the underprivileged small farmers' cause is observed, which is not present in the original. In the excerpt below, the commentator's voice is heard over the image of a meeting of the landowners, at which their union's new president is introduced. He is shaking hands with all the important and rich farmers.

Narrator: Landlose, das sind letztendlich nur einfache Kriminelle! Da ist sich auch der neue Präsident der Großgrundbesitzer dieser Region ganz sicher! Alle sind sie gekommen, ein General der Armee, der Polizeikommandant, sogar ein Abgeordneter der Regierungspartei. *Jeder hier hat Angst seine Ländereien könnten als nächste von Landlosen besetzt werden*

[Landless people, in the end these are simply criminals! This is what the new president of the big landowners of this region is sure of! All came, an army general, the police chief, even a deputy of the government's party. Each one here is afraid that his/her property could be the next to be occupied by the landless people]

Narrator: Les sans terres, de simples délinquants! Ce sont les propos du nouveau président des grands propriétaires fonciers de la région, *un groupe élitiste qui compte* un général d'armée, le commandant de la police, et même un député proche du gouvernement. *Tous ici craignent que leurs propriétés deviennent la prochaine cible, de la colère paysanne*

[The landless, the simple délinquents! This is the idea of the new president of the big landowners of the region, an elitist group that consists of an army general, the police chief, and even of a deputy close to the government. All here believe that their properties will become the next target of the farmers' rage]

In this fragment, the simple mention of a few members of the landowners' union in the original was not enough for the French translator to convey the power disparity in the conflict between the landowners and the landless people, so that *un groupe élitiste* [an elitist group] was added in the translated version. Thus, the positioning of the French discourse in favour of the underprivileged small farmers is emphasized even more in the translation than in the original itself. This can also observed in the last sentence of the fragment, where the translation of the neutral *Landlose* into the ironic *colère paysanne* [farmers' rage] emphasizes how the landless people's actions are interpreted by the landowners. In other words, the adjectives that have been added in the French version do make a point in the documentary perspective in that they provide some form of sympathy for the landless people. Although not changing the content drastically, the new commentary presents a free off-screen dubbing version. However, this is not a totally new and created one.

3.4 Translation layouts

The final product that the translator will deliver is a written text, which will be turned into an audiovisual product by the voice talent and the technicians working in the dubbing studio or for the television channel. As said before, the translator can be asked to perform different tasks (translation, spotting, linguistic control), involving different layouts. Let us investigate six different cases. The following examples do not have a back-translation because we are only concerned with format here and not content.

Example 1

On Catalan television the translator receives a documentary and has to render a translation with no time codes and no indications. Sometimes, the translator might add a footnote if that helps clarify the text, but the final product is a text with the following layout: the name of the character speaking on the left-hand side and the text on the right-hand side, occupying 60 characters.

"MYSTERIES OF EASTER ISLAND"

"MISTERIS DE L'ILLA DE PASQUA"

Traducció: Anna Matamala

NARRADOR En aquesta illa llunyana... envoltada per més quilòmetres d'oceà
que cap altre indret de la Terra... s'hi alcen monòlits enormes.

NARRADOR Durant gairebé mil anys l'origen i el significat d'aquestes estàtues
han estat un misteri i s'han fet múltiples conjectures. Un passat
catastròfic sotja el present. Quin significat tenen, aquestes
estàtues? Qui les va fer... i per què? Què va passar en aquesta illa
que la població indígena es va veure abocada al caos i a la mort?
Després d'anys de debats intensos, de teories i d'investigacions
arqueològiques, és hora de descobrir els misteris de l'illa de
Pasqua.

NARRADOR	El cinc d'abril de mil set-cents vint-i-dos a la tarda, una petita flota de naus holandeses, amb el capità Jacob Roggeven al capdavant, van perdre el rumb al sud del Pacífic. Sacsejats per la mala mar, el serviola va veure una petita illa, ben sola enmig de la immensitat de l'oceà. A les cartes nàutiques de Roggeven no hi sortia res.

Next, a linguist checks whether the language is adequate (i.e., conforms to client's norms even though this may not always be completely correct language) and creates a list of phonetic transcriptions of problematic words (e.g., proper names) to help the voice-talent. Finally, the text goes to the production department, where it will be prepared to facilitate the recording. There are two different procedures: (i) If there are different characters, the production department will cut the text into different takes, but the segments are longer than in fiction films (not only eight lines) (see example 1a), and (ii) If there is only a narrator, the production assistant includes time codes plus slashes to indicate pauses, as done in lip-synch dubbing (see example 1b).

Example 1a

THE CROCODILE HUNTER DIARIES. THE EARLY YEARS-7

TAKE 1

STEVE	(00.00) En aquest episodi dels diaris del caçador de cocodrils, la Becky, la Ilúdria, agafa una malaltia que ens trencarà el cor. El desfici de l'aparellament, i unes imatges impressionants dels rituals dels cocodrils. I en Wes, la llegenda, torna a entrar en acció. (00.17) Us convido a conèixer les interioritats del zoo d'Austràlia, amb la diversió, el perill i els drames quotidians que s'hi viuen.
STEVE:	(00.43) Els diaris del caçador de cocodrils. Els primers anys.
SUBT.	Parelles al zoo.

TAKE 2

STEVE   (00.47) Hem de salvar un animal i aquesta vegada és una serp perillosa i verinosa al bell mig de la ciutat. (00.52) Agafo això?

WES   (00.53) Sí. Per què no?

STEVE   Som-hi!

STEVE   (00.54) Aquest cop tinc els millors reforços del món. El meu millor amic, en Wes, ha tornat. La serp negra de panxa vermella és molt verinosa. De fet, és una de les vint serps més verinoses del món. (01.05)   De serps negres de panxa vermella se'n troben a les zones residencials, on tenen prou espai per sobreviure. Però aquesta ha arribat fins al bell mig de la ciutat, als jardins de la biblioteca pública. I això és un bon problema!

TAKE 3

STEVE   (01.20) És aquí. No em puc creure que en Wes, el meu millor amic, ja hagi tornat dels Estats Units. Ui, alerta! Hi ha anat a estudiar rèptils. A Austràlia ja era tota una llegenda en el món de les serps, però ara que ha tornat encara en sap més coses i és l'única persona del món que li confiaria la vida a l'hora de rescatar una serp. (01.46) Per aquí hi volta molta gent i no és lloc per una serp verinosa.

WES   (01.57) És de fa poc, oi?

STEVE   (01.58) Sí, de fa molt poc. Deu ser d'aquest matí. Quan l'ha trobat, la pell?

HOME ULL.   (02.03) Doncs quan m'han dit que vigilés la serp.

STEVE   (02.06) Ben fet! Aquí hi ha excrements... (02.10) El bibliotecari ha trobat una pell de fa poc i creu que la serp encara ronda pel jardí. Segurament no se n'ha anat gaire lluny. La serp té tanta por de la gent com a la inversa, o sigui que segurament encara està amagada enmig de les plantes. (02.27) No ha sigut gens agressiva, tot i que desenes, potser centenars de persones li han passat pel costat. Sort que ningú l'ha trepitjat sense voler! (02.41) És força important que trobem la serp abans que alguna criatura la trepitgi i hi hagi problemes. Ja l'he trobat. Surt i es mostra agressiva. Maleït sigui! No ho suporto, treballar amb aquestes serps tan petites! Et poden atacar tan de pressa que no tens ni temps de treure els dits. Vinga, cap a dins! Ja la tenim! Ben fet, bandarra!

WES   (03.06) Era sota la fullaraca, oi?

Example 1b

HIPPO BEACH

NARRADOR (00.28) Un hipopòtam de tres tones a trenta quilòmetres per hora... l'animal més perillós del continent africà. / Els hipopòtams són un niu de sorpreses. / Passen gairebé tota la vida a l'aigua, però no saben nedar. / (00.57) Tenen una aparença que convida a amanyagar-los, però amaguen un bon cop de geni. Els hipopòtams mascles són violentament territorials... i van armats amb ullals de trenta centímetres. / Per als hipopòtams mascles, l'èxit es mesura segons les propietats que tenen. (01.20) La vida a la platja és agradable, però, perquè sigui així, s'hi han de deixar la pell.

NARRADOR (10.01.23---10.01.28) LA PLATJA DELS HIPOPÒTAMS

NARRADOR (01.34) "Hipopòtam" significa "cavall de riu". Els rius són l'únic lloc on els hipopòtams se senten tranquils i segurs. / Tot i que respiren aire, se senten molt més relaxats sota l'aigua i poden aguantar la respiració fins a sis minuts seguits. / Als peus —que tenen parcialment palmats— hi tenen peülles, no ungles. / (01.59) Com que no saben nedar, als hipopòtams no els agrada no tocar de peus a terra. S'estimen més mantenir els peus ferms sobre el fons. / (02.18) Ara bé, no saber nedar no és un desavantatge tan gran com sembla... Els hipopòtams gairebé no pesen gens, sota l'aigua... És més fàcil aquesta mena de passeig espacial que no pas nedar contra corrent. / (02.34) El que sobta més és la rapidesa amb què es mouen a terra ferma. / No són corredors de fons, però poden fer una cursa prou ràpida en els cent metres. / (02.52) Quan un hipopòtam se submergeix, unes vàlvules especials li segellen automàticament les orelles i els orificis nasals, però això no implica que deixi de sentir-hi... o de comunicar-se... sota l'aigua. Aquests esclafits es produeixen dins les vies respiratòries tancades dels hipopòtams. S'assemblen molt als clics produïts pels dofins, i no és cap coincidència. / Investigacions recents demostren que els hipopòtams estan emparentats amb els dofins i les balenes, i que hi comparteixen un avantpassat comú. /

Example 2

Sometimes, the translator might be specifically asked to adapt the length of the speeches (in order to retain synchronization) and also to add time codes. This can be seen in the Spanish translation of *Ancient Voices. Cahokia: America's Lost City* (1999), directed by Jean-Claude Bragard, an example provided by the translator Judith Cortés. In this case, the translator was also asked to add a list of all the characters in the documentary at the end with an indication of their gender (male or female), and was also held responsible for the linguistic quality of the product, because no proof-reader checked it afterwards.

TÍTULO 2.54
VOCES DE LA ANTIGÜEDAD

NARRADOR 03.09
A las afueras de San Luis se construye una nueva autopista que tapará los secretos de una gran ciudad americana antigua. **03.18**

03.21
Antes de que sea demasiado tarde, unos arqueólogos de rescate investigan la zona. Sus descubrimientos son impresionantes. Tesoros como esta figurilla, o el cuerpo de un hombre encima de una capa de moluscos, rodeado por los cuerpos de más de 50 mujeres, que tal vez sean muestras de sacrificios humanos. **03.47**

03.53
A pesar de encontrarse a 16 kilómetros de San Luis, pocos conocen este lugar, llamado Cahokia. **04.01**

ABUELO 04.02
No tenía ni idea.

JOVEN 04.04
Es interesante, querría saber más. **04.07**

NARRADOR 04.09
A la mayoría de habitantes de San Luis les impactaría saber que viven encima de una de una metrópolis de 1.000 años de antigüedad. Mayor que las ciudades medievales de Londres o de Roma, Cahokia rivalizó con los centros rituales aztecas del sur. ¿Cómo era la ciudad de Cahokia? ¿Quién la construyó? ¿Por qué la historia la olvidó? **04.35**

TÍTULO 04.48
CAHOKIA. LA METRÓPOLIS PERDIDA DE AMÉRICA.

TIM PAUKETAT 04.56
Cahokia empezó como un *big bang*. Fue algo explosivo. La gente se desplazó hasta Cahokia en un período muy corto de tiempo, posiblemente en unos pocos años. Fue el inicio de un nuevo mundo. **05.15**

Example 3

In the third example, the translator received a VHS, in addition to a script which was sent by e-mail, containing the series *Egypt: Beyond the Pyramids*. She was told that someone would adapt the translation afterwards and that she simply had to take care of the translation indicating OFF when the speaker was not visible on camera and ON when the speaker was visible on camera. The result was the following: on top, the transcription of the original; on the left-hand side, the translation delivered and, on the right-hand side, the final product, which was recorded and which was transcribed from a DVD. Even for those readers who cannot understand Spanish, it is obvious that the adapted product differs considerably from the original, including not only stylistic changes but also modifications to the content. The 500 miles from the original (which is equivalent to 804.672 km) becomes 800 km in the translation and 680 km in the final adapted version that is broadcast.

Peter (off): Five hundred miles south of Cairo, a stunningly beautiful temple perches on the edge of the vast desert. Within its walls lies a toppled thousand-ton image of one of Egypt's greatest kings ... who left behind one of Egypt's greatest mysteries – the fate of his many children. It is a saga that some believe will end in a remote tomb in the legendary Valley of the Kings.

Peter (on): This jumbled pile of huge stones was once a statue of Ramesses the Second, ruler of Egypt over twelve hundred years before the Christian era. His face gazes toward the sky, and here's a shoulder. This was one of the greatest statues ever carved and it was erected here at the Ramesseum, Ramesses' mortuary temple close to present day Luxor.

Peter (off): In the fifth century AD, the Coptic Christians are believed to have pulled down the statue. And over the centuries, earthquakes further destroyed the fallen pharaoh's likeness. Of course, Ramesses had the last word. His image today is anything but a colossal wreck.

Peter (on): This statue better symbolizes the role of Ramesses the Second in Egypt's history. He was a king who led his armies to victory, who built the most astonishing structures all over Egypt. He ruled for sixty-seven years ...

NARRADOR (OFF)	**NARRADOR (OFF)**
A 800 kilómetros al sur de El Cairo, un templo extraordinariamente bello está suspendido al borde de un gran desierto.	A 680 kilómetros al sur de El Cairo, se alza un templo extraordinariamente bello situado al borde mismo del desierto.
En su interior, se encuentra una imagen derruida de mil toneladas de uno de los grandes reyes de Egipto, que dejó tras de sí uno de los grandes misterios de Egipto: el destino de muchos de sus hijos. Es una saga que algunos creen que terminará en una tumba remota en el legendario Valle de los Reyes.	En su interior, caída en el suelo, hay una imagen de mil toneladas de uno de los mayores faraones de Egipto, que dejó tras de sí un gran misterio: el destino de muchos de sus hijos. Misterio que algunos creen que podrá resolverse cuando se conozca mejor una remota tumba del legendario Valle de los Reyes.

NARRADOR (ON)
Este montón de piedras enormes en desorden fue en su tiempo una estatua de Ramsés II, el gobernador de Egipto aproximadamente en 1.200 A.C. Su cara mira al cielo y aquí tenemos un hombro. Es una de las mayores estatuas jamás esculpidas y se erigía aquí, en el Rameseum, el templo mortuorio de Ramsés, cerca de la actual Luxor.

NARRADOR (OFF)
Se cree que en el siglo V D.C, los cristianos cópticos derribaron la estatua y que con el paso de los siglos, los terremotos acabaron de destruir el retrato del faraón caído.

NARRADOR (ON)
Sin duda, Ramsés tuvo la última palabra. Hoy su imagen constituye unas ruinas colosales.

Esta estatua es la que simboliza mejor la función de Ramsés II en la historia de Egipto. Fue un rey que hizo vencer a sus ejércitos y que construyó las estructuras más asombrosas por todo Egipto. Gobernó sesenta y siete años.

NARRADOR (ON)
Este montón de <u>enormes</u> piedras en desorden fue en su tiempo una estatua de <u>Rameses</u> II, <u>que gobernó en</u> Egipto <u>hacia el</u> 1.200 <u>antes de nuestra era</u>. Su cara mira al cielo y aquí tenemos un hombro. Es una de las mayores estatuas jamás esculpidas y se <u>levantaba</u> aquí, en el <u>Rameseo</u>, el templo <u>funerario</u> de Ramsés, cerca de la actual Luxor.

NARRADOR (OFF)
Se cree que en el siglo V, los cristianos <u>coptos</u> derribaron la estatua y que con el paso de los siglos, los terremotos acabaron de destruir <u>los restos</u> del faraón caído.

NARRADOR (ON)
<u>De todos modos</u>, <u>Rameses dijo</u> la última palabra <u>y hoy</u> su imagen constituye una ruina colosal.

Esta estatua es <u>el mejor símbolo del papel</u> de <u>Rameses</u> II en la historia de Egipto. Fue un <u>faraón</u> que <u>llevó</u> sus ejércitos <u>a la victoria</u> y que construyó <u>grandes monumentos</u> por todo <u>el país</u>. Gobernó sesenta y siete años.

Example 4

Bowling for Columbine (2002) was a special documentary film directed by the well-known American Michael Moore which was released in cinemas and later on DVD. Voice-over was used for the interviews and the dialogues in the film, whereas Michael Moore's voice disappeared when he was off, in what we have called off-screen dubbing. In this case, as in the case with lip-synch dubbing, there was a translator and an adapter, who introduced the typical dubbing codes, as shown in the following examples.

Translation

BOWLING FOR COLUMBINE

HOMBRE: La Asociación Nacional de Rifle ha producido una película que seguramente hallarán de gran interés. Vamos a verla.

MICHAEL: Era la mañana del 20 de abril de 1999, muy similar a cualquier otra mañana en Estados Unidos. El granjero hacía sus tareas. El lechero hacía sus entregas. El Presidente bombardeaba otro país cuyo nombre no sabríamos pronunciar. En Fargo, Dakota del Norte, Kerry Mc Williams salía a dar su paseo matinal. En Michigan, la Sra. Hughes daba la bienvenida a sus alumnos a otro día de clase. Y en una pequeña ciudad de Colorado, dos niños iban a jugar a los bolos a las 6 de la mañana. Sí, era un típico día en los Estados Unidos de América.

INSERTO¿?:	BANCO NORTH COUNTRY
CAJERA:	¿Puedo ayudarle?
MICHAEL:	(ON) Sí, vengo para abrir una cuenta.
CAJERA:	¿Qué tipo de cuenta querría?
MICHAEL:	Quiero la cuenta por la que dan un arma gratis.
CAJERA:	Muy bien.
MICHAEL:	Había visto un anuncio en el diario local de Michigan en el que decía que si abrías una cuenta en el banco North Country te regalaban un arma.
CAJERA 2:	Hace un depósito y le regalamos un rifle. Ahí tiene el folleto, puede mirárselo...
MICHAEL:	Mjmm.
CAJERA 2:	En cuanto comprobemos antecedentes y todo eso, podrá llevárselo.
MICHAEL:	Bien. Bien. Muy bien. Em... esta es la cuenta que quisiera abrir.
CAJERA 2:	Tenemos una cámara acorazada que siempre contiene unas 500 armas.
MICHAEL:	¿Tienen 500 de estos en su cámara?

Adaptation

BOWLING FOR COLUMBINE

(JUGANDO A LOS BOLOS POR COLUMBINE)

PRESENTADOR: La Asociación Nacional del Rifle ha producido una película... que seguramente será de su interés./ Vamos a verla.

MICHAEL: (V.O) Era la mañana del 20 de abril de 1999, una mañana cualquiera en los Estados Unidos./ El granjero llevaba a cabo sus tareas./ El lechero hacía sus entregas./ El Presidente bombardeaba otro país cuyo nombre no sabríamos pronunciar./ En Fargo, Dakota del Norte, Kerry Mc Williams salía a dar su paseo matutino./ En Michigan, la Sra. Hughes daba la bienvenida a sus alumnos en el colegio./ Y en una pequeña ciudad de Colorado, dos niños iban a jugar a los bolos a las 6 de la mañana./ Sí, era un día típico en los Estados Unidos de América.

INSERTO: BANCO NORTH COUNTRY

CAJERA: (OFF) ¿Puedo ayudarle?

MICHAEL: (OFF) Eh, (ON) sí, venía para abrir una cuenta.

CAJERA: Claro. ¿Qué tipo de cuenta deseaba?

CAJERA 3:   (P) Voy a llamar a la agencia número 12, ¿vale?

MICHAEL: Ehm, quiero la cuenta por la que dan un arma gratis.

CAJERA: Muy bien.

MICHAEL: (V.O) Había visto un anuncio en el diario local de Michigan en el que decían que si abrías una cuenta en el banco North Country, el banco te regalaba una arma.

CAJERA 2:   Si hace un depósito, le regalaremos un rifle. (OFF) Aquí tiene el folleto. Échele un vistazo.

CAJERA 3:   (P) (OFF) No, eso fue ayer.

CAJERA:	(P) (OFF) Sí, enseguida.
MICHAEL:	(OFF) Hm-hm. Ya.
CAJERA 3:	(P) (OFF) Sí, exacto. Estaba buscando esa transferencia. Muy bien, ahora me quedo más tranquila.
CAJERA 2:	(OFF) En cuanto comprobemos (ON) antecedentes y todo eso...
MICHAEL:	Sí, sí.
CAJERA 2:	... podrá llevárselo.
MICHAEL:	Muy bien./ Ehm, ésta es... ehm, la cuenta que quisiera abrir.
CAJERA:	(P) (OFF) Sí, gracias, enseguida le paso. Un segundo, por favor.
CAJERA 2:	(OFF) Tenemos una cámara acorazada que siempre contiene... (ON) unas 500 armas.
MICHAEL:	(OFF) ¿Tienen 500 rifles en su cámara?

In view of the fact that the reader might not be able to read Spanish, some comments will be made about the adaptation and the final version which was broadcast:

1. In the adapted version, symbols used in lip-synch dubbing are used such as the symbol used to indicate that the speaker is off-screen (OFF) or on-screen (ON). The symbol (P) indicates an overlap and (V.O.) refers to an off-screen commentary. It is remarkable that in the professional world the term voice-over, borrowed from the field of Film Studies, is used to refer to an instance of off-screen dubbing.
2. In the adapted version, a slash is used to indicate pauses in the discourse, as also seen in example 1.
3. The adapted version contains more text than the translation, which did not include almost unintelligible words.
4. The adapted version includes hesitations *(ehm)* which, as is generally the case with voice-over, are eliminated in the final version that is broadcast.
5. In order to achieve voice-over isochrony, some sentences from the translation are shortened: *Bien. Bien. Muy bien* simply becomes *Muy bien*. The meaning is not altered *(OK. OK. Fine > Fine)* and synchrony is achieved.

Example 5

In the German company Titelbild[46] the translator is asked to deliver a translation with a special layout in order to facilitate the recording. Time codes – just those that are absolutely necessary and not too many –, information on pronunciation, notes on delivery speed and important visuals that coincide with the text are added on the left-hand side, but no ON/OFF symbols are used. On the right-hand side the name speakers' names are written in bold, next to the text spoken aligned with the time codes. Clear indications of speaker pauses are introduced by means of new paragraphs or the # symbol. A large font (at least 12 points) is used and no last-minute handwritten changes may be added, because they could confuse the speaker. Paragraphs are not split over consecutive pages and no hyphens are used.

Cues TCR	Name (bold): text with clear indications of speaker pauses (line break or #)
+ information on pronunciation	
+rhythm (delivery speed)	
+rel. images (important visuals that coincide with the text)	

Example 6

In the last example, which has been already pointed out as the future of this transfer mode, a translator working in the UK is asked to do a 'voice-over', meaning to both translate and record the translation. In this case the profile of the translator is extended to that of translator and voice-artist. In

---

46 This information was provided by Mary Carroll in a seminar on voice-over and commentary held at the 2005 MUTRA Conference in Saarbrücken (Germany).

cases, in which the material is available in digital format, the translator works with a special software program. Softel's audio description station (www.softel.co.uk), for example, can be used in voice-over or even a simple Windows Movie Maker, which allows voice-overs to be recorded.

The following picture shows the screen of the Softel software program, in which, during the recording stage, the spoken text is saved in WAV files. This software is completely Windows 2003 compliant and works with Windows XP software products. It allows for time coding, translation and recording and the final recording can also be done using this software.

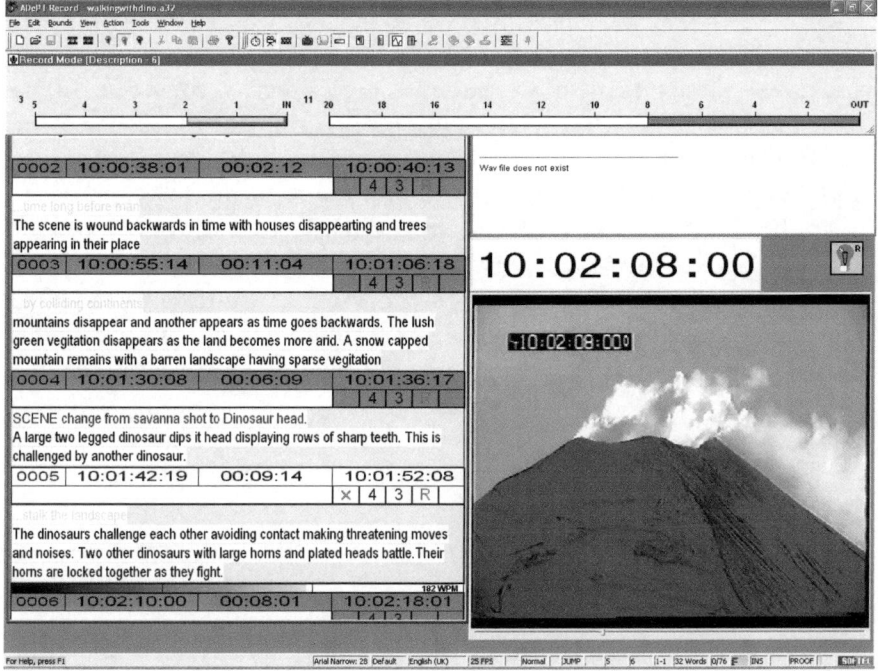

Figure 4. Screen taken from the Softel software program.

3.5 Conclusion *Summary*

In Chapters 2 and 3 we have seen the process of translating a postproduction product – mainly documentaries – for both voice-over and off-screen dubbing, which are the two main transfer modes used when translating this type of audiovisual text. The distinctive feature of postproduction is that translators are usually given a script or transcript of a varied nature, which corresponds to a finished product that usually gives voice to different speakers depicting different types of discourse that can include mistakes relating to both form and content. With regard to voice-over specifically, various types of synchrony have been identified, such as voice-over isochrony – achieved by means of language rewordings –, kinetic synchrony, literal synchrony and action synchrony, the last form of synchrony being a feature shared with the off-screen dubbing of commentaries. As far as the specific features of the translation of documentaries are concerned, tightly linked to voice-over and off-screen dubbing due to the relationship between this genre and these transfer modes in Western Europe, terminology and proper nouns have been recognized as two of the main hindrances, entailing an arduous documentation process, even more difficult when transcriptions are inaccurate. In the last section of this chapter, different translation layouts were presented that are used in different professional contexts.

3.6 Suggested exercises

1. Underline the changes that the original version has undergone in the voice-over. What type of units disappears in order to reach isochrony in the target-language version?

Original version	Voice-over	Back-translation
I guess my interest with this building starts with simple curiosity. I mean, it's so well preserved, and	El interés por este edificio empieza por curiosidad. Está tan bien conservado que sería estúpido no saber	The interest with this building begins with curiosity. It's so well preserved that I would be

it's silly not to know very much about what made it tick, why it was built. I'm interested in what it tells us about the religious mentality of the ancient Egyptians. The only safe way you can begin to understand what the significance of a building like this is to understand what they carved on the walls. *(Source: Egypt. Beyond the Pyramids. Mansion of the Spirits)*	con exactitud por qué se construyó. Me interesa saber qué nos puede contar sobre la mentalidad religiosa de los antiguos egipcios. La única forma segura de empezar a comprender la importancia de un edificio como este es saber qué esculpieron en las paredes.	silly not to know exactly why it was built. I'm interested in what it tells us about the religious mentality of the ancient Egyptians. The only safe way you can begin to understand what the significance of a building like this is to understand what they carved on the walls.

Now select an excerpt of a voiced-over interview in your mother tongue and try to identify the strategies used to reach voice-over isochrony.

2. Watch this excerpt from the BBC's *Newsnight*, broadcast on Tuesday, 15 May 2007. <news.bbc.co.uk/player/nol/newsid_6650000/newsid _6658900/6658981.stm?bw=nb&mp=rm>.

As you can see, the voice talent mimics the accent and intonation of the original. Discuss if this practice is also followed in your country and if it enhances authenticity and credibility.

3. Watch five different voice-overs in your mother tongue, either from interviews or documentaries, paying attention to the beginning and the end of each speech. You can find several examples or watch online television on the following websites:

   – <news.bbc.co.uk/2/hi/programmes/newsnight/newsnight_inter views/default.stm> (English)
   – <www.arte.tv> (French and German), <www.tv3.cat/seccio/3ala carta/> (Catalan)
   – <www.rtve.es/> (Spanish)
   – <http://globosat.globo.com> (Brazilian Portuguese)

Now answer the following questions:

a) When the original is heard, are the first and last words literal?
b) Do you think the translator should have been more/less literal?
c) Can you hear the original voice at the beginning? And at the end? For how long?
d) Is there really a need to hear the original voice?

4. Watch the news bulletins from three different television networks in your country and answer the following questions.

a) Has voice-over been used in all the news bulletins? Are there any differences depending on the television channel?
b) What types of speakers have been revoiced using voice-over?
c) Have any other transfer modes (dubbing, subtitling, simultaneous interpreting, etc.) been used? Can you identify any norms that dictate the use of any of these transfer modes?
d) Is voice-over used in the first person or in the third person? If both, are there any differences in usage?

5. Watch three different translated documentaries in your mother tongue: a historical documentary, a science documentary and a documentary on a popular and controversial topic. Several examples can be found on the following websites:

–   <www.bbc.co.uk/bbcfour/documentaries/>
–   <www.bbc.co.uk/sn/>
–   <www.channel4.com/documentaries/>
–
–   <http://www.bbc.co.uk/sn/tvradio/programmes/horizon/>

Now answer the following questions:

a) Are there any differences in terms of transfer modes used?
b) Are the same transfer modes used for the same types of speakers? For example, are all interviewees voiced-over?
c) Are the challenges in each documentary different? Why?

6. A significant number of documentaries contain names of fauna and flora. Try to identify these terms in the following excerpt, look for the scientific equivalents in Latin and then find the vernacular name in your own mother tongue.

After a stretch, he [the jackal] tries his luck at getting a sandgrouse for lunch. Their twenty minutes drinking time over, the last of the soundgrouse leave in a body: but there is another visitor to the pool – a lanner falcon. It is better equipped than the jackal to exploit this source of food. A puff adder comes down for a drink, gliding round the pool to the end where the tiny trickle of water emerges from the ground, the cleanest part of this popular watering place. All day, ostriches visit the spring, arriving in twos and threes, until there are sometimes as many as thirty-five there at once. A Ludwig's bustard joins the assembly. Gemsbok, true desert antelope, come to the spring in ones and twos, often from a great distance. The ostriches are plagued by biting flies and they take turns to relieve each other of the nuisance. His vigils at the spring revealed to Des the vital importance of this tiny, reliable waterhole in the vastness of the gravel plains. *Source: "The Skeleton Coast Safari". Broadcast on Televisió de Catalunya (TVC).*

4. Voice-over for production

The previous chapter dealt with translations which are done in the postproduction stage of the preparation of an audiovisual product, that is, once the programme has actually been created. While in the postproduction stage the audiovisual text is a finished product, the production stage usually deals with rough footage, different takes, unedited texts and, in general, materials which are still drafts. Hence, voice-over translations for production deal with unedited material – rough footage – which will go through many processes and changes before it is edited, voiced and broadcast. For this reason, the approach to this chapter is different from the previous chapter. While for postproduction translators are able to work from a final text – audiovisual and written – to be translated, for production translators find themselves confronted with a number of possibilities, which are reflected by the approaches to the translators' working practices and the translations. Translators may have at their disposal only excerpts from the original sent to be translated and which will subsequently be used and shown in the final programme. On some occasions, when an interview is performed through an interpreter, it may be that the target text (TT) produced by the interpreter is the same text that is used for the voice-over,[47] but in such cases there is no work for the translator.

All these features and variables will be described in this chapter using a selection of examples taken from authentic materials. The focus will be on the voice-over of interviews, paying special attention to both new challenges posed in this area and the off-screen dubbing of commentaries.

---

47   Many examples of this practice can be found in the BBC webpage, where journalists sent to foreign countries don't speak the language and use interpreters, such as with Evo Morales or Hugo Chavez.

4.1 Voice-over of interviews

Let us start with the most common case and situation, namely the translation of an interview, a press conference or some declarations that a famous character has made to the press, and where there was no interpreter involved. The process of translation is as follows: The translator receives the tape without a transcript – when writing this chapter, in 2005, in Spain we still worked with VHS – and this tape contains the ST interview. The source-text (ST) interview is seen in its entirety, documentation for terminology takes place at this stage, and then the translation can begin. By listening, rewinding and listening over and over again, the translator creates a document which will function as the continuity list along with the TCRs.[48] The translator will hand in the translation in rough – though much work will have been carried out to adapt the language from oral and colloquial language to a form of language that will be read aloud by a voice-artist and this is something which is neither written nor oral but somewhere in between the two modes.

This type of translation shares many features with postproduction voice-over. To start with, the text, as is the case with any audiovisual translation– has to be faithful to the image. This means that adjustments may have been made to the discourse to match the facial gestures or body language to what is said and translated (kinetic synchrony). That will happen, for example, when the thumb and index finger are used to express a given size of something that he or she is talking about, or when the interviewee touches his head to refer to the need of an intellectual process. In such cases the discourse must coincide.

In the following example from the *TVE* programme *Redes* (2004) we can see the TCR inserted in the main body of the text. This then functions as the indication given by the translator to synchronize the image with the translation.

---

48   As far as we have been able to check, there is no universal layout for continuity lists
     for voice-over for production.

Example:
To the question on how we learn to use the right and left hand the reply was as follows:

With much difficulty. Children confuse right and left all the time. By eleven is when they start distinguishing them. The problem between left and right is very subtle. If I look at myself this is my right hand, but if I look at you I see the hand on the same side as mine which is your left hand, because you have turned round. If your back was touching my back your right hand will be on the same side as mine, but this is not true. When you ask me: where is the right? I have to check if it's mine or yours. This is why we have to talk about the world view from the point of view of the subject, that is, from my point of view, or the point of view of the object: your right hand.

Translation
54:00
MacManus:

Con mucha dificultad. Los niños se confunden constantemente entre la izquierda y la derecha [54:07] y sólo cuando tienen unos 11 años comienzan a distinguirlos correctamente. El problema con la izquierda y la derecha es muy sutil. Si me examino a mi mismo, esta es mi mano derecha [54:31]. Si te miro a ti, y veo la misma mano en el mismo lado que la mía, es tu mano izquierda, y esto es porque te has dado la vuelta. Si me estuvieras dando la espalda tu mano derecha estaría en el mismo lado que la mía, pero no es así. Cuando me preguntas ¿dónde está la derecha? [56:23] tengo que aclarar si se trata de tu mano o la mía [57:01]. Por eso tenemos que hablar de la visión del mundo desde el punto de vista del sujeto, es decir, desde mi punto de vista, o desde el punto de vista del objeto: tu mano derecha.

And though synchronicity is not observed as in dubbing with lip-synch, it must be remembered that the professional voice-artist has to keep the reading delivery in line with certain special visual images (action synchrony). Moreover, while the translator produces a written text, the text will be delivered by a voice talent, hence it has to be a form of language written with that in mind. Therefore, a feature of this type of translation – shared with voice-over for postproduction – is the change from oral and colloquial language to a syntactically correct and precise discourse to be read aloud. Most elements which characterize conversational language are deleted. Repetition is one of the elements which disappear in order to allow the spoken translation to fit the original discourse, taking into account the initial seconds during which the original's speaker's voice can be heard in the original language (voice-over isochrony). Here is an example from an

interview with Ted Nelson, which was broadcast on the Spanish TV programme *Redes* (November 2005, La 2[49]).

Original: Yeah, right, this is an interesting sort of question, because as you know … you
know, this term, ehhh technology is in itself a perfect term because is definitive. Yeah:
what we call technology was invented by a guy who had something else in mind, sort of
competition in mind, someone who wanted to start a monopoly or something. So we
have to watch it and keep track of it because it's too fuzzy.

Voice-over: La palabra tecnología en sí es equívoca, porque sugiere que es definitiva, que
es correcta y que no se puede cambiar. Sin embargo eso que llamamos tecnología lo
inventó alguien que tenía algo en mente, con una ventaja competitiva, alguien que a
menudo quiere crear un monopolio. De manera que lo que llamamos tecnología es
algo con lo que deberíamos ser cautos.

Back-translation: The word technology itself is erroneous because it suggests that is definitive, correct and unchangeable. Nevertheless that which we call technology was invented
by someone who had something in mind, with a competitive advantage, and wants to
create a monopoly. Hence what we call technology is something we should be careful with.

The text in the example above shows some of the many transformations
which a colloquial answer may undergo. For example, the conversation
markers have disappeared *(because as you know … you know, this term,
ehhh).* Ted Nelson in Spanish does not hesitate and he does not use phatic
language *(Yeah).* His discourse has been tightened up, and in so doing the
expression *sort of,* for example, has been eliminated and the sentence *So we
have to watch it and keep track of it because it's too fuzzy* becomes *Hence
what we call technology is something we should be careful with.*

The previous examples correspond to first-person voice-over, which is
the general practice in countries such as Brazil, Catalonia and Spain. However, another possible scenario, which we also saw in postproduction, is
when the voice talent (or journalist) reports on what the speaker is saying.
Though we hear the speaker's voice in the background, the speech of the
celebrity incorporated in a comment in the third person *(third-person voice-
over* in Grigaravičiūté and Gottlieb's terminology (2001)). Following an
example by Franco (2000b: 184–185), in Troeller's documentary *Rechtslos
im Rechtsstaat* (1996) the director reads aloud all instances of commentary
that were originally written in German. These commentaries are interrupted by first-person monologues or dialogues. There is, however, one

---

49   La 2 is the second TV channel of the Spanish state-owned television broadcaster TVE.

instance of third-person voice-over, in the last scene of this documentary, in which we see a group of girls from the northeast of Brazil attending an English class. The commentary that precedes the scene suggests that the girls are learning English in order to improve their interaction with the thousands of sex tourists who come to the city every year. Then, we hear a woman's voice with a foreign accent off-screen, asking the girls if they would like to marry a foreigner. Their answer is expressed in the documentary as follows:

> Commentator: *Sie sollen aus ihrer Illusion erwachen, ein Sextourist könne der Märchenprinz sein. Dennoch, <u>auf unsere Frage, ob sie gerne einen Ausländer heiraten möchte, sagt keine nein</u>.*
> [They must wake up from their illusion that a sex tourist could be the enchanted prince. However, <u>to our question, if they would like to marry a foreigner, none said no</u>]

The first part belongs to the original commentary and the underlined part represents the girls' reported answers by Troeller. It can be said that one of the effects of third-person (reported) voice-over is greater manipulation of content. In this case, for example, the question put to the girls was not answered with a simple yes by all of them; most did say yes, others hesitated, and there was also a girl who answered: *acho que sem amor acho que num dá não casá assim … dependendo …* [(I) think that without love (I) think that it's not possible to marry then … (it) depends …]. The translation of such an utterance, however, would certainly spoil the view that these girls might do anything (including selling their bodies) to get out of their poor conditions that they find themselves in.

However, voice-over for production, as we have seen, differs from voice-over for postproduction in various aspects, especially in those aspects related to the characteristics of the source text and hence working conditions, which will be analysed in depth in the next section.

4.1.1 Faithfulness and manipulation

First of all, the translation offered tot he audience does not usually correspond to a fully structured text with various speakers but rather to excerpts which will be included in another programme. In fact, once the translation is finished, it is sent to the programme editor, who will decide on how much text from the translation is used, and on the context in which translation is used and this can give rise to contradictory situations. Although voice-over is used in order to create a feeling of authenticity because, in the background, the original voice can be heard and can even be listened to for a few seconds at the beginning (see Chapter 1), the reality is that by decontextualizing an utterance, the utterance can be distorted as far as both content and intention are concerned (Franco 2000b, Orero 2007b, Darwish & Orero forthcoming).

Franco (2000b) illustrated that the absence of preproduction / production scripts seems to reinforce the idea that documentaries 'mirror reality'. However, as she also demonstrated in her thesis, shooting never happens accidentally, interviews are generally planned and interviewees often prepared in advance.[50] Moreover, after shooting has been completed, the raw material goes through a series of editorial changes, which may result in a completely different product altogether. A good example of the manipulating power of editing became apparent in the interview with Thierry Michel, in which he said that only after frenetic filming for six months in Brazil,[51] he returned to Belgium and only then decided to make two documentaries using the material that he had gathered. One documentary was *Gosses de Rio*, although he did confess that the primary idea was to produce a fictional story. Regarding editing, Silverstone stresses the effect of the work done in the "cutting room":

> Much of the work of narrative and rhetorical construction is clearly complete prior to editing: images are shot and questions asked for their answers, and the manner of both to some extent determines the character of the final film. To some extent but by no means entirely. Most of the work of film-making is done in the cutting room, and the restructuring and rewriting of this film gives some indication of how much can be done, and how much can be changed, as a result of changes in its narrative and its rhetorical structure. (Silverstone 1986: 97)

As far as scripts are concerned Franco (2000a, 2000b) provides a reminder and states that the important points to bear in mind are that documentary

---

50   In a face-to-face interview with Thierry Michel (14 June 1998, Brussels) and phone and written interviews with Gordian Troeller (a telephone interview on 2 April 1998 and a written interview on 25 April 1998) it was clear that both interviewees were very specific about the reality of documentary preplanning. Likewise, the BBC's *Principles and Practice in Documentary Programmes* (London, 1972) mentions "preparation" as the first production stage, which is followed by "shooting, editing and finishing", according to Collins (1986: 133).

51   Two weeks of which with the boys of *Gosses de Rio*.

This discussion would have gained a lot from reference to critical theory / cultural theory and film theory, even manipulation theory / which

scripts are postproduction texts, and that, consequently, the videotaped *treat the film material as a (semiotic) text* film acquires a primary position as *the* source text from which transcriptions of the original and/or voice-over-for-production versions are derived.

A remarkable case is that of the Bin Laden tapes. The translations and broadcasts of Bin Laden messages are such a contradiction to our experience as voice-over translators that we have decided to investigate to the situation in detail. Since 9/11 Bin Laden has been issuing tapes containing messages. The authenticity of the messages has been questioned and this started as soon as the first tape was broadcast. Before undergoing any translation, these tapes are analysed by experts in order to establish evidence of authorship before being broadcast (Darwish 2006). Authorship in these cases is still a matter of study in the specialist area of Forensic Translation *Check this !* Studies, in which a special methodology has been designed to determine *It sounds far-fetched* whether the text which needs to be translated actually belongs to the author. For audiovisual texts, translation-driven forensic analysis of videotaped messages has to bring together both the audible and scripted texts, and as Darwish comments: "although features of elocution, enunciation and intonation play an important part in determining meanings and intentions of the discourse and in establishing evidence of communication, they play a rather secondary role in establishing evidence of authorship" (2006: 45). *inaccurate* We presume that after a thorough analysis the following Bin Laden tape was broadcast. The first surprise was that while in most cases the translator for the voice-over is transparent, on the Bin Laden tape the opposite is the rule. Moreover, we can find on the BBC website (www.bbc.co.uk) on 23 April 2006 how the translator is obviously marked on the screen using a subtitle.

━━ VOICE OF TRANSLATOR

Figure 5. News item screen captured from the BBC website (aired on 23 April 2006).

Also manipulation takes place not only in the cutting room, but also at the translator's desk

Going to the BBC *News Online* page we can still see the video and read the translated transcription of the tape with emphasis being made to the role of the translator:[52]

> The Pentagon has released a videotape of the terrorist suspect Osama Bin Laden, which officials say provides compelling evidence that he masterminded the hijacked plane attacks on New York and Washington. It shows bin Laden apparently celebrating the deaths of those who were killed on September 11. The tape, shot by an amateur cameraman, was found by US intelligence officers in a house in Jalalabad, in eastern Afghanistan. Downing Street says there's no question of its authenticity – and that it leaves no room for doubt about bin Laden's involvement in the attacks. Read the full text for yourself. (http://www.bbc.co.uk/radio4/today/reports/archive/international/binladen.shtml) [Retrieved on 24 April 2006]

> (Transcript and annotations independently prepared by George Michael, translator, Diplomatic Language Services; and Dr. Kassem M. Wahba, Arabic language program co-ordinator, School of Advanced International Studies, Johns Hopkins University. They collaborated on their translation and compared it with translations done by the U.S. government for consistency. There were no inconsistencies in the translations.) <http://www.bbc.co.uk/radio4/today/reports/archive/international/binladen.shtml> [Retrieved on 24 April 2006]

But Darwish (in Darwish & Orero forthcoming) analysed the text and discovered that while the first Arabic words of the excerpt below are audible the English, the voice-over does not match. The rest of the voice-over script is a condensed text of two segments in the original, which are barely audible under the voice-over. The voice-over script, which was reduced and edited by the journalist, lasts the duration it takes to read it out. There are usually no seconds left at the end in news items, so it is almost impossible to check if the speaker finished the discourse at the same time as the voice-over.

Original Arabic text (segment 1). The shaded text was not broadcast.

ومما يظهر ذلك أيضا رفضهم لحركة حماس بعد أن فازت في الانتخابات مع تأكيدنا على ما نبه عليه الشيخ أيمن الظواهري من حرمة الدخول في المجالس الشركية إلا أن رفضهم لحماس أكد أنها حرب صليبية صهيونية ضد المسلمين..

---

52 <http://www.bbc.co.uk/radio4/today/reports/archive/international/binladen.shtml> [Retrieved on 24 April 2006].

Is this production voice-over? [handwritten]

إن الحرب مسئولية تضامنية بين الشعوب والحكومات ، والحرب مستمرة والشعوب تجدد الولاء لحكامها وساستها وترسل أبناءها إلى الجيوش لقتالنا ، وتواصل الدعم المادي والمعنوي وبلادنا تحرق وبيوتنا تقصف وشعوبنا تقتل ولا يبالي بنا أحد ، ويكفيكم مثالاً على الانتهاكات الصارخة على ملتنا وعلى إخواننا وبلداننا ما قامت به حليفتكم إسرائيل من اقتحام وهدم لسجن أريحا بتواطؤ مع أمريكا وبريطانيا

Translation

<u>What shows this also</u> [fade out] is their rejection of the Hamas Movement after it has won the elections – with our assertion of Shaykh Ayman AZ-Zawhiri caution about the prohibition of entering into the infidel council. But their refusal of Hamas has confirmed it is a Crusade-Zionist war against Muslims.

[fade in, under voiceover, hardly audible] The war is a joint responsibility between peoples and governments. The war continues and the peoples renew their allegiances to their rulers and politicians [fade out] and send their children to the armies to fight us and continue to [their] financial and moral support, while our countries are being burned down, our homes bombed, and our peoples killed, and no one cares about us.

BBC's English Voice-over

It is an ongoing war against Muslims. The enemy continues to murder our children, our women, the elderly, and destroy our homes.

Interestingly, there is no explicit mention of "the enemy", "our children", "our women" and "the elderly" in the original message.

With this example – and the other Bin Laden examples – it is clear [*Unclear arguments* handwritten] that importance is given tot the text and its translation, which in most cases are overlooked either because the journalist wants to interpret the text differently (Aitken 2008) or because the language of the original was not suited for literal transcription and translation. In fact, Darwish (2006) and Darwish and Orero (forthcoming) have investigated the translation of news items for voice-over and they discovered that it is usually the team of journalists in the news programme who translate, and often deliver, the translated – and thoroughly edited – text as voice-over. What proof does the audience have to believe that the voice that we can hear reading the *why do we need a proof for that?*

translation of Bin Laden's text was the translator's voice? We do not have any answer to this question but a reasonable explanation is that, given the many *fatwas* issued in recent years (which in fact is part of the news item) to writers or journalists, the profession has probably decided to play it safe. When the news item is deemed 'sensitive', broadcasters generally want to detach themselves from the content and hence the translator (who in fact is only doing his or her job, as is the journalist) bears the responsibility for the translation. But, as we have already mentioned, this is a truly exceptional case.

4.1.2 Special features

The fact that no script is available is a distinctive feature of voice-over for production and deeply affects the translation process, as will be demonstrated in this section. Interviews are live and therefore there is no script apart from the journalists' questions, which are never sent to the translator. Since time and costs are always a priority in the media, no transcription of the interview is usually prepared, that is, translators always translate listening from the screen. This requires translators with high comprehension levels of oral language, a skill that can sometimes be compromised as a result of various elements that influence the spoken discourse in the source text. We can group the many variables which are intimately related to the delivery of the discourse into three categories: prosodic, paralinguistic and indexic elements.

Prosodic elements which are present in delivery speed may vary considerably from one speaker to the other. At one end of the spectrum, we find those speakers who speak extremely slowly and who gesticulate because they have realized that the interlocutor does not understand what is being said because of technicalities or because of speaking in a different language. At the other end of the spectrum, we find those speakers who are nervous because of the way that they speak, or because they want to squeeze all the information they can into the few seconds that they have. The result can be comical to listen to, but at the same time it is extremely frustrating if the information has to be translated.

Accent is another prosodic element which can make a translation extremely easy or difficult. The accent can be the result of several facts. Maybe it is the fact that the speaker is talking in a foreign language, or because the speaker originates from a remote or marked location (e.g., Glaswegians or Geordies). In fact, while it is true that 99% of the voiced-over interviews *inaccurate* are in English, not everyone in the world speaks English as a first language. Hence, the language most translated from is some form of *lingua franca*, which is English but generally as the speaker's second or third language. This may make the translation easier or more difficult, depending on the level of fluency with which the speaker speaks or the technicalities of the topic being discussed.

In the category of paralinguistic elements we have, for example, the voice and its many characteristics (tone, pitch, timbre, intonation, intensity, texture, etc.) Diction, which may be perfect without any accent, can be affected by problems of an acute temporary nature (e.g., a cold) or of a chronic nature (e.g., a lisp). In addition to the voice we also have the phenomenon of body language, which may affect the voice, for example, when the person who is speaking puts one hand over his or her mouth.

The third category consists of indexic features, which group all the aforementioned elements and are related to the voice and to the preference for certain prosodic or paralinguistic elements. These features include, for example, the use of interjections, colloquial markers and all expressions relevant to the phatic function of language.

Voice-over for production, as understood in this book, implies always delivering a written version, which will be later voiced by either a voice talent or a journalist. However, for some television channels, such as *Arte*, the term *voice-over* is applied to what interpreters do, that is, they receive a tape, with or without a preproduction script, and after watching a videotape a few times, they record a voice-over, which starts a few seconds after the original and finishes at the same time, as explained by Edith Voelker in a presentation of the *Arte* translation service for Euroconference delegates in 2005. In these cases, there is no written translation and the interpreters have to be able to deliver a fluent speeches which sound spontaneous and authentic and which are adapted to the target audiences. It is often the case that interviews are recorded in the morning, voiced-over in the afternoon and broadcast in the evening.

A similar case arises when time is really non-existent, and the translator has to travel to where the production team is working – usually a TV station or production company – and translate *in situ* as a member of the production team. The lack of an official, in-house TV station translator, who may offer his or her services on an ad hoc basis, may lead to the fact

This makes no sense

that the language spoken in the footage is not understood, and since no script is available, the presence of a translation is imperative. In this case, the translator views the footage together with the production team and offers a live interpretation of what is being said. The production team spots the time code of the frames which are of interest and the translator will then translate those seconds in a written form. With this translated material, the production team will then edit the translation to fit the context for the voice-over translation.

As far as the characteristics of the source text are concerned, technology poses various challenges to the translator. An example of this new technology is the feature of video-conferencing (see Figure 6). In addition to the previous problems already analysed (lack of time and script), we find that with the video conference the interviewee, who is away and perhaps on another continent, has the sound in asynchrony to his lips.

good screenshot

Figure 6. Frame taken from interview through videoconferencing.

The presenter in the TV room asks a question, and we always see how the journalist in the distant location listens to the question with a delay of some seconds because of the return of the signal. The problem of reception of the source text (ST) is highlighted with technical hitches, such as the eco effect, or the lack of synchrony between lip movement and sound reception. The slight delay in the broadcast of the image in relation to the sound makes listening to the interview more of an audio, rather than audio and visual, exercise. Here, we have pointed out only the quality of image and sound, and how the quality of these features affects the translator's task. The translator will have to rely solely on the soundtrack. We could add some further complications (already highlighted above) such as the topic of the interview which may lead to the use of highly specialized terminology and the interviewee's possible speech impediments.

As was the case with the previous example of videoconferencing, the translator may receive the material that needs to be translated with no picture whatsoever, or with extremely poor sound quality. The scenario in which the translator receives no picture arises, for example, when all that the translator gets to see are vertical colour lines. This could be the result of problem that arose when the format was changed (e.g., transferring from beta to VHS). An example of poor sound quality is when the translator receives the task of translating an interview which was held by the seaside. The landscape may be breathtaking, with the light of a golden late summer sunset, the topic of the interview may be relatively easy, but it there may also be slight breeze, which was picked up by the microphone and all that can be heard is a thumping noise, and from time to time some broken words. This is clearly a mistake on the part of the sound engineer. However, the whole tape was recorded and sent to the translator for translation. In this case – the opposite of the two previous cases – we enjoy lovely views but with no sound to be translated. From the broken words it may possible to write a text, but this task is more reminiscent of an exercise in creative writing than translation.

Another problem may arise when, for example, there is a hand in the way. This can be because the interviewees put their hands over their mouths, or as can be seen in the following frame, because of an unfortunate angle of the camera. As was the case with the videoconferencing example, the translator must rely exclusively on the sound even though there is also an image.

Figure 7. Frame taken from interview where a physical obstacle covers the speaker's mouth.

When translating interviews, a recurring practice which is annoying for the translator is the presence of two cameras. One camera – with one microphone – focuses on the interviewer, and the other camera – with e second microphone – focuses on the interviewee, as can be seen in Figure 8. Two different recordings with different images and soundtracks are produced. They will be edited and mixed by the production team, but the translator gets only one of the tapes. This means that the translator will get either the interviewee's face with the soundtrack of the interviewee's voice and no picture of the interviewer and the soundtrack of the interviewer's voice or vice versa. This is the commonest way of recording an interview but it also means that the translator has to struggle to understand either the questions or the answers. If time is not of the essence, a phone call to the production team may solve the problem and the translator may be lucky to receive both tapes. Since the translator works with the video of one of the two people in the interview, synchrony can be annotated only for the person who is on the video.

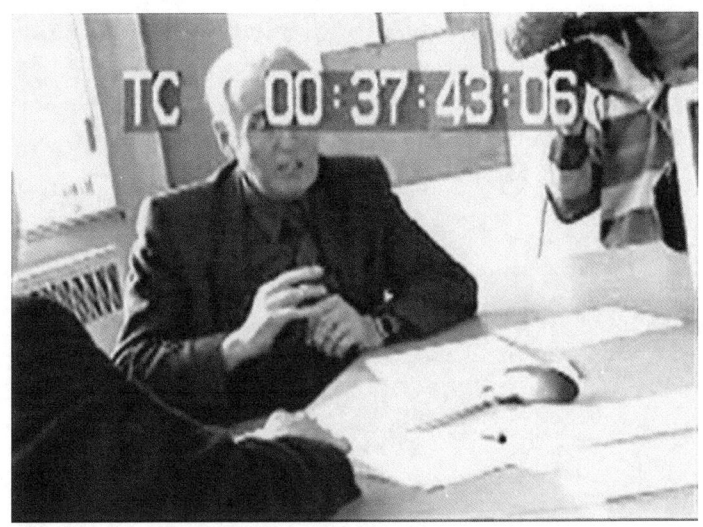

Figure 8. Two-camera recording, one camera has recorded the opposite.

4.1.3 Other influential features

[handwritten: English!]

On some occasions, several takes are made with the same question and/or answer. This is due to external factors such as a sudden noise (e.g., a mobile phone ringing), or because the question/answer did not meet the expectations set. In these cases, the translator has to translate each take, since he does not know which take will be used by the producer. When translating several takes of the same question/answer the effect of homoioteleuton tends to occur, and more so when the translator is tired as result of hours of translating or of being confronted with many difficulties.

The figure in rhetoric *homoioteleuton* (also *Homoeoteleuton, Omoioteliton, Omoioteleton*) is composed of Greek *homoios* "equal" and *teleute* "end". The definition of the term in paleography could be imported into the field of Audiovisual Translation, and even more so when dealing with the translation of voice-over for interviews in production. In this case, a *homoioteleuton* is an omission whereby the copyist – or translator – has accidentally skipped some small part of the text, having looked away from the text which was being copied and then looking back at a part of the text where the same small part of text occurs, and copying from that point on. This happens, for example, when the tape is rewound, when the question is asked more than three times with slightly different word order every time.

In the following example, taken from the programme *Redes* (a weekly programme which promotes science and state-of-the-art scientific issues), we have three similar texts taken from three different takes.

Take 1

> During billions of years life has been more or less predictable, so much so that scientists have been able to develop a framework which is called models of life. You were just saying that it would be possible to find bacteria in almost any place such as archea [...]

Take 2

> For billions of years life has been so predictable that scientists have managed to develop what is called models of life. You said it's possible to find bacteria almost anywhere. And that if there were water to swim some tiny protozoos would have invaded everything like predators. Would life be the same in the next billion years? Can be use models of life?

Take 3

> During billions of years life has been more or less predictable. Scientists, as yourself, have drawn what is now called models of life. You were just saying that it would be possible to find bacteria such as archea in almost any place, and that if there were water where they could swim protozoos could invade everything like predators. How would life be in the next billion years? Can be use models of life to make the prediction?

In these examples the first sentence is almost identical but not quite. When listening and rewinding it was possible – unless attention is paid to the Time Code – to move from one excerpt to the next, and in fact if tiredness is an issue, the translator may end up producing a text which is a fusion of the three takes, and which does not coincide with any of the visual images. In conclusion it can be said that media, and audiovisual media in particular, are becoming a complex communication system which offers a fast-growing number of broadcast possibilities in many formats. New challenges such as media accessibility, interactive and simultaneous delivery of different formats present many translation possibilities and modalities. Sophisticated and ever-changing technologies, together with more robust communication systems, define new formats for the contents of media along with the translation of such formats. The audiovisual translator has to adapt to these changes and go beyond the realm of the written word into the realm of the spoken word, honing skills traditionally required not only from interpreters, as has been demonstrated in the translation of interviews for voice-over, but also from journalists, as will be shown in the next section, in which the translation and creation of commentaries for production will be discussed.

4.2 The translation and creation of commentaries

Commentary for production takes place when the team of journalists which produce a TV programme (or a film for that matter) is planning the contents of the programme. The journalists may decide to use excerpts from some existing commentaries in (foreign) programmes (BBC *The Human Body*), sports personality interviews (David Beckham), sports events (World Swimming Championship, Formula 1, European Premier League football matches), awards celebrations (Oscars, MTV), which may be live or recorded. We have looked in the previous section at the use and translation of interviews. Let us now have a look at the translation of excerpts of commentaries taken from programmes which have already been produced, but which the added difference that these commentaries are now used to make new programmes.

In order to produce such programmes the team of journalists – within the production department – will buy a number of minutes of an existing TV programme. These excerpts will be used interspersed in the main body of the new programme, sometimes simply to provide images to illustrate the commentary (for example, some seconds on the human genome code). The translator will be sent the material which has been bought by the journalists but usually this material has no accompanying transcription. However, we have seen that in some cases scripts do exist and they can be of a high quality. The inclusion of translators in TV production teams may result from the fact that the journalists' general knowledge of foreign languages is still a major problem. This appears to be the situation in Spain and even though this change in the future, present university education programmes have not been modified accordingly to address the problem of foreign language competence. Another factor which may affect the inclusion of translators in TV production teams is the tight time schedule in force to produce TV programmes. It is faster to send a whole programme to a translator for translation within 24 hours or to call the translator in than for the team of journalists to translate, when they have other urgent tasks to deal with.

The translation process for excerpts of produced programmes is the same as the process already described in the previous chapter in which the translation of entire programmes was discussed. The challenges are also the same: synchronization with the images has to be retained (action synchrony) and the translation must fit in the space available (isochrony). As for the difficulties of working without a transcript, they have already been highlighted in the previous section. The only difference now is that commentators usually use more formal language and are therefore easier to understand. Thus, the only real difference can be found in the production process. The translation may suffer many and varied transformations from the moment it is handed over to the production team and the moment it is broadcast (Darwish and Orero forthcoming). The translation may be used or not. It may be used as a reference from which a new commentary stems and is written, or it may be adapted to suit the needs for illustrating a different topic (e.g., it may be condensed to fit a short news item). A typical example are the many programmes on in vitro fertilization (IVF) , in which they always use a sequence of three identical images when dealing with human reproduction, stem cell research, etc. The images are always the same but for each occasion the commentary changes, according to the programme requirements.

As mentioned before, the working profile for voice-over production translator is that of a journalist-cum-creative writer-cum translator and adapting (i.e., domesticating) or even creating a commentary may very well be one of the working practices. Let us investigate a few scenarios.

Example 1

The translator receives the material which needs to be translated – no script – from a live event, such as an international sports competition with different countries taking part. The material that the translator receives is footage which has been bought from a news agency. The country in which *examples are very helpful. But generalisations are necessary, since examples cannot cover all possible cases.*

the footage will be shown is represented by an athlete who is not one of the top three. Hence, the camera and comments are focused mainly on those who are expected to win. The translator faces the task of localizing the translation of the footage being presented, focusing on the national athlete, who is not in the expected top three, and to whom little or no reference are made by the commentator. As is the case with any news-related translation, there is little time available for the documentation and translation. This is actually what happened when, in 2001, we had to translate 13 episodes of the ballroom dancing competition *International Sport Dance Standard Championship*. The episodes were broadcast during the summer months on the Spanish national channel *RTVE*. This is an extreme example since no Spanish competitor was present.

Each episode had the same structure. The city in which the competition took place was presented, and then the dancing couples introduced themselves. The rest of the programme showed the different dance styles, in different stages of the competition. Commentaries which had to be *[English]* translated were very simple commentaries such as "lovely performance", "great step", "she's got a nice hairstyle", "the dress is stunning". Given the tight deadline, we contacted the Spanish Dance Sport Federation (Asociación Española de Baile Deportivo y de Competición), which gave us the names of some of the best couples and their recent achievements. This information was fractioned in 13 paragraphs to match the 13 episodes and was added at the beginning of each programme, when the couples introduced themselves.

Example 2

In our second example, the translator was asked to adapt the original commentary,[53] focusing on the Spanish athletes that took part in a competition. The result was a text which was completely different from the original. However, the text satisfied the expectations of the Spanish audience nonetheless.

> *English original version:* Here we see Iván Raña ready to take off. World Champions are plenty in this men's field. World Duathlon Champion from last year Tim Don and there former world champion Simon Lessing all out to get this man, number two in the world Greg Bennett.

53   We would like to thank Ricard Sierra for kindly sending us this example.

Translated commentary: Y ahí tenemos a Iván Raña, el gallego campeón de España, campeón de Europa y campeón del mundo, en una de sus primeras apariciones en la copa del mundo de este año. Su objetivo, al igual que el año pasado serán los campeonatos del mundo que se disputarán a finales de año. Ése es Greg Bennett, posiblemente, su mayor rival en esta carrera.

Back-translation: Here we see Iván Raña, the Galician who's won the Spanish, European and World Championships, in one of his first appearances in this year's World Cup. His aim, as last year, will be the world championship, which will take place by the end of the year. This is Greg Bennett, probably his main rival in this race.

Example 3

Though this may fall under the category of creative writing, on some occasions the translator is given a tape or file with some images. This was the case with the documentary *Isle of Wight*, shown at *Redes* in 2001. On this occasion, the tape which contained a documentary also contained declarations given by talking heads which were interspersed with clips of the beautiful features of a beach. The comments made by the talking heads could be heard, but the excerpts of landscapes had neither music nor commentary. The translator was asked to translate the speech given by the talking heads and to create a commentary which fit both the comments and the images shown.

In the following example we see a house (with no soundtrack) whose back garden has been eroded by the sea.[54] The house has been boarded up and signs with the word *danger* can clearly be seen.

Figure 9. Images taken from *Isle of Wight* (I).

54   Images from <http://www.isleofwightattractions.co.uk/Landslipgallery1.htm> [Retrieved on 1 June 2007]

After some seconds, the talking heads of a middle-aged couple can be seen saying:

> Five years ago we put our house up for sale. There was this lady who lived 100 miles away and was interested. She came with an agent from an insurance company, whose office was from nearby she was living, and asked him if they would insure the house. They say they wouldn't because it was too dangerous and the reason given was erosion.

After this intervention, some more silent frames were shown. This time a theme park was shown. With the next intervention the viewer is informed that this is *Blackgang Chine Fantasy Park*. The park manager says "These are the remains to the small path of the Model Village. Now this whole area has long been washed away. We had to dismantle the whole area and move it to a safer place which wasn't particularly cheap".

Figure 10. Images taken from *Isle of Wight* (II).

From the commentaries and the images we were able to create the following text:

– To the excerpt accompanying the house with no back garden:

> Spanish created commentary: *Las autoridades locales han reforzado con grandes piedras la base del acantilado para intentar salvar aquellas zonas que son importantes para la economía local, como por ejemplo las zonas de turismo. Otros terrenos simplemente se consideran irrecuperables y quedan condenados. Esta casa ha perdido el jardín y también su valor en el mercado inmobiliario. La erosión también está empezando a tener consecuencias socio-económicas.*

> *Back translation*: The local authority has used large stones to reinforce the base of the cliff in an attempt to save those areas which are important for the local economy, for example those areas important for tourism. Other areas are simply considered as impossible to save and are condemn. This house has lost its garden and its value on the housing market. Erosion is also beginning to have socio-economic consequences

– And the text created as a commentary to accompany the views of the park:

> Spanish created commentary: *Blackgang Chine Fantasy Park es el parque de atracciones más antiguo del Reino Unido. Fue construido en 1843 y durante los últimos 20 años el parque ha ido perdiendo 10 metros de terreno cada año y no podrá resistir 20 años más. Se encuentra en una zona de alerta roja, una de las zonas declaradas irrecuperables por las autoridades locales.*
>
> *Back translation*: Blackgang Chine Park is the oldest attraction park in the United Kingdom. It was built in 1843 and for the past 20 years the park has been losing 10 metres of land per year. It will not be able to withstand another 20 years. It is situated in a red alert zone, which has been declared as irrecoverable by the local authorities.

4.3 Conclusion

Good

Though it is an impossible task to make a watertight taxonomic classification of voice-over using different parameters, we have tried, for the sake of clarity, to group the most salient features presented in Chapters 2, 3 and 4. Table 4 presents the product that a translator may receive from various clients as well as the tasks that he can be asked to carry out and the material that he is given to deal with the translation.

Table 4. Taxonomy of voice-over features (based on Matamala (2008)).

Products	– Fiction: TV series, films, bonus materials, etc. – Non-fiction: documentaries (scientific, historical, travel, anthropological, technical, human sciences, etc.), interviews, sports events, making-of documentaries, instruction manuals, infomercials, corporate videos, news, current affairs programmes, docu-dramas, reality shows.

Clients	– Television – Dubbing Studio (cinema, DVD, television) – Distributors – Filmmakers – DVD authoring houses – Translation agencies – TV production companies
Tasks	– Translation (with different degrees of adaptation): voice-over of interviews and off-screen dubbing of commentaries – Creation of commentaries – Spotting – Linguistic revision – Voicing
Material	– Image and script (different degrees of quality) – Only image *? and sound (video) ?* – Only script – Image in an unknown language and script in English

The transfer modes applied to the previous products may vary according to the client's requirements or the tradition of the country in which the translation takes place. In the two previous chapters we focused mainly on non-fictional products, where interviews are usually voiced-over and commentaries are dubbed off-screen. This does not imply that other practices are impossible. It simply means that these are the practices that are of interest for the discussion in this book.

As far as the main challenges of voice-over and the off-screen dubbing of commentaries are concerned, they can be summarized as follows:

Table 5. Taxonomy of voice-over and the off-screen dubbing features.

Specific challenges: voice-over	– Adapting the length of the text, leaving a few seconds (voice-over isochrony) – Synchronization of body language and text (kinetic synchrony) – Orality of the original: rewording the language to create a comprehensible discourse.
Specific challenges: off-screen dubbing of commentaries	– Adapting the length of the text (isochrony) – Keeping the tone of the original, which is generally a formal discourse. *register*

Table 5. Taxonomy of voice-over and the off-screen dubbing features. (cont.)

Common challenges: voice-over and off-screen dubbing	– Synchronization of text and visuals (action synchrony) – Creating a readable translation ((written)> oral > written > oral). It will be a written text that will be delivered orally and will be received audiovisually, hence depicting a syntactically appropriate structure. – Creating, for example, a scientific discourse, with specific terminology. – Localization (adaptation) of text, if necessary.
General challenges in audiovisual translation with a special impact on voice-over and the off-screen dubbing of commentaries	– Comprehension problems, because of the absence of a transcript or because of mistranscriptions. – Content errors in the original – Terminology – Documentation process – Proper nouns and numbers – Working conditions: time – Working conditions: absence of image / script / etc.

4.4 Suggested exercises

1. As already mentioned, in this chapter and in previous chapters, one of the first steps when starting a translation is to check the script which needs to be translated and to check what appears on the screen. In this exercise we would like to exploit the ability of translation from the screen, that is we would you to listen to and watch an excerpt, and without a script, to proceed with the translation adding time codes or any relevant information.

    Watch an excerpt of any audiovisual product with the language combination that you usually work with. If your source language is English, you may want to go to the BBC webpage for live interviews and current affairs <http://news.bbc.co.uk/2/hi/video_and_audio/default.stm> or to the FourDocs website <http://www.channel4.com/fourdocs/>, where a wide selection of quality material and an archive for classic documentaries <http://www.channel4.com/fourdocs/archive/> can be found.

Previous exercises can be prepared, with transcription where some key-words have been taken away, and students have to fill in the gaps, such as any English listening exercise. *No meaning + consistency*

Different degrees of difficulty can be prepared before attempting a 3 minute excerpt.

2. Though voice-over translators are usually not asked to synchronize their texts to the screen, on some occasions, as we have seen in this chapter, care must be taken to make sure that the visual text coincides with the translation delivered. Since there is a shareware revoicing programme which you can download from <http://www.techsmith.com/snagit/accessories/dubit.asp>, a good exercise is to choose an audio-visual excerpt, and ideally it should be an interview. First listen to the original text, do the translation and then revoice your translation, en-suring that the translated text does not exceed the duration of the source text.

3. Often, when translating spontaneous oral texts, we find repetitions, hesitations, etc. Below you will find the transcription of an interview. Edit the text to achieve a syntactically correct discourse but make sure to maintain the oral register.

Peter:
Correct me if I'm wrong, but there are some traits which are characteristic of hu-mans, such as yawning? Have you ever seen a chimp yawning? Do primates yawn, all of them?

Jane:
Yeah, 'course they do.

Peter:
All primates, or all animals?

Jane:
I can't say if goldfish yawn, but I can tell you all right my dog yawns, and often.

Peter:
Some palaeontologists and physiologists from Maryland University say that have stud-ied the function of the brain, well, actually, the function of the yawn in the brain. Their conclusion is that it has been inconclusive, they haven't found a thing. They say yawn-ing is a pre-human habit men inherited from the chimps. What function has yawning in chimps?

Jane:
None.

Peter:
None?

Jane:
Naaaaaah, yawning has to do with breathing, yeah?

Peter:
They measured the level of oxygen in their lungs before and after yawning and nothing. So why it is contagious?

Jane:
It's not likely.

Punset:
But we do it, right?

Jane:
Wow, yeah, you are right, yeah. It's funny when you do it 'cause someone else does it, funny, yeah.

Peter:
mmmmmmmYou have discovered that chimps are very good at using tools. How did you come about that?

Jane:
Yeah it was kind of incredible, yeah. And let me tell you the story because one day in the jungle I went by a termite nest, and I sat down to rest in a nearby tree. All of a sudden a big chimp sat down by the termites, took a blade of grass, like that, and doing this he started to get ants from the nest and use the grass as an eating tool.

Peter:
This is an amazing finding, because for years the difference between us and animals was the use of tools.

Jane:
But that's not true at all.

Peter:
Yeah, it's not true, and then they CAME and said it was language, communication, and I suppose that's not true either ...

Jane:
Yes and no. Chimps communicate beautifully through a wide repertoire of voices, facial expressions, gesture codes, body language, you know, sounds and routine movements, yeah. But we can do things like tell events that took place in the past, a long time ago like, or histories, and memories, and even plan the future, what we'll do, what's going to happen or wishful thinking, you know? That only to do with us humans, yeah, its different, yeah.

Peter:
You also discovered chimps are not completely vegetarians, isn't it?

Jane:
Yes, I saw once a chimp on top of a tree eating a piece of meat. All of a sudden a female chimp jumped on the treetop and asked him to share. That's clear, I mean, if the female wanted some meat, that means it's not only one chimp that eats meat, but it was new to us. We took it for granted they were beiges, and never challenged that. It's strange why we are happy with some ideas with no base, nonsense actually.

4. Go to a website specialized in sports (e.g., <http://news.bbc.co.uk/sport/>, <http://www.worldscreen.com/searchresults.php> or <http://www.tv3.cat/>). Look for an international event in which your country participated. Write a commentary which could be read as a voice-over of the news.

Perhaps the book should have been written in the languages of the authors and then translated professionally into English.

5. Training in voice-over

This chapter looks at training in voice-over translation at a university level, focusing on our experience at the *Universitat Autònoma de Barcelona*, where the first course on voice-over was launched as a postgraduate in the academic year 2001–2002. After some years of teaching in two formats (both face-to-face and online) and from the experience gained and the adjustments made to our methodology, we can now present the aims and outcome of our project in this chapter. First of all, we would like to take into consideration some issues which are at the basis of our approach to training. Though we have not followed any methodological school, the learning materials, the learning environment, and the teaching staff have been tested for their adequacy in each and every step of the design, creation, implementation and development. We would like to highlight that voice-over, or the broader field of audiovisual translation, is not what is widely considered to be a specialist training even though it may seem that way. Voice-over training is a complex form of training (Nord 2005: 211) which is heavily based on technology and the translation itself does not relate to a specific area of knowledge as economic or medical translation generally do. We have seen in the previous chapters that any topic in every genre lends itself to being translated by voice-over, so voice-over training has three levels of specialization: the subject matter, the format (audio and visual) and finally the technical specificities which support the audiovisual material (software programs, audiovisual formats, translation templates and the clients' requests).

Bearing in mind the magnitude of the enterprise and the need for efficient and holistic training, the team opted for a 'deep learning approach' (as opposed to a surface approach) (Harris 1994: 203, Morgan 1995: 7), in which the interaction and dialogue in learning (student-teacher/student-student) helps the students to think critically in their study and encourages them to construct meaning. The encouragement that students experience to adopt a deep approach to their learning is a key issue in our course and it allows us to teach the many skills within a context and taking into consideration the discourse of each form of subject material.

A whole variety of articles has been published, some looking specifically at training for audiovisual translation in general (Bartrina & Espasa 2001, Díaz Cintas, Mas López & Orero 2006, Izard 2001, Kovačič 1998, Yagolkowski 2006), for subtitling (Brondeel 1994, Carroll 1998, Díaz Cintas 2001a, Gottlieb 1993, 1996, James 1998, Klerkx 1998), for dubbing (Bartrina 2001, Chaume 1999, Espasa 2001), for new technologies in audiovisual translators' training (Chaume 2003a, Mas López & Orero 2004a, Santamaria 2003, Matamala 2005c, 2006, Orero & Santamaria 2002), for AVT in language teaching (Díaz Cintas 1995, 1997, Neves 2004, Taylor 1996), for online training in AVT (Amador, Dorado & Orero 2004, Bartoll & Orero 2008), for script analysis in AVT teaching (Remael 2004, Mas López & Orero 2004b) and for voice-over (Agost & Chaume 1996: 210, Batrina & Espasa 2003, Matamala 2004, 2008).[55] In addition to the many approaches and different traditions on training for AVT, we have also looked at general translation training in order to compare and contrast our beliefs with more scientific (or at least more formal) approaches to translating.

While we have tried to cater for a wide and different number of teaching materials, the fact is that little attention has been paid to the voice-over translation of fictional products, that is, of films. While this practice is in use in some countries, it is alien to us (in Brazil, Catalonia and Spain) academically and, thus, we have decided not to venture into the unknown as a result of practical considerations. Nevertheless, we have attempted to include and look at the widest variety of cases, so as students are trained to cope with diverse and complex scenarios in future projects.

5.1 The background

Teaching voice-over translation at a university level was a challenge presented to us some seven years ago when we decided to start a postgraduate course in AVT (Díaz Cintas & Orero 2003, Mas López & Orero 2003).

55   Bartrina and Espasa propose an exercise in voice-over as a drill previous to dubbing. They write: "We include voice-over as a preparatory exercise for dubbing, with the main emphasis in isochrony; or equal duration of original and the voiced-over translation" (2005: 89–90).

We did not know of any courses in voice-over translation at any other university or private institution in Europe (Moreno 2003, Sponholz 2003, Malmkjær 2004, Tennent 2005, Moreno 2005, Díaz Cintas, Mas López & Orero 2006) so we had no orientation or guidelines to inspire us or to adhere to. Hence, we were faced with the task of preparing the syllabus content, its teaching approach and methodology, along with the teaching aids and materials (Thorpe 1995, Chesterman 2005). We consulted four of the most representative books on translation training: Baker's *In other words: A course book on translation* (1992), Kussmaul's *Training the translator* (1995), Hatim and Mason's *The translator as communicator* (1997), and Tennent's *Training for the millennium* (2005) in addition to the two special issues in evaluation and training published by *The Translator* 6(2) (2000) and *Meta* 46 (2001). On the whole, these publications deal with the professional profile (of the generic 'translator'), which is useful but the text typology and the translator's functions and skills are clearly focused on the written media. Occasionally, the translation of specialist texts is mentioned but, as we have already mentioned, this is not the case for voice-over.

While it is true we are no longer in the infancy of Translation Studies, we are still in the phase of setting up the terminology, organising more training and competence development for some specialities within Translation Studies, such as AVT or Media Accessibility, which are a growing academic field and industry mainly given the fact that are an intrinsic part of the Information Society. Legal, commercial or medical translations are specialized translations which could be analysed by an umbrella methodological and hypothetical framework given the fact that these translations all belong to the same media: the written text. AVT has as many topics and genres as translation in general. The many concepts and norms which were once drawn up for Translation Studies no longer apply for AVT. Concepts such as *faithfulness*, *equivalence*, or *norm* have new and shifting definitions, which must be studied again, taking into consideration that AVT is a dynamic field which is of epigonic nature to that of industry. New formats, new genres, new software, new hardware, and ever-changing technologies require that the audiovisual translators be professionals who must be in constant contact with the industry for which they work and must be aware of the industry's development. They must be professionals who have to have a thorough knowledge of the formats and technologies behind the documents being translated. With all these factors in mind, we created a team of industry experts who were prepared to think about the translator profile which would meet the market trends and needs. The experts were also prepared to come and teach at the university and together they helped to create the syllabus, the teaching materials and the general course setup and they started to run the face-to-face course.

5.2 The translator for voice-over

The translator for voice-over does not differ from any other profile in audiovisual translation, and in order to avoid reinventing the wheel, we depart from Nord and her description of the *functional translator*.

> S/he is aware of the fact, in today's translation practice, translations are needed for a variety of communicative functions which are not always the same as the intended function of the corresponding source text (= professional knowledge). S/he knows that the selection of linguistic and non-linguistic signs which make up a text is guided by situational and cultural factors and that this principle applies to both source and target-cultural text productions (= metacognitive competence). S/he is able to spot the "rich points" (Agar 1991: 168) where the behaviours of the representatives of a particular pair of cultures or diacultures in a given situation is so divergent that it may lead to communication conflicts or even breakdowns, and finds ways and means to solve cultural conflicts without taking sides (= intercultural competence). S/he knows that, due to culture specific conventions, apparently similar or analogous structures of two languages are not always used with the same frequency or in the same situation (= distribution) by the respective culture communities and that the use of the wrong set of signs may severely interfere with the text's functionality. S/he has the ability to produce a target text serving the desired function, even though the source text may be badly written or poorly reproduced (= writing abilities) and knows how to use both traditional and modern (i.e. electronic) translation aids and knowledge sources (= media competence). S/he has a good general education and a better specific knowledge of the topic dealt within the source text – or knows how to compensate efficiently for any lack of knowledge (= research competence). DS/he works fast, cost-efficiently, and to perfection, even under high pressure (= stress resistance) and knows what her/his translations are worth (= self-assertion, from the practitioner's point of view and self-assurance or self-confidence, as the trainers see it). (2005: 210)

In her list, Nord reflects on the profile that academics and practitioners agreed upon at the 1999 Leipzig Conference on Translation Quality, but interestingly for voice-over she adds:

the practitioners uttered a few more requirements such as skills in specific forms of translation, e. g. dubbing, voice-over […] management and leading competence, the ability to work in a team and to constantly adapt to changing working conditions, revision skills, and the like. (2005: 211)

Complementary issues such as competences dealing with the identification of work environment, job organization, personal planning, and the set of abilities which makes a person ready to face the new 'information society', such as: creativity, flexibility, adaptability and the capacity to learn and solve problems, employability and adequacy to market needs, were also taken into consideration when setting up the profile and when designing the syllabus and its implementation (Mas López & Orero 2004a, Wilss 2004: 10, Mackenzie 2004: 33).

5.3 Setting up the course

During the first year feedback from students and lecturers was crucial to adapt, sometimes on a weekly basis, the way in which the course was taught. One example was the original idea of splitting the three-hour class into three different exercises with separate objectives. The first part of the class was used for correcting, as a group, the homework produced individually from work set the previous week. The second part of the class would introduce a particular issue or set of issues, practical or theoretical, which would be exploited in the third part of the class. The work given was designed in such a way that it had to be taken away as homework. Two decades ago, VHS was the only format that we had for working with audiovisual media. With this in mind material for each student was prepared in advance, not realizing that students perhaps did not have easy access to a VHS player, as it turned out to be the case. This meant that working individually with a VHS player and computer had to be done exclusively at the university, while more descriptive and theoretical activities had to be set up as homework.

After three years and some adjustments we felt confident about the course, so we thought it was time to transfer the experience to the online format. An interesting fact which illustrates beautifully the dynamic nature of audiovisual translation and its challenges is the fact that while in the first year we were using VHS tapes for teaching and working, now we are working on the intranet server. Back in 2001, digital technology was not widely available and the change in audiovisual formats from analogue to digital had not taken place. Within a year, VHS tapes and video recorders had become obsolete and had been replaced with CD-ROM players and CD-ROM players were used as media support. Two years later, DVDs were the only thinkable format on campus, while memory sticks or portable hard disks were just beginning to be used.

At present, students bring their own portable memory hardware to class, downloading the audiovisual material from the server on the intranet server. The ever-changing world of technologies no doubt poses a challenge to the audiovisual translator but also to the course lecturers, organizers and institutions which have to update facilities at a record-breaking pace. Teaching methodology has many approaches and we opted for a 'deep learning approach' within the Bologna paradigm. The deep learning approach is a communicative approach which promotes a shift from the teacher to the student and from teaching to learning. The student is responsible for the process of learning skills, through exercises and hard work and the assistance and tutoring provided by the teacher. In addition to that, the student is also believed to reap the rewards from the benefits of the interaction between. The approach taken was thought to be adequate given the nature of the course, its vocational application, the technical requirements, and the subject matter, as Wilss points out "one of the characteristic features of translation teaching is the combination of knowledge and skills" (2004: 13).

5.3.1 Voice-over translation: Face-to-face format

The course we set up here was originally taught in three-hour sessions, once a week for a period of ten weeks. It is interesting to note that postgraduate teaching at the *Universitat Autònoma de Barcelona* (UAB) is placed in the evening section of the time-table schedule. Classes had to be organized between 4:00 p.m. and 9:00 p.m. Being a postgraduate course, the students who attended the course usually held day-time jobs, which fits in perfectly with the times, but possibly reduced performance concentration taking into account that these long sessions were organized at the end of the day and that most postgraduate students also work. This is why we have decided to shorten the teaching hours but extend the sessions from ten to fifteen weeks.

As far as the technical requirements are concerned, students work in a multimedia room with individual computers connected to the intranet server. The software used is RealPlayer or Media Player with a split window and a word processor (generally MS Word). Although in certain countries (e.g., the UK) translators are required to act as voice talents and have to learn to use specific software (see Chapter 4), this is not the case in Catalonia and, therefore, students are not trained in this area and Windows Movie Maker is used only to raise the students' awareness of voiceover isochrony.

In fact, technical requirements are one of the thorny issues when organizing AVT courses because substantial (time-related and financial) investments are required to set up a state-of-the-art teaching room and to make all the materials available in digital format. Audiovisual material, whatever format, can be downloaded worked online or installed on each of the computers in the teaching lab. It can also be given to the students on a CD-ROM or memory stick at the beginning of the year and then brings us to the issue of copyright.

Copyright on AV material, its formats and limitations, should be observed when using such material for research, teaching and training purposes. Each country has different copyright laws and the laws that are in force in, for example, Spain may not necessarily be in force in other countries. Nevertheless, a big step forward for the field of AVT would be to achieve some sort of universal dispensation of copyright when excerpts of audiovisual material are used for research or training. At present, legislation is rather ambiguous and little is known because of various reasons: the many available formats in which media can be supported, how long an excerpt is, or the percentage of volume that the work represents as part of the overall work from which it comes from. With the many media campaigns against piracy there is an overall feeling that copying audiovisual material is banned. While this may be the case for public use and home distribution, there is some leeway for research, and it is up to researchers to find out which regulations apply in the country in which the research is being carried out.

In our case, we opted to buy from some twenty films an authoring firm and these films which would cover most of the genres which would be investigated. That gave us some material which we could digitize and copy for students to work with at home.[56] Given that in Spain an indeterminate portion of an original audiovisual work, also in an indeterminate format, can be used for teaching purposes and can be quoted in research, we decided to work with limited intranet access, with which video clips could be downloaded for work during the class. Moreover, the lecturers, who are professional translators, usually bring excerpts of translations done by themselves and already broadcast to discuss with the students.

Each class/week focuses on an exercise which poses different challenges for voice-over translation. There are some specific features, such as the importance of the image or documentation processes which are found in the entire curriculum (Matamala, 2004, 2008).

Each week the class focuses on one of the many cases described in Chapters 3 and 4. Classes and exercises are graded according to level of difficulty and are centred around the tasks that are needed to carry out the translation as if it were an actual job. On some occasions, for example when the translation has to be done from the screen, students have experienced difficulties because there is no written script from which they can translate. Even though we wondered whether exercises should not be based on real translation cases so as students would be better at coping exercises, we finally settled on giving the students more time to do exercises, but not on lowering the level of complexity. In addition, we favoured examples taken from real life.

a) *Theoretical sessions*

The first session is devoted to theoretical aspects of not only voice-over but also of off-screen dubbing, since these transfer modes are often related. The process of translation is explained and the differences between translating for production and for postproduction are highlighted. After this first theoretical session, a professional from a dubbing studio is invited to show how voice-over is recorded in a dubbing studio and to explain what happens to the translation once they are delivered. Although the students are taught that voice-over is used in Eastern European countries to revoice fictional products, the course tackles only the translation of factual programmes and this because of the language combinations in which

56   In the meantime, we have reverted to the old system of teaching, asking students to do some work at home with audiovisual files, which they take home on their memory sticks.

students generally work (from English into either Spanish or Catalan). However, if this module was to be taught in a centre with other language combinations, some sessions should be devoted to the particularities of audiovisual translation.

b) *Translating for postproduction with a script*

The next set of classes focus on translating documentaries for postproduction, and here students work with a script. During six weeks students translate different types of documentaries which present different challenges, starting with the off-screen dubbing of commentaries and slowly moving on to more complex voice-overs of interviews. Apart from the difficulties related to each transfer mode, clips are carefully selected so that students are confronted with a wide variety of recurrent problems: wrong transcriptions, content errors, terminological problems or documentation problems. During the first weeks the products chosen contain fairly formal language, but by the end of this session the standard language of narrators is combined with the informal language of interviewees, forcing the students to reword interventions which otherwise would not be understandable. Finally, a last session is devoted to the translation of products in unknown languages translated through an English pivot translation.

Once the students master the translation of commentaries and interviews with a script, they take a step further and start translating without a script, mainly bonus materials for DVDs. During four weeks they have to improve their listening comprehension skills, an important competence in audiovisual translation. This makes the students aware of the idiosyncrasy of this type of transfer mode, which is halfway between written translation and interpreting. The students also learn to introduce time codes in translations and create character lists, which some dubbing studios ask their translators to deliver.

c) *Translating for production*

Finally, in the last three weeks, the students work with rough unedited material which presents even more comprehension difficulties. In addition, they translate for voice-over and create commentaries introducing time codes and dealing with all sorts of accents, language varieties and topics.

The degree of difficulty of the products increases gradually and by the end of the year students are able to translate for both production and postproduction, with and without a script. Students are also faced with a wide range of topics (cinema, current affairs, history, travel documentaries, science, wildlife, etc.), which impels them to find information about topics unknown to them and to do so in a extremely short period of time, thus experiencing real-life working environments.

5.3.2 *Voice-over translation: Online course*

Before turning to the syllabus and exercises, which form the teaching core of the online voice-over translation course, the online methodology that we apply must be explained.

Articles have been published on the specificities of the Virtual Learning Environment (VLE) adopted in this course (Amador, Dorado & Orero 2004, Amador, Dorado & Orero 2004 forthcoming). A major difference between the online course and the traditional face-to-face course is that the online course has been designed to be taught by linear development. This means that students follow only one module at a time. Each module consists of ten units, which have a theoretical framework, although the emphasis is predominantly on practical aspects. A unit takes place over one week – Monday to Monday. Students hand in their work on Monday, the same day on which they receive the marked work that they handed for marking the week before. The process of linear development also means that while all the students are able to work at the same pace and receive general weekly feedback from the teacher, they can also participate in group discussions either via chats or forums. A further benefit is the possibility of incorporating new students, who can join the course every 11 weeks, and that teachers are employed for a 12-week period.

The VLE has a section for curricular content on an intranet server. In this section materials are created in a multimedia format, which can then be exploited individually by each student.

Figure 11.
Screen of Dubbing Module where Voice-over *(Voces superpuestas)* is located.

Completed exercises are sent to the teacher every week and the teacher corrects the exercises and returns them to the students with feedback the following week. Comments are made individually, though some more general issues that seem to be recurrent in exercises in general tend to be focused on in weekly group discussions.

The communication area (highlighted in orange in Figure 12) offers students the following facilities: personal e-mail, a forum where general topics are posted (Figure 13), a chat service for those connected synchronically or those who wish to carry out a group activity, and a resource area, (also located on the intranet), where the course bibliography is kept for student to download together with some general links which may be of interest to (audiovisual) translators. The job-offer area is also located here, together with a diary of events such as seminars, conferences, etc.

Figure 12.
Screen of different services available on the Intranet.

Figure 13. Forum screen.

The course was designed to be run and taught by a team, brought together to offer a similar course as the course on offer with the traditional face-to-face postgraduate audiovisual content. This was done to follow the approach for creating materials which focus on the process of creation rather than evaluation. For this approach, the experience of previous face-to-face experience was important since it was the team work which seemed to work in the case of the face-to-face course. There was also an understanding and a feeling of empathy among the team members.

The team opted to create high-quality material rather than to test already created material since "good quality can be built in, rather than bad quality being inspected out" (Koumi 1995: 341). Koumi (1995) also lists the following recommendations which taken into consideration for this course:

– recruiting high-quality staff for the materials creation.
– training of staff striving to retain staff so that they will become experienced
– working in well-established teams
– teams permitted plenty of thinking time to re-draft and refine materials
– teams working to a student-centred set of design principles, which are frequently line reappraised.

While in the face-to-face course voice-over is a course with its own identity, in the online format voice-over is taught in only one week and it is placed in the module of dubbing. The reasons behind this difference lie, first of all, in the organization of the online material and the time limitations of the module. While in the face-to-face course voice-over started as a subsidiary, it has now become a fundamental course, the online course does not offer any choice of courses. Hence, we decided that voice-over needed to be present, but we did not have the possibility to offer any additional credits. Financial difficulties are another reason why voice-over does not have its own module. Designing, preparing and creating online materials are taxing activities both time-wise and money-wise. Postgraduate courses must be self-financed, which means that subsidiary courses can be implemented only when the course has some benefits. After two years of running the online course two new modules were developed: intralinguistic subtitling and video-games. Two years later, audio description and subtitling for the deaf and hard of hearing was added, and we are now in the stage of thinking of the new modules that we will be able to create next.

Although only lasting one week, in this unit students are given a wide view of both voice-overs and off-screen dubbing (Matamala 2004, 2008). There is a theoretical unit with a whole variety of examples (available on the intranet), which students have to read in order to get a general idea. Subsequently, the teacher introduces new topics and addresses any doubts that students might have in the forum area and during the weekly chat. To assess their evolution, students are asked to do two exercises which summarize the main characteristics of both transfer modes in non-fictional products. These exercises will be discussed in the next section.

5.4 Exercises

The online version of the master's degree, which currently lasts a week, condenses in two exercises the main difficulties of translating interviews for voice-over and commentaries for off-screen dubbing, for production and postproduction respectively. Whereas the interview is a rough product without a script and with many proper names and historical references, the commentary that the students are asked to translate is an excerpt from a wildlife documentary, with an extremely accurate script, which contains a whole variety of terms.

The face-to-face format, with a longer syllabus, includes a wider range of exercises. A selection of these activities is presented in the following charts. Further exercises can be found in Matamala (2008).

Exercise 1	
Activity:	– Translate a commentary from English into Spanish. – Transfer mode: off-screen dubbing.
Aim of the activity:	– Be aware of the presence of transcription errors and of the need to spell-check all proper names.
Materials:	– Clip from the documentary *Swimming With Giants*, from the series "The Quest" (25 seconds). – Transcription from the script provided to the translator: "Each winter most of the North Atlantic hump back population migrate up to 4,00 miles from their northern feeding grounds to three nurseries in Dominican waters. Samana Bay, Navidad Bank and Silver Bank, a thousand square mile patch of reef."
Challenges:	– Translating proper names which have a Spanish equivalent (Samana Bay, Navidad Bank and Silver Bank, North Atlantic). – Unit conversion (square miles, miles). – Correcting errors in the original (4,00 miles) – Terminological problems: "humpback whales", "nurseries". – Reaching isochrony.

Exercise 2	
Activity:	– Translate a commentary into Catalan. – Transfer mode: off-screen dubbing.
Aim of the activity:	– Learning to solve terminological problems and dealing with formal language.

Materials:	– Ten-minute clip from a wildlife documentary – Postproduction script with an accurate transcription.
Challenges:	– Creating a commentary which fits the space available (isochrony). – Reproducing an oral formal language (not a written one). – Looking for terms in the target language: in some cases, no equivalent might exist and students have to create terminological proposals. – Interaction text-image: they have to be careful so that the commentary is synchronized with the image (action synchrony).

Exercise 3	
Activity:	– Translate an excerpt from an interview for production from English into Spanish. – Transfer mode: voice-over.
Aim of the activity:	– Creating an understandable discourse in the target language from a hesitant unplanned interview without a script.
Materials:	– Clip from the interview to a world leader scientist whose discourse is characterized by: many oral markers, scientific content treated with a colloquial register and vocabulary, names of other leading scientists, strong local accent.
Challenges:	– Need to reword the language. – Comprehension of the original – Translating for voice-over: need to adapt the length of the speeches (voice-over isochrony). – Introducing time codes (spotting).

Exercise 4	
Activity:	– Translate an excerpt from a documentary with different types of speakers / discourses, using different transfer modes: voice-over for interviews, subtitles for spontaneous language and off-screen dubbing for commentaries.
Aim of the activity:	– Mastering different transfer modes in a single product
Materials:	– Clip from a documentary from the series "Pathfinders", on travel adventures, which includes a narrator (on-screen and off-screen), improvised shots and talking heads. – A postproduction script is provided.
Challenges:	– Combining different transfer modes in a single product. – Proper names. – Adapting different types of language: from the narrator's formal language to the hesitant interviews and the totally unplanned shots with informal language. – Detecting content errors.

Exercise 5	
Activity:	– Translate interviews from a documentary and create a commentary.
Aim of the activity:	– Creating a commentary from scratch, applying journalistic skills.
Materials:	– Clip from a documentary on the Isle of Wight. There are a series of interviews in English and the original narrator is not heard. – No script provided.
Challenges:	– Translating interviews for voice-over. – Creating of a commentary from scratch: students have to improve their journalistic skills and create a text gathering information from the interviews, the image and using other resources such as the Internet. – Specific terminology on erosion.

Exercise 6	
Activity:	– Translating an excerpt from an interview for production from English into Spanish. – Transfer mode: voice-over.
Aim of the activity:	– Creating a syntactically correct discourse in the target language from an interview with abstract language without a script. The translation should fit the length of the speech.
Materials:	– Clip from the interview to a world leader scientist whose discourse is characterized by: many oral markers abstract and lose information with a colloquial register and vocabulary. Short interventions with open answers.
Challenges:	– Need to reword the language – Comprehension of the original – Reduction of discourse – Translating for voice-over: need to adapt the length of the speeches. – Introducing time codes.

Exercise 7	
Activity:	– Translating an excerpt from an interview for production from English into Spanish. – Transfer mode: voice-over.
Aim of the activity:	– Creating an understandable discourse in the target language from an interview without a script where the speaker is not fluent in English.

Materials:	– Clip from the interview to a world leader mathematician whose discourse is characterized by: many false starts, oral markers from other language which is not English, use of very concrete technical terms imbedded in chaotic English which is hard to understand, the speed of delivery is very fast.
Challenges:	– Need to research terminology – Understanding the original – Rewording the language. – Translating for voice-over: need to adapt the length of the speeches. – Introducing time codes.

Exercise 8	
Activity:	– Translating an excerpt from an interview for production from English into Spanish. – Transfer mode: voice-over.
Aim of the activity:	– Creating an understandable discourse in the target language from an interview with many takes of same question and many body language which need synchronization of discourse. The speaker uses precise academic English full of passive constructions.
Materials:	– Clip from the interview to a world leader marine scientist whose discourse is characterized by: sentences always start with much hesitation then launching at great speed into the answer. The personality of speaker and the subject matter forces the interviewer to decide to make several takes for each question. The speed of delivery is very fast.
Challenges:	– Need to research terminology – Understanding the original – Rewording the language from English academic to Spanish oral and conversational. – Need to adapt the length of the speeches. – Many similar answers from different takes: need for concentration. – Introducing time codes and description to match discourse with body language.

5.5 Assessment

In the field of Translation Studies dealing with the topic of evaluation is a thorny issue as a result of the number of approaches (House 2001) and is itself the object of evaluation. As late as 2005, 35 years after beginning training translators, Christiane Nord (2005) presented her insights into and experience in training, which goes to show that there is a monumental lack of systematic and scientific approach to training and evaluating all the areas of evaluation: selection of learning material, teaching and learning methods, and quality assessment.

Since we are dealing with the realm of humanities and very much detached from the pure sciences, objective assessment is a remote possibility. To complicate matters even further we also have to take into consideration the recent shifts in the paradigm, that is the shift from teaching to learning to learn and the definition and testing for competence rather than traditional translational abilities. We are dealing with a course aimed at specialization and set in an academic environment geared towards life-long learning, and where translation is one of the many skills needed to train a successful intercultural and multi-skilled multimedia communicator.

Carol Meier (2000) was advancing this reality when she wrote:[57]

> Today, however, the growing demand for translations in such fields as technology and business and the increased scrutiny of translators' work by scholars in many disciplines is giving rise to a need for more nuanced, more specialized, and more explicit methods of determining value. Some refer to this determination as evaluation, others use the term assessment. Either way, the question is one of measurement and judgement, which are always unavoidably subjective and frequently rest on criteria that are not overtly expressed. This means that devising more complex evaluative practices involves not only quantitative techniques but also an exploration of the attitudes, preferences, or individual values on which criteria are established.

Training evaluation is "the systematic collection of descriptive and judgement information necessary to make effective training decisions related to the selection, adoption, value, and modification of various instructional

---

57 This quote is from BITRA: <http://cv1.cpd.ua.es/tra_int/usu/vercompleto.asp> [Retrieved on 18 March 2007]

activities" (Goldstein 1980: 237), Lee-Jahnke (2001: 258) dealing with the issue of quality further emphasizes that "true quality can only be achieved if the goal is made perfectly clear to the student", and thus in the previous section each activity has been presented along with its aim.

Having said all of the above, quality assessment in audiovisual translation essentially differs from assessment in the field of Translation Studies because of the importance that Translation Studies allocates to the process of translation as opposed to the quality of the product. A process-oriented assessment (Gile 2004) is recommended throughout the training syllabus in view of both the psychological advantages and the efficiency of the process in guiding students. Nevertheless, product-oriented assessment is necessary in order to increase the efficiency of the teachers' intervention in helping students optimize the product and to facilitate entrance onto the real market. We try to strike a balance between theoretical and practical (read academic and professional) features, but before going into the evaluation of students' performances in each teaching format, we must emphasize the importance that we pay to the evaluation of the materials, lecturers and their reception by students. This evaluation is carried out at the end of the course and using a questionnaire. Gabr (2001) favours this methodology and lists the following advantages:

– It is the best tool to be used for large numbers of respondents;
– it provides quantitative data for analysis;
– it gathers in-depth information on the training students need;
– it can be completed and analyzed quickly;
– it is relatively inexpensive;
– it is more accurate if anonymous and is convenient, because the respondent sets the pace;
– it also provides a variety of response options and thus is easier to answer.

We have designed the following questionnaire, in which students assess the topics referred to in each of the items below. They do so by giving a mark on a scale of 1 to 5 (with low marks representing bad qualities and high marks good qualities) for items 1 to 7 and by answering the open questions (8 and 9).

1. The appropriateness of the course objectives to the actual needs of students.
2. The progression of the content has been adequate.
3. Achievement of the course objectives.
4. Quality of the materials.
5. The degree of difficulty of the topics has been adequate.
6. Relevance of the course to market needs.
7. The overall performance of the instructor
8. Suggestions/comments about the course content.
9. Other suggestions/comments.

5.5.1 Evaluation in the face-to-face format

In the face-to-face module on voice-over, students are required to attend 80% of the course and their participation in class is taken into account, promoting a lively debate and interaction between teachers and students. In fact, each week the teacher provides short task to be done at home, which is then analysed in class. Although not compulsory, those students who wish to hand in the task are invited to do so, and lecturers send the students personal feedback. The students are also asked to hand in three different longer assignments, which correspond to three different steps of difficulty: translating a commentary from a documentary for off-screen dubbing, translating an interview for production and creating a commentary from scratch. In our opinion, the combination of three compulsory assignments plus the possibility to have a short weekly task corrected allows those students who are really interested in this modality to improve gradually and achieve a good command of voice-over and other related transfer modes by the end of this 15-week course.

5.5.2 Evaluation in the online format

For the online unit of voice-over the tutor marks every student's translation and posts the answer to each and every student. Subsequently, a general comment is made in the forum about the general difficulties found in the translations handed in. If students want to, they can have another try and do the translation again taking into account the personal comments and the comments posted on the forum. The students may also look at the clip of the commercial version which is always posted. With all that background information, and after having done the translation again, the students can once more send their translations to the tutor for marking or they can simply reply to the tutor to discuss the comments and corrections suggested. This way, there is active communication between the students and the tutor, sometimes even more dynamic and personal than in the traditional face-to-face courses. Students are evaluated taking into consideration active participation on the chat, the proposed translation and the many interventions in the forum.

5.6 Conclusion

We would like to conclude this chapter by pointing out that we have presented two innovative courses (face-to-face format vs online format), developed at the *Universitat Autònoma de Barcelona*, where students are trained in translating non-fictional products for both voice-over and off-screen dubbing. Learning to translate for voice-over – face-to-face or online – is now a reality. After eight years of observing steady numbers of students who took the course and who were satisfied with the course contents, we can safely say that we have managed to design, develop and successfully run a course (face-to-face and online) on voice-over within an MA in Audiovisual Translation. The rate of success can be measured by many standards: level of student satisfaction with the teaching, which can be measured by the number of students who recommend the course in email distribution lists, and personal communication. It can also be measured by the number of students who manage to secure full-time jobs as translators. While the first students in the course enrolled thanks to systematic and much programmed marketing, the course now uses word of mouth advertising and we enjoy a steady flow of students who make teaching online a highly enjoyable experience.

We have tried to design courses which mirror the market reality and needs (Arango-Keeth & Koby 2003) and aim at a wider profile than the general translator. When we set up the course, we had in mind a person who will perform a variety of communicative functions with a life-long learning attitude to upgrading multimedia and IT skills, and perform these tasks working to tight deadlines and in adverse situations. For us, this is the profile of the audiovisual translator today, voice-over being an extremely relevant translation experience needed for other audiovisual translation transfers. Let us think of the common need for having to check the continuity script with the audiovisual text on the screen. We hope that the approach and exercises will be a useful point of departure for someone setting up new voice-over courses.

5.7 Suggested exercises

1. Look online and see if there are any voice-over courses available. Now answer the following questions:

   - Do they include translation?
   - From what perspective is voice-over considered?
   - Are courses academic or professional?
   - Can you see any issues related to analysis or study in the course description?

2. Search in the internet for academic institutions in your country.

   - Do they offer any audiovisual course?
   - At what level: undergraduate or postgraduate?
   - Is voice-over a course?
   - What are the main audiovisual modalities on offer?
   - Where will you place voice-over? Justify your answer.

3. Why do you think that voice-over is not (usually) studied at university? Why do you think academics have not paid much attention to this audiovisual translation modality?

   After studying the course, do you think it should be studied based on its own merits? Or do you think it should be part of another translating modality, such as dubbing?

1. In his book *Can we trust the BBC* (2008) former BBC journalist Robin Aitken writes:

   If you are an Ulster Unionist, or a Eurosceptic, or an evangelical Christian, or a member of the Bush administration, or a pro-life campaigner, or even a plain old Tory, you have very good reason for not taking at face value everything the Corporation tells you. But it would clearly be wrong, and absurd, to say that *everything* the BBC says is wrong and tainted. Much of its output is excellent, as good as anything available; it's just that so much of it is coloured by a set of political and cultural assumptions which many do not share.

   Go to <http://www.bbc.co.uk/> and choose some news related to your country, or an issue you are familiar with. Does Aitken's comment sound reasonable?

   What is this ???

6. Giving voice to practitioners and academics: A global survey on voice-over

Who was the questionnaire sent to? The answer on p. 165.

From the onset of this book we, the authors, wanted to write something which the largest possible audience would be able to relate to but at the same time we were aware of certain limitations. We wrote this book from two distinct, geographical perspectives: a Catalonian perspective and a Brazilian perspective, which could be considered two extremes both in size and politically. We looked at bibliographies in Catalan, French, German, Italian, Polish, Portuguese, Spanish and Polish, and we are fully aware that much more has been written in other languages that we could not access. We tried to compensate this imbalance by designing a questionnaire (see Appendix 1), which we sent to more than one hundred people. Half of the questionnaires came back, but only 43 contained relevant information which we processed and used to write this chapter.

When this book was conceived, satellite television was in its infancy and we did not realize that only a few years later it would not matter where in the world you were to enjoy British Sky TV. We sent the questionnaires to as many different countries that we could think of and in our e-mails we also asked our respondents to forward the e-mail and questionnaire to anyone they might think could help us out. This explains why we sometimes got two replies from small countries and relating to minority languages. The idea behind the questionnaire was that respondents would be able to give us a state-of-the-art overview of voice-over in their countries of residence.

Badly written, bad argument

We received questionnaires from a wide variety of countries, even though there are European countries missing (e.g., France, Netherlands) and no input was obtained from the Middle East and from North and Central America. In addition, there are entire continents (e.g., Africa) which are not represented (with the exception of South Africa), as shown in Table 6.

Table 6. Number of respondents by countries.

	01	02	03	05	06
Austria	✓				
Canada					✓
Catalonia			✓		
Croatia	✓				
Czech Republic	✓				
England UK	✓				
Germany	✓				
Greece		✓			
Israel	✓				
Italy			✓		
Latvia	✓				
New Zealand	✓				
Norway	✓				
Peru	✓				
Poland			✓		
Portugal		✓			
Republic of China (Taiwan)	✓				
Romania	✓				
Scotland UK		✓			
Slovenia	✓				
South Africa	✓				
Sweden			✓		
Turkey	✓				
Venezuela	✓				
Wales UK	✓				

Despite not presenting a detailed overview of the practice of voice-over around the globe, there is no doubt that the results of these questionnaires will help us corroborate, reject or expand the ideas developed in the previous chapters. Hence, we have decided to summarize the results obtained, being fully aware that these results are neither systematic nor fully representative.

The results of the questionnaires can be grouped under the following sections:

a) personal and professional questions, which will design a profile of our respondents (6.1);

b) questions related to voice-over terminology, usage and reception (6.2);
c) questions related to aspects dealing with voice-over features (6.3);
d) questions related to the teaching of voice-over (6.4);
e) questions related to professional aspects of voice-over translation (6.5) and
f) questions related to the practice of creating commentaries (6.6).

As already suggested, answers to the questionnaire were not systematic. Respondents sometimes chose more than one alternative in questions, sometimes they did not answer a question at all. There were even times when they answered only parts of the questions. Therefore, compatibility between the number of answers and the number of respondents is rarely achieved and cannot be expected.

6.1 Personal and professional questions

We asked a couple of questions in order to have a general idea of who are respondents actually were. Of the 43 respondents, nine were academics, 22 were professionals and 12 ticked both options. This gives us a marked professional slant to the replies, which is, in fact, what we had in mind since we were interested in national practices from those individuals with hands-on experience.

Within academia we found universities from across the globe,[58] but we received considerably higher input from European institutions, which was what we had already expected considering the respondents' countries of origin. Independent academics came from Croatia, Greece, Portugal, Slovenia and Sweden. Of the 22 respondents belonging only to the world of industry, the vast majority (16 respondents) work as free-lance translators while ten were from mainly state-owned TV channels, and more interestingly from small communities. The remaining respondents indicated

58 Universitatea Babeş Bolyai, Cluj-Napoca (Romania), Bar LLan University (Israel), University of Vienna (Austria), Stockholm University (Sweden), Ming Chuan University (Taiwan), Roehampton University (UK), Universitat Autònoma de Barcelona (Spain), Łódź University (Poland), Instituto Superior de Contabilidade e Administração, Instituto Politécnico do Porto (Portugal), North West University, Vaal Triangle Campus (South Africa), University of Montreal (Canada), Hellenic Open University (Greece) and University of Bologna (Italy).

that they were working for private translation companies.[59] As a whole, out of the 34 respondents that belong to the industry only (22) and to both the industry and the academia (12), those that do voice-over translation for television work mainly for the following channels mentioned in Table 7:

Table 7. Channels for which the 34 voice-over professionals work.

	Channels per country						
Canada	Télétoon	TF1	France 2 France 3	VRAK	YTV	TVA	TQS
Catalonia	TV3	C33					
Croatia	HRT-Croatian Radio and TV	Nova TV	RTL Croatia	HBO Croatia			
Czech Republic	Public Czech channels						
Germany	WDR Cologne						
Greece	Public Greek Channels						
Israel	Israeli TV	First Channel	Educational Channel	ARTE France			
Italy	RAI	Mediaset					
Latvia	Public Latvian channels						
New Zealand	Māori TV						
Norway	TV2						
Poland	TV1 TV2 TV4	Polsat	Ale Kino!	TCM	BBC Prime		
Scotland UK	BBC2						
Slovenia	Slovenia National TV	National Geographic	BBC International	CNN International	Discovery		
Sweden	TV4	TV4+	ZTV	Sveriges TV 1–2			
Non-identified country of professional	EITV-Entertainment TV Satellite						

59   The companies cited were: Alliance Atlantis Vivafilm (Canada), Argos Company Ltd. (Eastern European Translation and Localization Experts, Poland), Etcetera C.A. (Venezuela), Itfc (London, UK), JARP (Canada), Softtitler, Språk Centrum AB (Stockholm).

As far as the 43 respondents' working languages are concerned, Table 8 below indicates the percentages of source and target languages they work with.

Table 8. Source and target languages with which respondents work.

Percentages	Source Languages	Target Languages
83.7%	English	
39.5%		English
30.2%	French	
23%		French
18.6%	German Italian	
11%	Spanish	
9.3%		Italian Spanish
7%	Danish European Portuguese Swedish	Catalan German Swedish
4.5%	Norwegian Russian	Greek Polish European Portuguese
2.3%	Afrikaans Catalan Croatian Hebrew Japanese Māori Polish Welsh Unspecified Eastern European languages	Afrikaans Brazilian Portuguese Chinese Czech Latin American Spanish Latvian Māori Romanian Scottish Gaelic Slovenian Turkish Welsh Unspecified Eastern European languages

As can be observed, English and French scored highest as both source languages (English with 36 respondents (83.7%) and French with 13 or 30.2%) and target languages (English with 17 or 39.5% and French with

23%), followed by the source languages: German and Italian (18.6% each), Spanish (11.5%), Danish, European Portuguese, and Swedish (7% each), Norwegian and Russian (4.5% each), Afrikaans, Catalan, Croatian, unspecified Eastern-European languages, Hebrew, Japanese, Māori, Polish and Welsh (2.3% each). These were also translated into Italian and Spanish (9.3% each), Catalan, German and Swedish (7% each), Greek, Polish, and European Portuguese (4.5% each), Afrikaans, Brazilian Portuguese, Chinese, Czech, unspecified Eastern European languages, Latin American Spanish, Latvian, Māori, Romanian, Scottish Gaelic, Slovene, Turkish and Welsh (2.3% each). The highest figures also suggest that originally English-speaking audiovisual output still occupy a central position in international programming.

When asked about the experience they had as translation teachers/researchers/practitioners, only three (7%) out of 43 had been working for less than a year, the same number had been working for over 30 years and another group of 3 respondents (7%) did not reply. The largest numbers of respondents had worked for 10 years or less (44%) and from 11 to 20 years (23%). Other 11% is in the activity from 21 to 30 years. Based on these figures, we can say most respondents (78%) are in general highly experienced professionals that have been in the activity from around 10 to 30 years. Though they were not asked for either age or gender, it is easy to work out the average of the former.

Concerning the audiovisual transfer modes respondents teach/do research on/work on and the frequency they perform these activities, the answers elicited demonstrated that open subtitling is taught, researched and practised more often than any other mode by 22 respondents (51%) with dubbing and voice-over scoring second in frequency (34.8% each), followed by closed subtitling for the deaf and hard-of-hearing (28%). The least marked were, in decreasing order, live interpreting, surtitling for the theatre/opera and the most recent audiovisual translation type, audio-description.

6.2 Specific questions on voice-over terminology and usage

In this part of the questionnaire, respondents were asked two main questions. The first question related to whether they referred to voice-over as "an audiovisual mode of transfer where firstly the original version is translated, and then its target language version is recorded (no lip-synch) on top of the original speech, which in turn remains audible" was largely discussed in Chapter 1 of this book. As a main conclusion, 35 respondents (81.40%) answered positively whereas the remaining eight respondents (18.6%), most of them from small linguistic communities, tended to associate the term voice-over with oral texts delivered by an off-screen speaker and without the co-presence of the original, such as *speakning* in Swedish, *sinkronizacija* in Croatian (similarly in Slovenia), *cteny komentar* in Czech. Except for one Catalonian respondent, who named voice-over also as "the interviewee's speech", all associations reveal the impact of Film Studies for the conceptualization of voice-over in Translation Studies.

In terms of usage, the second question of this section confirmed another issue introduced in Chapter 1 of this book, that is, the apparent close connection between the voice-over mode and the so-called factual genre, at least in the Western world. This is so because, when asked which audiovisual products were voiced-over, documentaries (with the narrator either off or on) scored a total of 59 answers (40.9%), documentaries' interviewees or talking heads scored 33 answers (22.9%), TV news 29 answers (20.13%), commercials 10 answers (6.9%), promotional materials or infomercials, multimedia presentations and software scored a total of five answers (3.4%), with a total of 136 references to non-fictional audiovisual products against only eight references (5.5%) to fiction films (from Catalonia, Israel (Israeli Russian TV), Latvia, Poland, Scotland and Turkey) and two (1.3%) to children's programmes (Sweden). Although the frequent use of voice-over in factual output seems clear, it is worth reiterating that, from the authors' perspective, off-screen narrated documentaries as well as all types of advertising material and programmes for children are in fact dubbed off-screen, the name adopted in this book to differentiate from voice-over, when the original voice remains audible at the background of the translated voice.

Once more the impact of Film Studies or the view that off-camera speech or what we call off-screen dubbing is a sort of voice-over translation can be observed in a few of the respondents' comments it is observed. Such an example can be seen in the following comments:

> Since we are a subtitling country, we always subtitle when people are on screen. For documentaries this means that the translation consists of both voice-over and subtitles. We sometimes get programmes where the whole programme is voice-overed, not only the narrator. In those cases SVT insists on getting an M & E-track (with syncs and effects only), so that we can subtitle the on-screen passages. Swedish viewers are used to have any on–screen person subtitled and would be very irritated to see that person voice-overed. Thus the translation of a documentary always implicates voice-over AND subtitles, preferably by the same translator. (Sweden)

> The usual pattern in documentaries is to voice-over the narration ('off' sections) and to subtitle 'talking heads' ('on' sections) – unless there is a smooth off-on or on-off transition for the same speaker or the same dialogue. (Slovenia)

Other respondents share a more Translation Studies-oriented concept of voice-over, which can be observed in:

> Voice-over with original speech audible is only used in documentaries and news. (Catalonia)

> For me, in French, narrator off-screen is "voix off" and not voice-over. (Israel)

Once respondents had indicated the audiovisual products which made use of voice-over translation most frequently, they were asked to identify the potential reasons why voice-over was used in these programmes. The most evident reasons for respondents were 'tradition' and 'sense of authenticity', which were ticked 24 and 23 times respectively. Whereas tradition may have been imposed throughout history by any type of censorship or economic situation, sense of authenticity is related to the co-presence of the original, as in subtitling, and the (false) idea of literality or little manipulation that seconds left of the original at the beginning of the voice-over translation is also kept. Sense of authenticity did serve respondents to justify the large use of voice-over in factual audiovisual products.

Another popular reason was the use of voice-over translation as a money-saving measure (19 respondents), which, as suggested, may have defined tradition in some countries. Finally, eight respondents (from Canada, South Africa, Sweden, Peru, Poland and Wales) stated 'other reasons' for the preference of voice-over instead of the alternative use of subtitles, which can be grouped into time-saving measure and reading speed/ability.

6.3 On voice-over features

As mentioned at the beginning of this chapter, this book has presented various features of voice-over as used in the authors' countries of origin, but the answers provided in the questionnaires will help us gain a wider knowledge of this practice throughout the world. The questions posed in this section refer to the presence/absence of the original sound, to the seconds left at the beginning and at the end of each voiced-over segment, to literal synchrony, to singular accents and gender, and to the relationship between voice-over and simultaneous interpreting.

a)　Presence/absence of the original sound

To the question "Is the original soundtrack volume eliminated or reduced", 27 respondents ticked "reduced" and 12 found that "both cases are possible", whereas 4 respondents (one respondent from Greece, one from Turkey, and two from Sweden) replied that the original soundtrack is eliminated. For the latter, voice-over is probably viewed in the Film Studies sense, that is, as narration coming from an invisible source speaker, without the co-presence of the original voice. The same is true for those respondents who said that both possibilities are used, that is, having the original soundtrack eliminated or reduced. We asked them what the choice for one or the other would depend on, and the replies we received can be summarized as follows:

- Some of the academics or professionals have not been able to establish a pattern and, hence, cannot account for any specific reason (Croatia and England).
- Quite a few respondents mentioned client's preferences.
- Producer's decision (Venezuela)
- It depends on the economic resources and the studios you work with (Catalonia).
- It depends on the kinds of programmes and also on the broadcasting channels (Italy). A similar reason is given by another respondent from Catalonia, who said that the original is eliminated in fiction and reduced in documentaries and news.
- It depends on the genre (Slovenia): "In documentaries, the original dialogue is not always heard; if it is, it is usually hardly audible or

audible only when it does not start or end in synchrony with the voice-
over; in TV interviews, it is usually at a very low level; in commercials
either eliminated or at a very low level; in radio news, the original
sound track frequently begins with the original speech full volume,
which then fades off and is first briefly "covered" by the translation,
and then for the major part only the translation is heard, and it ends
with the original sound track".

The important conclusion is that those who see the possibility of the original
being eliminated in a voice-over translation are clearly approaching voice-
over from a Film Studies perspective. Eliminated original speech in documentaries or on the news are, for the authors, instances of "off-screen
dubbing".

b) Seconds left at the beginning and at the end

As we have explained in previous chapters, the general practice in voice-
over is to leave a few seconds of original speech audible at the beginning
and sometimes at the end while delivering the translation. Yet, there seems
to be some variation. That is why we asked our respondents whether voice
talents actually practice this, and in most cases the answer was "yes" (31
out of 43 respondents) or "sometimes" (9 respondents). The length of the
translated segment (i.e., the time available), studio criteria and personal
taste seem to be some of the factors adduced to explain the absence of
these initial seconds. On the other hand, in Poland it seems that this practice is used by the voice talents simply to check if what they hear is what
they will read.

Regardless of the general practice in their countries of origin, our respondents were asked whether, in their opinion, a few seconds should be
left at the beginning. This question was answered positively also by 31 respondents, followed by five negative answers, three ticks for 'sometimes',
and very few who ticked "I don't know" or who did not tick any option.
Those who answered "sometimes" believe that a few seconds should be
left when it is otherwise difficult to realize who the speaker is, for credibility purposes and also on the radio, since on television the picture is a
sufficient indicator of the original situation. On the other hand, according
to one of our informants, it is better not to leave a few seconds in short
sentences.

As for the seconds sometimes left at the end of each speech, 22 of the 43 respondents answered that this is a general practice in their countries, whereas seven answered this is not, 12 ticked "sometimes", one respondent did not know and another did not answer at all. Again, the length of speech, personal taste, studio criteria, time and the particular features of each scene are the reasons which explain the absence of final seconds of audible original, in spite of the fact that a few translators did not identify a systematic and obvious pattern behind this decision. As explained by some of our respondents, it sometimes happens that the translation ends up being longer than the original. Hence, a few extra seconds of the original are impossible to be left at the viewer's disposal.

On the other hand, when asked about their personal opinion, 23 respondents consider that a few seconds should be left at the end, contrary to 11 who answered "no", five who ticked "sometimes" and four who did not tick any option. Some respondents consider that this is not a necessary practice because "it might be disturbing for the audience" and sometimes it is simply impossible because speeches are too short or subtitles follow.

c) Literal synchrony

Another controversial issue is what has been called literal synchrony in Chapter 3. This is why we included the following question in the questionnaire: "Do you think that translators tend to be as literal as possible at the beginning of the intervention when the original soundtrack is heard?" The answer was "yes" in most cases (21 respondents), whereas others replied "no" (nine respondents), "sometimes" (six respondents) and "I don't know" (six respondents), and one respondent did not answer at all. In our opinion, most respondents are advocates of this literality because of the sense of authenticity provided by voice-over. However, there are some constraints to literality: some respondents consider that "you can be literal if the length of the translated version permits you to be so", in other words, "when the target language structure allows it". Another respondent adds that "there is no unique rule" since it depends on each particular project, on the subject and target group. In conclusion, as proposed in the book and confirmed by a Slovenian respondent, "priority must be given to the natural rhythm and word order of the Slovene language".

d) *Singular accents and gender*

The reproduction of accents in voice-over was another issue dealt with in Chapter 3. To the question "In your country: does the voice talent have a slight accent of the people who are talking in the original product?" the vast majority answered 'no' (33 respondents), whereas four respondents replied 'yes': respondents from France, the UK and Turkey. One respondent did not know and five respondents ticked 'sometimes'. These rare occasions correspond to some "dramatic actions" (Venezuela), to specific words in the original language that cannot be translated and are pronounced according to the phonetic rules of the source language (Italy), to excerpts where a comic effect is desired (Italy), to TV ads (Italy) and to situations when "there's logic to it" (Canada). Another Canadian respondent replied that it depends on the client's or director's choice, but the general pattern in this country seems to be the reproduction of accent whenever the original speech presents such a feature.

Another recurrent practice in the countries of origin of the authors of the present book is that gender is kept in voice-over versions. This means that if a woman speaks in the original product, an actress will be used to revoice the product, whereas an actor will do the voice-overs of male speakers. When asked about this, 29 respondents answered that gender is maintained, whereas 10 respondents mostly from Eastern European countries replied that gender is not kept in their countries, three answered 'sometimes' and one did not know. Many gave further details such as a respondent from Canada who said that gender is kept whenever possible, depending on the client's or director's choice, or even on the product type, as added by an informant from Romania. Another respondent from Poland explained that in feature films they always have a male voice talent, whereas in nature documentaries female voice talents are sometimes found. In Sweden, on the other hand, they rarely have women voice talents, according to one of our respondents from this country. Finally, it is interesting to stress that a respondent from Slovenia explains that gender is kept in on-screen sequences of documentaries, TV and radio interviews and in commercials, whereas sometimes it is not kept in off-screen sequences of documentaries. There is no doubt that in the latter instance the respondent is referring to the narrated parts of documentaries, whose transfer mode is called off-screen dubbing in this book. Finally, another respondent from Catalonia explains that in live interpreting of interviews gender cannot be kept. Although sharing similar characteristics, live – either consecutive or simultaneous – interpreting is not to be considered an instance of voice-over because the latter is always pre-recorded. The relationship between these two transfer modes will be tackled in the next section.

e)   Pre-recorded / live

In order to observe whether respondents differentiated between voice-over and live interpreting, they were asked if voice-over had always been pre-recorded in their country, to which 22 respondents answered 'yes' and 12 replied 'generally yes', whilst three respondents – one from Croatia and two from Catalonia – answered 'no', eight did not know and one did not answer. These answers highlight that there is still some confusion about the terminology being used. A clear example of such confusion is one respondent from Catalonia who answered that voice-over is never pre-recorded despite the fact that the authors of the book are able to confirm the contrary based on extensive practice in the field. In Latvia and Slovenia, on the other hand, it seems the difference between voice-over and live interpreting is pretty clear, as the Slovenian respondent explained that "live interpreting is sometimes used in TV interviews that are part of news pro-grammes, where it is read by the news presenter (time pressure) or in live interviews during sports events."

With a more theoretical approach in mind, we asked the following question: "Although (there is no universal consent) not everybody agrees on that, do you think live interpreting of interviews on television should be included within the voice-over mode?" The majority of answers were 'no' (20 respondents), but a remarkable number of replies were positive (12 respondents). In fact, some respondents said that they did not understand the question, so we had nine respondents who ticked 'I don't know' and two who did not answer this question. Those who gave a positive answer considered that the resulting product in voice-over and live interpreting is very similar in terms of authenticity, purpose, features (the original language is heard) and, thus, both modalities should be closely related. As for those respondents whose replies were negative, both transfer modes are viewed very differently because of various reasons, which can be summarized as follows:

–   "the working conditions and constraints are particular" (Canada),

because it was not clearly phrased.

- time restraints are not the same, hence "live interpreting [is] a different mode" (Austria),
    - despite some similarities (both languages heard/perceived at the same time), the difference in the procedure significantly influences the outcome: translation first, then recording, then broadcasting (in the case of voice-over).
    - "The other great difference is the control of synchrony in voice over (absent in live-interpreting)", says a respondent from Italy, an opinion shared by a respondent from Portugal, who teaches both modes and has detected different mental and physical processes for each modality;
- "voice-over is always pre-recorded while interpreting is always live" (Czech Republic),
- interpreters are not considered voice talents (Poland),
- "voice-over translation allows for manipulation/rewriting of the original text" (Italy),
- live interpreters don't usually have the text to be translated, so the result is a less-cohesive text with more hesitations than a voice-over translation (Catalonia), and
- a prepared translation (as in voice-over) allows for a better quality version than does interpreting (Slovenia)

6.4 On voice-over teaching

Before going into the teaching aspect, respondents were asked if they knew of any study on voice-over reception and the respondents' unanimous answer was negative (35 answered 'no', six ticked 'I don't know' and two did not answer), which reveals the need for further research on this specific transfer mode.

Regarding voice-over teaching, 16 respondents from ten countries (Canada, Catalonia, England and Wales (UK), Israel, Italy, Poland, Portugal, Slovenia, Sweden, and Turkey) answered that voice-over was taught in their countries as opposed to almost the same amount of respondents (15), who said no voice-over was taught in their countries. In addition, there were also 11 respondents who did not know of any course on this type of translation and one respondent who did not answer.

In the countries where voice-over is taught, training is offered at universities, sometimes in short courses on audiovisual translation at an undergraduate level (Austria, Slovenia, Turkey), but generally at a postgraduate level (Catalonia, Israel, Italy, Poland, Portugal and the UK). Training is also offered by companies and agencies that provide the service (Israel, Italy, Sweden and Wales (UK)). However, it is often a secondary transfer mode, as explained by a Swedish respondent: "Since 1964 it is [*sic*] part of the Swedish Television subtitler training but as a minor issue, since it is only used for documentaries". Maybe for viewing voice-over in a Film Studies sense, the respondent considers indeed that voice-over is not a special mode of translation at all and states that, "if the translator has got the talent [...] and has developed sense for stylistics and nuances, he can translate voice-over as well as subtitles. For voice-over he doesn't need any special training, just a few practical instructions". This confirms the opinion of another respondent, who says that "people seem to learn by watching and listening". The apparent ease with which voice-over is produced is a recurring theme in the scarce literature on voice-over, but this book has provided proof to show that voice-over presents some peculiarities that require specific skills.

The same may also be said about the programme of drama courses in Canada, whose respondent, an actor, highlights the fact that voice-over is a specialization within the theatre programme or in voice-oriented schools, although there is no doubt that he is referring to voice-over in the Film Studies sense, in other words, not from the point of view adopted in this book.

Of our 43 respondents, 11 are actually teaching voice-over translation. When asked about the main elements that they want their students to master, they put forward different issues that can be grouped into four general categories: synchronization, comprehension skills, production skills and other skills.

Issues related to synchronization

– Synchronization with the visuals and the rhythm of the source language.
– Timing and introduction of time codes (spotting).
– Condensing ability: reduction and editing, and the importance of rhythm of the speech in the target language.

- Understanding the relations between cinematographic grammar and human language grammar so that they know what to omit (or add) because of time or space constraints.
- Echoing what is said on the screen: place names in the translation at about the same time they are said in the original.
- Maintaining the illusion that they are hearing a simultaneous interpretation.
- Reaching text-picture synchrony.
- Taking into account pronunciation, gestures, mimics, etc.

Comprehension skills

- Understanding speech rhythms, different tones and voices
- Translating without script

Production skills

- Faithfulness to the original, although not copying exactly what the speaker says: rephrasing the original with a flawless language, no hesitations, no false starts or grammatical mistakes unless they serve a purpose.
- Writing a translation which is coherent, communicative and adequate.
- Creating a discourse which is defined as "false oral language".

Other skills

- Being able to do research fast.
- Relationship with other transfer modes: combination of subtitling/voice-over.
- Delivering a reader-friendly graphically-organized text.
- Acting or voice skills

In fact, all these challenges have been dealt with when describing the main challenges of voice-over as well as when presenting the course designed at the *Universitat Autònoma de Barcelona*. The only peculiarity is the acting or voice skills required from some professionals who are asked not only to translate but also to put their voices in the final product.

6.5 On professional aspects

Another part of our questionnaire was exclusively addressed to practitioners (a total of 22 respondents). It dealt with the types of clients and the products to be translated, and with the main challenges that the practitioners face as professional translators. The respondents work for a wide variety of clients:

– dubbing and subtitling agencies,
– dubbing studios whose clients are television channels,
– television networks directly,
– businessmen,
– corporate, government, associations,
– producers, and
– documentary directors.

Sometimes they do not know who the final client is and sometimes they are not aware of the fact that they are translating for voice-over. As a respondent in Catalonia says, "They don't ask for that, basically they want a documentary to be translated where there is some voice-over".

As for the products professionally translated by means of voice-over, the answers mainly correspond to non-fictional genres, which once again reinforces issues of authenticity that the relationship transfer mode – genre implies. The audiovisual products mentioned were:

– documentaries (19), specifically documentaries with interviews (two),
– corporate communication (two)
– infomercials (three),
– internal communications (one),
– news (three)
– radio programmes (one),
– sports interviews (one),
– technical courses (one), and
– TV reconstitution shows (cops, accidents, etc) (one).

However, as already mentioned previously in this chapter, respondents from Eastern European countries (such as Latvia and Poland) answered that they also translated fictional products such as:

- fiction films (two respondents from Latvia and Poland)
- shows (one from Poland)
- sitcoms (one from Poland)

Concerning the kind of product the translators generally work with, five out of 20 respondents are used to production materials such as unedited interviews, but the vast majority (15) usually translates finished products, that is, postproduction audiovisual output in the exact format in which it will be broadcast. One of the respondents, from Sweden, explains that the manuscript is given to the voice talent, who "usually edits it a little bit", although "some voice talents rewrite the scripts entirely", which seems a rather unusual practice.

Most voice-over translators-respondents (18) usually work from a VHS tape plus a script, probably because of the fact that they work for post-production, and approximately a third work exclusively from a VHS tape. It must be noted that the questionnaire was sent in January 2005. We have kept the reference to VHS tapes in this chapter although most translators are now probably working with video files. Another, albeit less frequent, situation is translating from a script and without image, which has been experienced sometimes by three respondents. There are still two slightly different situations described by respondents: 1) working from the original final master on digital Betacam plus the final corresponding "as broadcast" script, plus the list of all subtitles, titles, inserts and credits (Canada), and 2) (as explained by our Israeli respondent) working also from other linguistic versions of the product and a VHS plus translated voice-over and/or subtitles plus script (in English, Spanish or other closely related languages).

As for difficulties faced while translating, we asked our respondents different questions depending on their working conditions.

a) Working from screen

Those working from screen were asked to qualify a list of difficulties as 'very often', 'often', 'sometimes', 'rarely' or 'never'. The list contained the following items: adapting the length of interventions, documentation process, language rewording, literality at the beginning, slang, speaker's accent, speaker's delivery speech, speaker's errors, speaker's speech impediment/particularity, speaker's style, terminology, text-image synchronization, tight deadlines, and translating proper nouns

Very analytical, rich in concepts and information

In spite of the fact that speaker's accent, errors, impediment/particularity were expected to pose major problems for those working from screen only, the respondents' answers did not confirm our expectations. Terminology and literality at the beginning seem to be the difficulties most often found by translators in this modality, followed by language rewording and documentation processes. On the other hand, speaker's speech impediment/particularity and text-image synchronization are considered minor difficulties, followed by speaker's errors, speaker's style and the adaptation of the translation length/duration. Curiously, six people considered "tight deadlines" a frequent or very frequent challenge and six other translators indicated that they rarely or never had problems with deadlines, which demonstrates the various possible scenarios present in a single modality. As for the rest of the items – slang, speaker's accent, speaker's delivery speech –, most of the respondents chose "sometimes" as an answer.

A difficulty not included in the list but added by a respondent from Sweden who works both from screen and with a script is the fact that sometimes you have to bring in a native speaker to listen to fragments with low sound levels or difficult dialects. On the other hand, an respondent from Slovenia tells us that when doing voice-over translation of documentaries without a script, most of the text is edited and delivered by professional readers, so that the most annoying aspects of translating spoken language are spared.

b) *Working from a script or transcript and a VHS tape*

Those working from a script or transcript plus a VHS tape were required to qualify the following list: terminology, language rewording, adapting the length of interventions, slang, literality at the beginning, tight deadlines, translation of proper nouns, documentation process, text-image synchronization, script errors, narrator's style, content errors in the original.

Terminology also ranked first, next to the length of interventions, tight deadlines and script errors, whereas the least found difficulties in this group were content errors in the original, literality at the beginning, the translation of proper nouns, text-image synchronization and narrator's style. Documentation processes and script errors were not considered items which were especially challenging. As for language rewording and slang, they were viewed as difficulties found "sometimes" by translators.

Regarding those professionals who work with a script or transcript plus a VHS tape, various additional comments were included in the questionnaires. A respondent from Catalonia stated that, although working with a script, the transcript of interviewees' parts was often missing from the script, and she added: "When interviewees are non-native English speakers, it can become a bit of a challenge to make out what they're saying. Also, because of the editing process, interviewees' parts are sometimes incomplete, incoherent, etc. Captions including titles and names of institutions can be tricky as well, since no context is usually given and this kind of terminology varies a great deal between countries." This opinion is shared by a respondent from Canada, who considers that "the worst problem is that most originals are badly written, not clear". In the case of working from pivot language versions, our respondent who translates into Scottish Gaelic points to the fact that pivot translations in English are generally used, which might entail the loss of some nuances.

c)   Working from a script or transcript without the image

For those working exclusively from a script, we listed the same items found in the previous point, and added just another one: the absence of visual reference which implies ambiguity. This was indeed one of the main difficulties in this variety, next to text-image synchronization and adapting the length of interventions, which is to be expected taking into account that no image is available in this modality. Script errors and tight deadlines were also ticked as recurring difficulties, whilst content errors in the original and language rewording are found to be difficult "sometimes". As for the rest of the items selected – terminology, slang, literality, translation of proper nouns and documentation processes –, they are rarely found to be problematic according to the translators in this group. It seems contradictory that for these translators terminology ranks as a "rarely" found problem, yet for the other groups it is one of their worst nightmares, but the problems inherent to the working conditions of this group – that is, the absence of visual reference – might have pushed this issue into the background. Another reason could be that translators who face vast amounts of terminological problems usually translate scientific documentaries, and a script and a VHS are usually available for such programmes.

   Despite the great variation that is imposed by the type of material available and the peculiarities of each genre, one could say that, summarising all the results from the various groups, the three main difficulties for translators are tight deadlines, adapting the length of interventions (isochrony) and terminology, whereas for the majority of professionals literality at the beginning and the translation of proper nouns rarely pose problems. Language rewording and slang are challenges found sometimes by the practitioners who answered the questionnaire.

Although a wide list of difficulties has been presented, most of them are not considered unique to voice-over. As stated by an respondent from Latvia: "I do not think any of those are unique to voice-over. I truly find it difficult to point out any issues *exclusive* for voice-over and tend to look at it as a mode that in a way combines the characteristics of subtitling as written mode and dubbing as spoken". Nevertheless, a few issues could be mentioned as unique to voice-over:

- Adapting the speech lengths/synchronization with final master's time code
- Reference of correct orthography of names and locations
- Literality at the beginning
- Text-image synchronization
- Narrator's style

Professionals were also asked about specific tasks related to voice-over translation, namely isochrony, inclusion of time codes and revision of the translation and the findings related to these three issues which will be described below.

a) Isochrony

As for isochrony, or the length/duration parallelism between voice-over versions and their originals, 23 respondents said they themselves check it as opposed to only three who said they do not. This somehow reinforces the importance of synchronization in voice-over, as explained in previous chapters. A comment by a Slovenian translator rightly points to the fact that "it does not help if the reader does not adopt the same rhythm as I do". In order to reach this synchrony, only one respondent uses specific software by Softel. The vast majority read the text aloud (16 respondents) and/or rely on their experience and instinctively fit the translation into the slot available by practice (13 respondents). Eliminating oral features is also the technique used by four respondents, and another translator explains that the dubbing studios may take care of these issues and that "short excerpts allow pacing".

From those three professionals that do not take care of isochrony, two explain that someone else is in charge of this task and one respondent from Sweden has never been asked to do so and the respondent comments: "It is very rare that we are asked to control the lengths of a voice-over script. However, it might be interesting to know that there are two different fees for voice-over translation". The fees referred to by the respondent are a lower fee for non-adapted translation and a higher fee for a translation with adapted lengths.

b)   Time codes

Concerning the inclusion of time codes, answers indicate that it is not a regular practice among our respondents since 17 out of the 24 respondents who answered this question are not required to do so. As the respondents inform us, in most cases someone working at the dubbing studio does the job, like the dubbing director or editor or assistant (Italy), or even a technician may include time codes. In Israel, time codes are inserted by channel workers in charge of postproduction.

As for the seven respondents who have to include time codes, they do it manually and no specific software is used. It is worth mentioning though the observations of two respondents who do not have to insert time codes. The respondent from Slovenia says "I sometimes indicate time codes in the text at certain 'orientation points' to help the reader, especially when the picture cannot guide him/her or when voice-over is combined with subtitles." The respondent from Israel always includes time codes (even though they are not required). In addition, the Israeli correspondent teaches students to do so as well.

c)   Revision

Regarding the revision of voice-over translations, 12 out of the 24 respondents who answered this question affirm that their versions never go directly to the voice talent without any previous checks, whilst nine affirm that their translations are checked and two why say that they their translations are sometimes checked. Once the translation for voice-over is delivered and before its recording, different agents can take part in the voice-over/translation/recording process, according to the answers compiled:

− Someone who checks the translation and, if something is not OK, improves it. This person is called by one respondent the "quality assurer", whereas the Croatian informant calls this person the "proofer."
− In Latvia, an editor "checks whether all utterances required for uninterrupted and understandable dialogue have been inserted in the translated version as well as their correspondences with the original, as [*sic*] appropriate s/he deletes redundant translation or requests additional [*sic*] if s/he considers this is needed for the target version"
− Linguists (also called "language revisor" by the Slovenian respondent and "philologist" by the Polish respondent) check for grammatical/lexical errors, calques and the readability of the text.
− Other respondents mention the producer (Wales, UK), the client, the voice director and actors, who can suggest minor changes.

After these additional changes, around half of the respondents affirm to be allowed to check the final version, whereas the other half never has control over the revised version or only sporadically, when major changes are to be introduced, as observed by the Latvian respondent.

An exceptional case of power over one's own translation is reported by a respondent from the UK who wrote that when the company itfc in London commissions a translation, he is in charge of the whole process, including giving voice to the translation which, in our opinion, asks for specific vocal skills. —↘ However, one may have these skills . . .

6.6 Other modalities: created commentaries

Apart from voice-over, we wanted to know if any of our respondents had been asked to create a commentary, an unusual practice described in Chapter 4. This practice is applied to sequences where no original commentary exists and the translator is asked to make up a commentary based on images and the whole context of the programme. Taking into account that the terminology is not well established, we asked our respondents if they had been asked to create a free version, totally adapted to the target audience from an original product and, as expected, only two respondents (from Venezuela and the Republic of China) answered 'yes', confirming that this practice is uncommon. When asked what they had to adapt, the Venezuelan respondent replied "humour, because of cultural differences, and also filter offending language in drama material." According to her answer, it is possible to say that the question was not understood in the sense discussed in Chapter 4, but as regular adaptation procedures that are defined by the translator and the client and that depend on the type of programme to be translated.

6.7 Conclusions

To conclude our questionnaire, we asked our respondents to add any comments concerning voice-over that they found interesting, especially regarding voice-over difficulties, job contexts and specific tasks that they are asked to perform. Many were already inserted in the present chapter, whenever we found this information to be relevant. Nonetheless, we chose the observations of our Latvian respondent to close this chapter because they stress the importance of this rather underestimated transfer mode and in so doing we hope that these observations will improve the status of voice-over, thus achieving the main objective of this book:

> Overall, it seems to be a bit underestimated mode of translation lacking such serious study, as e.g. subtitling. It is sometimes also thought of as inferior to the other modes of audio-visual translation. Yet, this mode of translation is widely used in some countries, like, for instance, the Baltic countries, Poland, Russia, one reason being the relative economy of resources, another, the very strong tradition of voice-over which prevents the audience to accept the other modes, at least in television translations. It is interesting that, for instance, in Latvia, subtitling is widely accepted in film translations for movie theatres whereas reacted negatively against by the TV audience. Although this cannot be seen as a study project leading to any serious conclusions yet, last year the Latvian public television was practicing a strategy where the same fiction film on Sunday nights was shown with subtitles on one channel of the public TV and voiced-over on the other. The percentage of audience consistently differed considerably in favour of the voiced-over version.

The main objective of this book

6.8 Suggested exercises

1. Do some research on professionals of voice-over translation in your country and answer:
   - How can you define the profile of the voice-over translator there?
   - Do professionals use other terms for voice-over translation?
   - Does the definition of voice-over as "an audiovisual mode of transfer where firstly the original version is translated, and then its target language version is recorded (no lip-synch) on top of the original speech, which in turn remains audible" apply to your country?
   - Do professionals translate mainly from the image? Or from a script or transcript and the image? Or from a script or transcript only?

2. By observing audiovisual output that makes use of voice-over, can you say that professionals reproduce the accents of original speakers? If so, in which cases? Do you agree with this practice?

3. Search for the syllabus of courses on voice-over translation in your country. What are the skills emphasized in these courses? If voice-over is not taught there, comment on the skills that you think are most important for voice-over translators to acquire.

4. Do you think voice-over translations should be revised? By whom?

7. A commented bibliography on voice-over

This chapter presents the first commented monographic bibliography on voice-over. It includes only those publications, in print and digital form, which deal with voice-over, and those which comprise or contain discussions of individual works or authors commenting on voice-over. Works which are mainly bibliographical references and which have been used in previous chapters have not been added but are listed in the References section. We did include unpublished PhDs and substantial research work such as term papers. Consequently, this selection is fairly complete. The annotations are subjective.

AGOST, Rosa (1999)
Traducción y doblaje: Palabras, voces e imágenes, Barcelona: Ariel.

The objective of this introductory book is to discuss dubbing in Spain. Before doing so, the author describes four modes of audiovisual translation: dubbing, subtitling, voice-over and simultaneous interpreting. With regard to voice-over, or *voces superpuestas*, the book defines this mode as a transfer mode characterized by the simultaneous broadcast of the original and the translated tracks. The translated version (which the author calls the "dubbed version") begins after a few words from the original soundtrack have been heard. Agost considers the creation of a translation that can be easily read to be the most difficult issue, since synchrony is not as strict as in lip-synch dubbing. The author highlights that voice-over is the transfer mode used in documentaries in Spain. Most importantly, the book treats voice-over as a single translation mode, without turning it into a category of dubbing or into a type of simultaneous interpreting.

ALEKSONYTE, Zivilè (1999)
Comparative analysis of subtitles and voice-over in Danish and Lithuanian respectively as compared to English (based on the Danish film Breaking the Waves) [term paper]. Vilnius: Faculty of Philology, University of Vilnius.

As stated by the researcher, the comparison of Danish subtitles and Lithuanian voice-over of the English-speaking original is meant to look for flaws, for the amounts and kinds of information that "the recipient does actually lose" in both translated versions. In order to do so, Aleksonyte makes use of Gottlieb's theory of subtitling strategies. No matter how biased the objective or efficient the analysis and conclusions might be, one of the strengths of Aleksonyte's work – presented in the second part of the article – is the discussion surrounding the concept of voice-over as opposed to dubbing and subtitling, and especially as opposed to commentary and narration. Finally, Aleksonyte acknowledges that the phenomenon of voice-over needs further investigation, and closes the text in sympathy with the authors of the present volume by saying that "the point is not to compete, but to 'drag' voice-over out on the equal basis among the other techniques of film translation." (p. 23).

ALLOUBA, Esmat (1992)
"Translator investigator: A discussion of the problems of translating voiceovers". *Professional Translator & Interpreter* 1, 9–10.

The article is written from the point of view of the translator who hands in a text to be edited and then broadcast. It presents questions and some answers to issues such as copyright, translation fees, the translator as a voice artist, the process of translation and the many agents involved in voice-over from translation to broadcast.

ANTIA, Bassey (1996)
"Situation audiovisuelle dans un pays multilingue: le Nigéria", in Yves Gambier (ed.) *Les transferts linguistiques dans les médias audiovisuels*, Villeneuve d'Ascq: Presses Universitaires du Septentrion, 61–72.

The article opens by stressing the importance of audiovisual translation in Nigeria, firstly because of the country's complex multilingual situation, and secondly because of the country's high percentage of illiterates (58% of the population). As a consequence of illiteracy, Antia claims that many people in the country are dependent on translated audiovisual media, and she describes the three instances or activity domains where translation takes place: the information (TV and radio), advertising (TV and radio) and entertainment (theatre and cinema) domains. With regard to the "forms and techniques of audiovisual translation" applied in these domains, the author says that 'narration' is used in report interviews during the news, which reports back to the problematic nature of 'narration' being considered a mode of transfer, or of Luyken *et al.*'s definition of "narration as an extended voice-over" (1991: 80). For the translation of advertising, Antia provides six cases to illustrate the myriad possibilities of linguistic transfer. Voice-over appears in three cases that address both the translating voice recorded on top of the audible original (the definition of voice-over in this book) and the translating voice on top of images, replacing the original that disappears completely (the definition of off-screen dubbing in this book).

ÁVILA, Alejandro (1997)
El doblaje. Madrid: Cátedra.

This is the first monographic book on dubbing in Spanish. In the book, Ávila devotes two pages to documentary revoicing, which is called *sonorización* in the original Spanish. He highlights two main elements often combined in this genre: narrative documentaries and simultaneous translation, in his own terminology. In narrative documentaries, dubbing actors reproduce the information contained in a script following the image and in a neutral tone, since what really matters is what is said rather than who says it. According to Ávila, the process consists of three steps (translation, linguistic adaptation without lip-synch and artistic direction) and it is less expensive than dubbing a film. In documentaries in which the simultaneous translation system is used (voice-over in the TS sense), the actor can imitate the original voice and the key issue is not only what is said but also who says it. Hence, in order to prove the authenticity of the translation, the actor leaves a few seconds at the beginning (less than four seconds). Ávila uses the term 'simultaneous translation' for what we, the authors of this book, call voice-over. Likewise, Ávila's narrative documentaries fit into the concept of off-screen dubbing as suggested by the authors of this book.

BAKER, Mona (ed.) (assisted by Kirsten Malmkjær) (1998)
The Routledge Encyclopedia of Translation Studies, London: Routledge.

Without deserving its own entry and following Luyken *et al.* (1991), voice-over is mentioned in passing in the entry devoted to dubbing. Voice-over appears as a type of revoicing (together with narration and commentary) and is subsequently compared to dubbing in terms of the acoustic output. Apart from that, we do not find anything else on the topic, not even an entry on revoicing.

BARANITCH, Vladimir (1995)
"General situation with electronic media in Belarus", in Yves Gambier
(ed.) *Communication audiovisuelle et transferts linguistiques. Audiovisual
communication and language transfers* (International Forum, Strasbourg,
22–24 June 1995). Special issue of *Translatio* (FIT Newsletter / Nouvelles
de la FIT), 308–311.

This brief article talks about audiovisual transfer and translation techniques
in Belarus, in a post-Soviet Union period. This means that censorship has
left its marks in the 1995 audiovisual translation scenery described by
Baranitch, where methods that covered the original voice – completely or
partially – were predominant. As described by the author, the few methods of film translation in Belarus were: (1) dubbing and dubbing-with-
voice-over (the latter as a comparatively new technique), meaning that
"four or five actors are used to narrate the translation and the original
voice is heard as well" (p. 309). Both forms were broadly used under the
Communist regime on state TV, and remain popular among the older
generations; (2) voice-over, the main translation technique for home video,
which was introduced in the country at the beginning of the 1980s. As a
curious fact, Baranitch tells the reader that voice-over translators were per-
secuted by the Communist regime, which led to the distortion of their
voices (see the entry on the Gavrilov translation). Baranitch also describes
two methods for doing voice-over translations, one for simple films and
another for more complicated ones, and he adds that voice-over translation is the preference of the younger generation, precisely because the original voices can be heard and (3) subtitling. The author describes the third
and least used translation method, subtitling, aimed at deaf people. In
addition, he makes some considerations about the translator's role as intermediary and the translation of swear words and politically-incorrect
words.

BBC Broadcasting Research (1985)
Spoken translations and subtitles in documentaries. Special report provided
by the BBC Written Archives Centre.

This special report by the broadcasting research department presents the
results of two questions included in the BRD (Research and Development) Omnibus Survey carried out in 1985. A representative sample of

adults who watched documentaries about foreign countries (880 in all) were asked whether they preferred subtitles or "spoken translations" (i.e., voice-over) and whether they preferred a British voice or one with a slight foreign accent when using voice-over. The results show a preference for voice-over (56%) with a British accent (60%). The report details the method used and presents the results according to age, education, gender and social grade.

BOGUCKI, Łukasz (2004)
A relevance framework for constraints on cinema subtitling. Łódź: Wydawnictwo Uniwersytetu Łódzkiego.

As stated in the title, the focus of this volume is on the subtitling mode, whose examples come mostly from the film *The Lord of the Rings*. Voice-over is touched upon in the introduction and in the second chapter of the volume, where the author discusses the conceptual framework in which subtitling is embedded. Although Bogucki divides screen / audiovisual interlingual translation into subtitling, dubbing and voice-over (p.11), on a note he restates the concept of former AVT scholars who say that voice-over is a type of dubbing as is the case with narration and commentary. According to the author, the main difference would be based on the absence and presence of lip-synchronization respectively. Only two pages are devoted to the voice-over mode.

CARROLL, Mary (2004)
"Translation: A changing profession", *Translating Today* 1, 4–7.

Though the article deals mainly with the role of the translator and the fast shifting requirements for adequate and efficient training, the author describes, in particular, some of the features for the two language transfer modes in which her company specializes and provides in-house training: subtitling and voice-over. Some important remarks on voice-over are made such as the fact that the fidelity of the translation to the screen is emphasized. A new topic is dealt with and it is the physical appearance of the translation for voice-over which has to be read by a narrator. And finally, some notes on the synchrony of the translation to two rhythms: the rhythm of the actors' speech, the rhythm of the images and, for subtitling, also the reading rhythm of the audience.

CHAUME, Frederic (2003)
Doblatge i subtitulació per a la TV. Vic: EUMO.
CHAUME, Frederic (2004)
Cine y traducción, Madrid: Cátedra.

These books – written in Catalan and Spanish respectively – offer an analytic and descriptive study of two major audiovisual modes: dubbing and subtitling within a TV context. However, a short description is also provided of all other practices such as voice-over. The books combine both theory with practice, and address issues such as audiovisual genres, audiovisual text, why dubbing or subtitling, how and who dubs or subtitles, etc. A proposal for an analysis of audiovisual texts is also offered, taking into consideration the fields of Linguistics, Translation Studies and Film Studies. Voice-over – in Catalan *veus superposades* – is considered by the author as the third manifestation of audiovisual translation. The definition offered focuses on the technical side of voice-over: the technician lowers the volume of the original soundtrack and increases the volume of the translated ("dubbed") soundtrack so the original text can be faintly heard underneath the translated text.

CHAVES, M. José (1999)
La traducción cinematográfica: El doblaje. Huelva: Universidad de Huelva.

Although the book is on dubbing, a recurrent chapter on audiovisual translation types is found. Following Luyken *et al.* (1991), Chaves separates two main methods: subtitling and revoicing (in Spanish, *reexpresión*), which includes lip-synch dubbing, voice-over or *voix hors champ*, narration and free commentary. A section of the book is reserved for each modality and voice-over is granted two paragraphs under the heading "simultaneous interpretation", following Ávila's terminology (1997), although the author acknowledges voice-over to be different since it is pre-recorded, whereas simultaneous interpretation is live. However, Chaves seems to contradict herself later on because, when talking about narration ("an extended voice-over", in Luyken *et al.*'s terms), she says that narration, as voice-over, can be delivered live, provided the translator has been previously given the text.

CRONE, John (1998)
"The role and nature of translation in international broadcasting: An Asian-Pacific viewpoint", in Yves Gambier (ed.) *Translating for the Media*. Papers from the International Conference (Berlin, 22–23 November 1996), Turku: Centre for Translation and Interpreting, 87–96.

Crone discusses the role of what he calls "translation functions" in the programming activities of Radio Australia's North Asia Department, the international shortwave and satellite service of Australia's national broadcasting organization. Out of the six translation functions that he describes, we find "the translation of commentaries of television or video features for subtitling or recording as voice-overs" (p. 88). Although he points to interesting requirements that should be taken into account (for example, the localization of content and style) in the translation of commentaries, none of them seem to be specific to voice-over translation. Therefore, it is possible to conclude that Crone uses the term voice-over in the Film Studies sense, as the position of a faceless voice over images. However, if looked from the perspective studied in this book, the localization of commentaries to be recorded as voice-overs means, using the terminology that is used by the authors in this book, the 'off-screen dubbing of commentaries', when no trace of the original is left in the final product.

DALY, Albert F. (1985)
"Interpreting for international satellite television", in Hildegrund Bühler (ed.) *Translators and Their Position in Society / Der Übersetzer und seine Stellung in der Öffentlichkeit*. X[th] World Congress of FIT / Kongressakte X. Weltkongress der FIT. Viena: Wilhelm Braumüller, 203–209.

The article describes the *Eurikon* project, in which some broadcasting experiments were held in 1982 to test the potential appeal of a European programme for simultaneous satellite television broadcasting. The language transfer modality used was simultaneous interpreting. This choice was due to time and money limitations. The article does recognize the superiority of subtitling, dubbing and voice-over as the traditional language transfer modes. Still, when pushed for any of the aforementioned constraints of time and cost, simultaneous interpreting may be used, mainly as an experiment and not as a long-term project. There is an interesting section in which the "authenticity problem" is analysed, that is, the prob-

lem that arises when a face and a voice are linked, and the article says they
have to be convincingly matched through lip synchronization and accents.
The article is concluded with a comparison of voice-over to simultaneous
interpretation and the benefits of using any of the two transfer modes
when neither dubbing nor subtitling can be used.

DARWISH, Ali & ORERO, Pilar (forthcoming)
"Rhetorical dissonance of unsynchronized voices: Issues of voiceover in
news broadcasts", *Translation Watch Quarterly*. Melbourne: TSI.

This paper looks at the translation of TV news through voice-over. The
manipulation and deviation from the original text through translation has
already been the object of study in documentaries (Franco 2000). Orero
(2007) has also analysed some formal aspects of voice-over which help in
the creation of hyper-reality. Technical and content infidelities are rendering the broadcast actualities into sexed up copies of the original, which –
to all intents and purposes – are in sheer contravention of what translation
is for as a faithful reproduction of the original and of objective and factual
news reporting. Using some examples from TV this paper evaluates the
many modifications which the contents of the original texts undergo to
give a different translation from the source texts.

DAVID, Valentina (2004)
Il voice-over: Una proposta di traduzione del documentario F. Scott Fitz-
gerald: Winter dreams [unpublished thesis]. Università degli Studi di
Trieste.

In the first part of her work, David presents different audiovisual translation modalities taking into account Gambier's (2004) proposal and
adopting his definition of voice-over. Subsequently, she devotes the second chapter to audiovisual translation theory. It is in the third chapter
that David focuses exclusively on voice-over. She compares different definitions of the term *voice-over* (Gambier 1994, 2004, Mailhac 1998, Franco
2001, Orero 2004), exposes its usage in the world and in Italy in particular, and analyses some of the genres in which this translation mode is
used, namely documentaries, interviews and commercial videos. David
also points at tradition as the main element for using voice-over to revoice
fiction films in Russia and Eastern Europe and explains that, in fact, when

subtitling (an even cheaper alternative) was introduced, the complaints from the audience put a stop to the experience. From a more theoretical point of view, the author adapts Lambert and Delabastita's model (1996), Mayoral, Kelly and Gallardo's proposal (1988), and Gottlieb's classification (1994) to voice-over. The fourth chapter deals with technical aspects of voice-over: David adapts Luyken's model describing the different steps followed in voice-over, and presents Orero's difference between production and postproduction. She finishes the first part of her thesis by describing the use of voice-over in documentaries, commercial videos and interviews, and reproducing Luyken's estimates of costs. The second part of her work has a more practical approach and its aim is to propose a voice-over translation of the documentary *F. Scott Fitzgerald: Winter Dreams*. An initial presentation of the documentary is found in Chapter 5, which also offers a wider view of the genre "documentary films" and of the transfer modes used in documentary translation. Then, a voice-over translation is proposed as an alternative to the subtitled version available (Chapter 6), a translation which is aimed at keeping an adequate register, at coordinating text and image, and at observing time constraints derived from this transfer mode. In Chapter 7, the author presents a general comment on the previous translation, specifically on fidelity and synchrony, and on style and register. Finally, the subtitled version is compared to the translation created by David, and different advantages are detected for the voice-over transfer mode.

DEL ÁGUILA, María E. & RODERO ANTÓN, Emma (2005)
El proceso de doblaje take a take. Salamanca: Universidad Pontificia.

In this step-by-step manual on dubbing, voice-over is never mentioned. However, in the description of concepts related to dubbing in the first chapter, we can find some characteristics which are similar to the transfer mode in question. The related concepts are *autodoblaje, sonorización en sincronía, postsincronización, sonorización* and *traducción en sincronía*. Although these concepts may be considered somewhat confusing because of their similarity, the distinguishing parameters among these concepts are the identity of the original actor and that of the voice talent, the correspondence between original and translating languages (are they the same or different?), and lip synchronization. Taking into account these parameters in the definition of the concepts mentioned, it can be said that *sonorización* corresponds to our concept of off-screen dubbing, that is, when translation may or may not have occurred and text-image synchrony is the case rather than lip synch. *Traducción en sincronía*, in turn, seems to be our mode in focus, the voice-over, because it is said to always require a translation and a parallelism between speech delivery by the voice talent and what is going on visually. Later on in the book, however, the authors affirm that dubbing is a mode for fiction, and that in documentaries *traducción simultánea* will be found. Considering the fact that documentaries are not live audiovisual products and that the authors use the word translation instead of interpreting, one may think that 'simultaneous translation' means voice-over. This is reinforced by the fact that terminology used by Del Águila already appeared in Ávila's work above (1997), where any type of revoicing was called *sonorización*, and voice-over was described as simultaneous translation.

DÍAZ CINTAS, Jorge (2001)
La traducción audiovisual: El subtitulado. Salamanca: Almar.

In this book on subtitling, Díaz Cintas has a chapter centred on different audiovisual translation modalities, following Gambier (1996) and Luyken *et al.* (1991). Voice-over (*"voces solapadas"* in Spanish) is found, next to narration, commentary and other modalities, which are briefly described. Díaz Cintas points out voice-over as a modality similar to simultaneous interpretation situated between dubbing and subtitling and, apart from its typical characteristics (i.e., seconds left at the beginning, original sound reduced, no lip-synch, low cost), Díaz Cintas adds a particular feature found in the UK: voice-overs in English imitate the accent of the original talking head.

DÍAZ CINTAS, Jorge (2003)
"Audiovisual translation in the third millennium". In Gunilla Anderman & Margaret Rogers (eds) *Translation today: Trends and perspectives*. Clevedon: Multilingual Matters, 192–204.

Díaz Cintas emphasizes the explosion in publications in the field of translation studies and specifically in audiovisual translation, due to the dimension of the cinema, video and television industry, and stresses the evolution followed by the terminology of the field (from film translation to audiovisual translation, screen translation and even multimedia translation). After this introduction, the author focuses on dubbing, voice-over and, more particularly, subtitling. The typical features of voice-over are briefly defined and this transfer mode is associated with countries such as Poland, the three Baltic States and some members of the Commonwealth of Independent States. However, in a changing world, Díaz Cintas envisages encouraging future prospects for voice-over because it is less expensive than dubbing and it is a more immediate way of delivering information – for example, in commercials or corporate videos – than the written text. Finally, the article points at the challenges audiovisual translation will have to face at different levels (educational, academic, professional, social and cultural) in a millennium in which it will be *the* translation sub-discipline.

DÍAZ CINTAS, Jorge & ORERO, Pilar (2005)
"Screen translation, voice-over". In *Encyclopedia of languages*. London: Elsevier, 473.

This is an encyclopaedia entry solely dedicated to voice-over from an Audiovisual Translation Studies perspective – including not only audiovisual products but also radio programmes – which starts by pointing out the terminological confusion with the term "voice-over". The article describes this language transfer mode from both professional and academic perspectives and compares it to dubbing and subtitling. It is considered by the authors an example of voice-over translation when two main professionals interact: the translator and the voice-talent or voice-artist. The article finishes with a description of the main features of this neglected translation mode, including quotes from a relevant and up-to-date bibliography.

DRIES, Josephine (1994)
"Slightly out of synch", *Television Business International*, 62–63.

The article analyses the use of voice-over as a language transfer preferred for broadcasting because of its financial cost. On the other hand, the article also suggests that voice-over is not necessarily the cheapest mode or a mode which shows a programme to its best advantage. The study looked at the broadcasting in Eastern European countries which experienced an influx of foreign programming along with the increased cost of translating all the imported programmes.

DRIES, Josephine (1995)
Dubbing and subtitling: Guidelines for production and distribution.
Düsseldorf: The European Institute for the Media.

As the title suggests, this work is meant for producers and distributors of television programmes in Europe. It presents the requirements of language transfer that should be taken into account in the preproduction stage of programmes, so that their marketing and distribution become more effective, and language transfer becomes an investment. By language transfer, the author means dubbing and subtitling. For her, voice-over is a dubbing technique. Dries differentiates lip-synch from non-lip-synch dubbing, that is, voice-over. Although she focuses on the former, Dries highlights the fact that some requirements for lip-synch dubbing may be applicable to voice-over so that the researcher may want to have a look at them. Also, Dries's definition of voice-over encompasses its prior meaning in Film Studies ("a background voice").

DRIES, Josephine (1996)
"Circulation des programmes télévisés et des films en Europe", in Yves Gambier (ed.) *Les transferts linguistiques dans les médias audiovisuels.* Ville-neuve d'Ascq: Presses Universitaires du Septentrion, 15–32.

This article examines the factors that influence and characterize the import of international audiovisual products by the European market. It does not mention anything specific about voice-over translation. However, when discussing the cost of imports in relation to language transfer modes and programme genres, the author leaves the impression that voice-over is the easiest mode to deal with. The same impression goes for the documentary genre, which often makes use of voice-over translation in Europe.

ELIAS, Caroline (2006)
"Live voice-overing for film festivals", Book of Abstracts of the International Conference *Languages & the Media* (Berlin, 25–27 October 2006), 39.

Elias writes about her experience as a translator for film festivals, a practice that she refers to as live translation or live voice-overing, which should be considered a first step towards film synchronization. Live translation or live voice-overing, she says, is practised at festivals such as the Berlin International Film Festival, the Cannes Film Festival, and the Venice Film Festival. Elias affirms that live voice-overing for film theatres and festivals requires a lot of skills that are undefined by the academic world so far. She compares LVO (T) and interpreting for the media in many ways (e.g., preparation time, number of people involved, number of speakers, duration of work, breaks, percentage of original conveyed, listening experience, character of speaker's voice) and main differences remain the communication channels (movie theatres and the audiovisual media); breaks during work (like TV commercials for media interpreting); the amount of original conveyed (80–90% in interpreting, 60–100% in live voice-overing) and voices used (journalists, anchors and animators in the case of interpreting and actors in the case of live voice-overing). In fact, differences pointed out by the author are mainly due to the channel of communication and do not seem to justify calling the activities performed in theatres and on television different names. Voice-overing, in Elias's terms, acquires then the reception/delivery perspective only. Finally, she affirms that due to specific stress, interference of other grammatical structures, phonetic similarities and working conditions, there is a multitude of specific situations and problems which are faced by translators and ignored by film festival organizations.

ESPASA, Eva (2004)
"Myths about documentary translation". In Pilar Orero (ed.) *Topics in audiovisual translation.* Amsterdam: John Benjamins, 183–197.

After debating the myth "a documentary is not a film", Espasa breaks a second myth: "documentary translation is not specifically audiovisual". In this article, which departs from *Traducir documentales: Paisajes híbridos* (Espasa 2002: 29–39), different discursive aspects are considered in order to characterize documentary translation as specifically audiovisual: field, mode, translation mode and textual function. Lip-synch dubbing, voice-over and subtitling are linked to documentary translation and a few lines are devoted to the description of voice-over, a transfer mode which is considered to be similar to simultaneous interpretation – because the voice does not replace totally the source text – and also to subtitling due to the coexistence of two codes. This comparison, which is inspired by Gambier (1996) and Díaz Cintas (2003), just reinforces the role of voice-over as delivery technique. Espasa points emphasizes the paradox in using a trans-

lation mode which fosters the illusion of authenticity when current theo-
ries debate on reality construction in documentaries, and makes some remarks considering its use in Spanish TV. Finally, the characterization of
target audiences, a key element when tackling terminology and information translation problems, is shown as one of the main challenges in documentary translation.

FAWCETT, Peter (1983)
"Translation modes and constraints", *The Incorporated Linguist* 22(4), 186–
190.

This must be one of the first articles dealing with AVT from a Translation
Studies perspective. Only two types of AVT are identified: subtitling and
dubbing, and it is within dubbing that voice-over is mentioned. Dubbing
is divided into two types: "standard" and "voice-over", with voice-over
already being acknowledged in the article as a "daily occurrence on our
television sets". The article is written from a UK perspective, hence voice-
over is a more recurrent AVT mode for TV than subtitling or dubbing. An
example of voice-over locution is given to introduce and illustrate the choice
of a voice-talent who reads the translation of a Polish documentary with
Polish accent. This instance is the first mention in AVT literature to the
topic of accents and delivery. It questions the adequacy of "a documentary
on African tribal life with voice-overs in impeccable "Oxford" English".

FAWCETT, Peter (1996)
"Translating film". In Geoffrey T. Harris (ed.) *On translating French literature and film*. Amsterdam: Rodopi, 65–88.

The article deals with dubbing and subtitling in films. It starts by making
a comprehensive analysis of the existing bibliography on audiovisual translation within Translation Studies, in search of a suitable theoretical framework which will take into consideration the many and varied features of
subtitling and dubbing. It is interesting, considering the many research
avenues presented in the article, that though voice-over is only mentioned
in passing, the comment is worth this entry since it is one of the few
articles dealing with the accent of the voice-talent who reads the translation and the shift from standard pronunciation to English with the appropriate foreign accent.

FRANCO, Eliana P. C. (2000)
"Documentary film translation: A specific practice?", in Andrew Chesterman, Natividad Gallardo & Yves Gambier (eds) *Translation in context: Selected contributions from the EST congress, Granada 1998* (Granada, 23–26 September). Amsterdam: John Benjamins, 233–242.

This article reports on the initial results obtained in the investigation of documentary translation that culminated in the PhD thesis described below. Its aims is to demonstrate that the activity of documentary translation constitutes a specific practice, firstly, because of some aspects considered typical of the factual genre (i.e., the material to be translated, the translation models and the transfer modes, with emphasis to voice-over); secondly, because of cultural aspects revealed by three documentary sequences and their French/German voice-over versions.

FRANCO, Eliana P. C. (2000)
Revoicing the alien in documentaries: Cultural agency, norms and the translation of audiovisual reality [doctoral thesis]. Leuven: Katholieke Universiteit Leuven. Available as PDF file at <http://tede.ibict.br/tde_arquivos/1/TDE-2005-02-23T06:09:47Z-94/Publico/ElianaPCFranco.pdf>.

This is the first systematic study on voice-over translation that tries to provide a consistent definition of the concept and a description of its dynamics. Through the analysis of 22 documentaries about Brazil produced in Western Europe and voiced-over from Brazilian Portuguese into French and German, the author tries to answer three main questions: 1. what people talk about, 2. how much people talk, and 3. how people talk in the voiced-over versions. The comparison between French and German versions of the same documentary made clear that, besides general norms related to the factual genre, cultural agency played an important role in defining the content and form of voiced-over versions. Results made it possible to establish voice-over as a translation mode in its own right, as well as to refute the belief that the translation of factual audiovisual output is objective and unproblematic.

FRANCO, Eliana P. C. (2001)
"Inevitable exoticism: The translation of culture-specific items in documentaries", in Frederic Chaume & Rosa Agost (eds) *La traducción en los*

medios audiovisuales (Col·lecció "Estudis sobre la traducció", no.7). Castelló de la Plana: Publicacions de la Universitat Jaume I, 177–181.

The author examines the treatment of culture-specific items in translated (voiced-over) documentaries, that is, to which extent foreignization plays a part in the voice-over translation of factual output. One of the main conclusions is that, due to genre, a certain level of exoticism is very welcome in documentaries because it contributes to the target viewers' understanding of informative content about a different culture.

FRANCO, Eliana P. C. (2001)
"Voiced-over television documentaries: Terminological and conceptual issues for their research", *Target* 13(2), 289–304.

This article is a summarized version of the second chapter of the author's thesis above (2000). It discusses conceptual and terminological inconsistencies found in the literature of audiovisual translation, especially related to the term 'voice-over'. It also tries to identify some of their causes and to delineate some consequences for research. It may be helpful for students embarking on a study on the topic.

GAMBIER, Yves (ed.) (1996)
"La traduction audiovisuelle un genre nouveau?", in *Les transferts linguistiques dans les médias audiovisuels*. Villeneuve d'Ascq: Presses Universitaires du Septentrion, 7–12.

As an introductory article in the volume, Gambier puts forward important questions about audiovisual translation within today's multi-faceted globalization context. One of these questions refers to the diversity of linguistic transfer modes, which the author tries to enumerate and define in the second part of the text. Already commented on in two works by Franco (2000b, 2001b), definitions of voice-over provided as a mode similar to consecutive interpreting, simultaneous interpreting, or even to oral subtitles, do not always help to understand the concept or the perspective from which Gambier is making the comparison. Nevertheless, such definitions helped to open up the debate about terminology related to voice-over.

GAMBIER, Yves (2000)
"Comunicación audiovisual y traducción: Perspectivas y contribuciones",
in Lourdes Lorenzo & Ana M. Pereira (eds) *Traducción subordinada (I): El doblaje (inglés-español/galego)*. Vigo: Servicio de Publicaciones, Universidade de Vigo, 91–101. Originally published in *Parallèles. Cahiers de l'École de Traduction et d'Interprétation*, 19 (1997–1998), 79–86.

In this article Gambier proposes a classification of audiovisual multilingual transfers, in which voice-over is defined as simultaneous interpretation. As an example the author points out the Gulf War. He distinguishes voice-over from narration because, whereas the former is mainly used for spontaneous interactions, the latter is usually based on a text which has been prepared, translated and summarized and which will be read by a voice talent or by a journalist. Needless to say, voice-over is never produced live, this being the main distinguishing feature when compared with simultaneous interpreting. Moreover, what Gambier calls narration is called 'off-screen dubbing' by the authors of this book.

GAMBIER, Yves (director) (2004)
"La traduction audiovisuelle: Un genre en expansion", *Meta* 49(1), 1–11.

This is an updated version of Gambier's 1996 article above, in which the author refines and redefines his previous list of audiovisual translation modes, besides adding other important points that concern the present context of audiovisual translation, especially the European context. Contrary to the 1996 classification, two observations are important as far as the voice-over mode is concerned. Firstly, the term voice-over is no longer presented as being interchangeable with simultaneous interpreting, but with half-dubbing *(demi-doublage)*. Secondly, Gambier differentiates between the use of the term in French and in English. In French, the term refers to the superimposition of the translation voice on the original voice, whereas for in English, it refers to the same concept as the term 'voice off', or the invisible commentator's single voice over images. Therefore, the French use would apply to interviews and the English use would apply to documentary commentaries, according to the author. In our terminological discussion, this view would reflect the Translation Studies perspective (the French use) and the Film Studies perspective (the English use). Not less important is the fact that 'narration' disappears from the list of AV translation modes, whereas 'free commentary' remains as a mode of adapting the programme to a new audience. In this sense, we end up with two concepts of commentary: (1) documentary commentaries that are meant to be voiced-over in the English fashion, and (2) the commentary mode of transfer, which is meant to localize the same documentary commentaries. Finally, talking about accessibility related to the different modes, Gambier questions the translator's ethics in voice-over, among others, since the translator deletes traces of the *other*. In fact, this view contrasts with many others that defend voice-over as an authentic mode for the co-presence of the original voice, one of the reasons why it is applied to documentary translation as well as to subtitles.

GARCARZ, Michał (2006)
"Polskie tłumaczenia filmowe", *The Journal of Specialised Translation* 5, 110–119 <http://www.jostrans.org/issue05/art_garcarz.pdf>.

Originally written in Polish, this article provides a brief description of television film translation in Poland, which consists of three modes: subtitling, voice-over and dubbing. Voice-over (*wersja lektorska* – reader's version; or *szeptanka* – whispered version) is the most popular mode of audiovisual transfer in Poland. According to the author, it is characterized by an average level of manipulation of the source text. Equivalence and reception seem to be major concerns in voice-over translation: the translated version must not only transfer the meaning of the original but also sound technically impeccable, in terms of reading/recording effectiveness and timing between recording and speech sequences. The reader (voice-talent) of the translated version is given enormous importance as the intermediary between translator and audience. Compared to dubbing, the author states that voice-over has a less arbitrary character because it is not meant to naturalize or domesticate foreign items. Compared to subtitling, voice-over and dubbing offer an advantage for audience members with reading difficulties, (e.g., children and the elderly). For attending to all sorts of audiences, the author names voice-over as "the universal translation method". However, because voice-over is the most popular mode, applied to fictional and non-fictional programme genres, and to different discourse types (such as interviews, monologues, commentaries, etc.) equivalence and faithfulness to the original do not always apply in the strict senses of the words. For example, according to one of the scholars mentioned by the author, voice-over translation is the process of linking facts and re-structuring them into a new context. Another scholar, referring to the audience with poor or no reading skills, says that voice-over can summa-rize and comment on the meaning of the story on the screen. As a way of conclusion, Garcarz states that voice-over will continue to be the predomi-nant audiovisual translation mode in Poland since television viewers do not feel willing to reading subtitles, commonly found in movie theatres.

'Gavrilov translation' (2007)
Wikipedia. [Retrieved on 7 May 2007] <http://en.wikipedia.org/wiki/ Gavrilov_translation>.

This text talks about a translation type practised since the early years of the Brezhnev era in the former Soviet Union until the Russia of today: Gavrilov translation. It has received this name from one of its three lead-ing performers in the last decades of the 20th century – Andrey Gavrilov. Gavrilov translation is described as

> very fast paced, though fully intelligible, usually trailing the original dialogue by a few seconds. The original audio can thus be heard to a large extent, allowing the viewer to grasp the emotions in the actors' voices, as well as hear the actors' musical performances if the film contains singing [...] Any text appearing on the screen is also read out by the interpreter.

Although the description makes us believe that Gavrilov translation is sim-ply the Russian name for voice-over, dubbing and simultaneous interpre-tation are indeed the terms associated with it, as in the definition of the activity: "Russian language localizations of foreign movies where dubbing is done by a single, usually male, voice artist", or in the explanation of its process:

> Many of these dubs were made using simultaneous interpretation due to time con-straints caused by competition among the distributors [...] Whenever possible, how-ever, the interpreters preferred to watch the films a few times first, making notes on the more difficult parts of the dialogue, and only then record a dub.

Clearly, 'dubbing' appears here with the meaning it has in Film Studies, that is, the mixing of different soundtracks (original and translation) of a film, whereas 'simultaneous interpretation' points to first-hand (non-re-searched) recordings of the translation. In fact, simultaneous interpreting marks the origins of Gavrilov translation when closed-door screenings of Western films were simultaneously interpreted to the USSR State Committee for Cinematography.

GRIGARAVIČIŪTÉ, Ieva. & GOTTLIEB, Henrik (2000)
"Danish voices, Lithuanian voice-over: The mechanics of non-synchronous translation", in Henrik Gottlieb, *Screen Translation 2000: Six studies in subtitling, dubbing and voice-over*. Copenhagen: Centre for Translation Studies, Department of English, University of Copenhagen, 75–114. Also published in Henrik Gottlieb (2000). *Screen Translation 2000: Seven studies in subtitling, dubbing and voice-over*. Copenhagen: Center for Translation Studies, Department of English, University of Copenhagen, 87–124.

Originally published in *Perspectives: Studies in Translatology* 7(1), 1999, 41–80, voice-over is presented as a cheap way of rendering dialogue in audiovisual translation widely used in Eastern Europe's television and video industry, although little scholarly attention has been given to it. It is considered to be a non-synchronous type of screen transfer which demands a skilled translator despite the relative lack of constraints. Since there is no established terminology in the field, the authors introduce two distinguishing elements: narrative function and semiotic representation. The former distinguishes between a third-person voice-over (reporting) and a first-person voice-over (recital), whereas the latter distinguishes between isosemiotic voice-over (voice replaces dialogue voice) and diasemiotic voice-over (voice translates displays and captions). Next, the article concentrates on Lithuania and analyses an episode of a Danish TV series translated into Lithuanian through a pivot translation in English. The aims of the study are to shed light on voice-over, to discuss the effects of pivot translation and to establish the relationship between semantic and stylistic loss and type of translation, translator's involvement and target culture setting. Specific details on the voicing-over of the series *Charlot & Charlotte* are presented and differences with theoretical descriptions are stressed. In the thorough analyses, structural aspects (full translation, reduction and elimination) and semantic aspects (full correspondence, partial correspondence and no correspondence) are considered and two important conclusions are reached: the voice-over is unnecessarily condensed and the vast majority of the sequences analysed are fully correspondent from a semantic point of view. However, when this is not the case, irony, figurative speech and differing linguistic norms in both cultures are problematic issues. Finally, the authors draw attention to what they call the "centripetal effect in translation", which moves the text away from its original through explicitation and standardization strategies which are found not only in the Lithuanian version but also in the English pivot translation.

KARAMITROGLOU, Fotius (2000)
Towards a methodology for the investigation of norms in audiovisual translation. Amsterdam: Rodopi.

This book develops a methodology for the investigation of norms in audiovisual translation aimed at verifying two main claims made by some scholars in the field: firstly, that Greece is a predominantly subtitling country, and secondly, that despite being a subtitling country, its children's television programmes are invariably revoiced. What might interest the researcher on voice-over translation the most, however, is the author's preliminary discussion in the introduction of the book, in which he defines audiovisual translation, subtitling and revoicing, as well as gives a brief account of their history. For the author, audiovisual translation means recorded audiovisual material only, which includes, in his terms, "subtitling, (lip-sync) dubbing, narration (including voice-over) and free commentary, with the last three categories constituting a broader category of revoicing" (p. 4). The letdown comes when Karamitroglou describes revoicing modes as opposed to subtitling. Contrary to Luyken *et al.*'s (1991) definition of narration as "an extended voice-over", the author decides to "subsume 'voice-over' under 'narration'" (p. 6) and banishes the term from the rest of the book. His findings, though not focused on voice-over, confirm the use of voice-over mainly for the translation of documentaries and sports programmes.

KAUFMANN, Francine (1995)
"Formation à la traduction et à l'interprétation pour les médias audiovisuels, in Yves Gambier (ed.) *Communication audiovisuelle et transferts linguistiques. Audiovisual communication and language transfers* (International Forum, Strasbourg, 22–24 June 1995). Special issue of *Translatio* (FIT Newsletter / Nouvelles de la FIT), 431–442.

The author examines the question whether there is already a need/demand for academic training to be oriented towards audiovisual translation

as a result of the specificities of the medium. In trying to convince the
reader that such a need does exist, Kaufmann describes the types of audiovisual translation and the requirements necessary for each type. These are
divided into *l'interprétation in situ* (simultaneous and consecutive interpreting, on the spot), and *l'adaptation en aval* (subtitling, dubbing, voice-
over and voice off, all pre-recorded). In addition to providing a precise
description of the types of audiovisual translation and their requirements,
Kaufmann makes us aware of French professional terminology related to
translation in voice-over. In French, voice-over is also called *doublage* by
TV voice-over practitioners. The comparison of voice-over to synchronous dubbing *(doublage synchrone)* made by the author has to do with
original and translation audio parallelism as far as speech duration and
specific words are concerned such as proper nouns and international terms
that can be recognized by the viewer. In addition, Kaufmann explains the
difference between voice-over and voice off *(voix hors-champ)*, useful for
our understanding that narration and commentary are discourse types,
and not translation modes, delivered by a voice whose source is located off
the film frame, although it is heard over the film images. In this sense, the
Anglicism *voice-over* as used in France refers to every speech superimposed
over the film visuals.

KAUFMANN, Francine (2004)
"Un exemple d'effet pervers de l'uniformisation linguistique dans la traduction d'un documentaire: de l'hebreu des immigrants de "Saint'Jean"
au français normatif d'ARTE". In Yves Gambier (org.) *Meta* 49(1), 148–
160.

Above all, this article confronts translation acceptability with original authenticity. It questions the extent to which the linguistic homogenization
practised by the francophone television channel *Arte* in documentary translation may impair the meaning conveyed in the original version. The corpus analysed is a documentary that tells the adaptation process of six poor
immigrants from different countries into Israeli society. This adaptation
process is reflected in many linguistic aspects which the author finds vital
to the understanding of the immigrants' conflicts, but which are strongly
requested to be suppressed in the French version by *Arte*. Examples of
French language standardization come from the documentary subtitled
sequences (scenes *d'ambiances*, such as songs) and voiced-over sequences

(interviews, on-screen monologues). Throughout the article, Kaufmann makes clear references to the concept of voice-over in use, which reiterates and, at the same time, reviews the concept in her 1995 article as an audio-visual translation mode that marks "the co-presence of the original and the translation" (p. 157) where an actor's voice is superimposed on the on-screen speakers' voice in dialogue and monologue sequences. Commentary and narration discourse differentiate from discourse in voice-over in terms of the source of the voice, that is, in the former, the voice is in *off* superimposed over images, and belongs to a commentator/narrator that no one can ever see. In general, this text is localized to the reception culture. A further terminological explanation is provided in an endnote where Kaufmann says that voice-over is also called *doublage voix off* in French. In this case, the speaker himself/herself may be off-screen, as well as the source of the translating voice, so that every instance of voice-over translation is an instance of voice-off speech. The term *doublage* is used as opposed to simultaneous interpreting, or translation on the spot. Finally, according to *Arte* formal instructions, audio synchronization remains an issue in *doublage voix off* (as identified in Franco's 2000b work), not only for the sake of speech length, but also for the sake of speech credibility, that is, the translation of proper nouns and foreign terms that can be recognized by the audience is kept parallel with the original.

KOVAČIČ, Irena (1998)
"Language in the media: A new challenge for translator trainers", in Yves Gambier (ed.) *Translating for the Media*. Papers from the International Conference (Berlin, 22–23 November 1996), Turku: Centre for Translation and Interpreting, 123–129.

The objective of this article is to assess the usefulness of traditional training for audiovisual translators as well as to suggest the need for research in the area. Kovačič goes on to discuss the necessary components of training, especially for subtitling translators, but she does devote one section to training requirements for voicing-over and dubbing. The good point in this publication is that Kovačič acknowledges voice-over as an audiovisual translation mode different from dubbing.

KRASOVSKA, Daina (2004)
"Simultaneous use of voice-over and subtitles for bilingual audiences",
Translating Today (1), 25–27.

The article looks at the Latvian commercial TV channels which offer – to
satisfy a bilingual audience – two modes of audiovisual translation: Latvian
voice-over and Russian subtitles. After defining the characteristic features
of subtitling, the analysis of voice-over results in the questioning of the
popular belief that voice-over disregards synchronization. It has been found
that – as in subtitling – reduction also takes place in voice-over. Krasovska
also describes the strategies taken by translators to synchronize the text
narrated to maintain original intonation aspects such as gasps, sighs, etc.
The analysis is based on the film *City of Ghosts* (2002) and it starts with
the many English idiomatic expressions which have a high rate of occurrence, such as "Are you OK?". Another recurrent problem is the use of
singular/plural-formal/informal register which luckily coincides in both
Latvian and Russian. The use of swear words and taboo language is also
analysed resulting in the observation that a watered down translated version is used in both subtitling and voice-over in an attempt to meet audience expectations: if the obscene language were to be kept in translation,
the result would be too vulgar to be accepted. In conclusion, the article
looks at reduction in both subtitling and voice-over through the strategies
of ellipsis, omission or deletion as well as periphrasis. Subtitling shows
more reduction than voice-over, which is usually achieved by syntax sim-
plification. It is remarkable that both subtitled and voice-over versions
have a semantic correspondence, which is sometimes achieved even at the
cost of the original screen dialogue.

LOCKE, Walter (1998)
"Translating MTV-speak. From PO through VO: A video translation postproduction timeline", *Language International* 10(4), 40–42.

Locke talks mainly about cultural differences in multilingual versions of
promotional videos. In a separate section of his article, Locke describes the
steps of a video translation meant for voice-over. His concept of voice-over
is clearly related to the recording of the translated version. The interesting
detail is the feedback that voice talents are required to give about script
length and style.

LUYKEN, Georg-Michael, HERBST, Thomas, LANGHAM-BROWN, Jo, REID, Helen & SPINHOF Herman (1991)
Overcoming language barriers in television: Dubbing and subtitling for the European audience [Media Monographs no. 13]. Manchester: The European Institute for the Media.

This publication is the starting point in much research on audiovisual translation. Though it provides a wealth of factual information, audiovisual translation is always portrayed from the realm of Media Studies and from the reception of the translated media programmes, and not from a translator's point of view or the field of Translation Studies. It is still one of the most reliable sources of fundamental information. Voice-over is defined as

> the faithful translation of original speech, approximately synchronous delivery, used only in the context of monologues such as an interview response or a series of responses from a single interviewee. The original sound is either reduced entirely or to a low level of audibility. A common practice is to allow the subsequently reduced so that the translated speech takes over [...] alternatively if the translation is recorded as part of the original production, it may follow the original speech exactly. (p. 80).

Many responses to "faithful translation" have already been discussed by many studies (Franco 2000, Karamitroglou 2000, Orero 2004, 2007). It is also interesting to provide Luyken's definition of narration since it is closely linked to the definition of voice-over and may explain later voice-over misunderstandings and possible misclassifications:

> Narration is basically an extended voice-over. If the original narrative is simply an extended monologue the narration is used to describe the revoicing technique adopted to translate it [...] the only difference which is likely to occur between voice-over and re-voiced narration is linguistic. The original narrative is likely to have been prepared in advance. Consequently it will usually have a more formal grammatical structure than the more spontaneous structure characteristic of casual speech. (p. 80).

Though now dated, there is useful information regarding the percentage of dubbed, voiced-over and subtitled products in different European countries, costs, "information programmes" and "sports" (off-screen commentaries). Comments can also be found on voice-over suitability for interviews and current affairs programmes.

MAILHAC, Jean-Pierre (1998)
"Optimising the linguistic transfer in the case of commercial videos", in Yves Gambier (ed.) *Translating for the Media*. Papers from the International Conference (Berlin, 22–23 November 1996), Turku: Centre for Translation and Interpreting, 207–223.

The article aims at bridging the gap between audiovisual specialists and translators when voice-over is the preferred linguistic transfer and when orality is crucial. Mailhac shows the specificity of voice-over translation with a descriptive approach to the whole translation and recording process. The article focuses on voice-over for commercial video material and starts by pointing out five facts regarding such a specific form of audiovisual translation and some problems faced by the translator. Though the article deals with the language pair French/English, many of its conclusions can be extrapolated to other language pairs, offering appropriate strategies for the translator to optimize the linguistic and cultural transfer. The author also calls upon the educational institutions to train their students in translation programmes in the appropriate skills to face translations of such a nature.

MAILHAC, Jean-Pierre (2000)
"Translating commercial video material", in Michel Ballard (ed.) *Oralité et traduction*. Arras: Presses de l'Université d'Artois, 401–423.

Using the previous article by the same author as a departing point, this article shows the specificity of translating commercial voice-over texts compared to the two traditional language transfer modes of subtitling and dubbing. The specificity of the commercial voice-over text is given by the fact that its purpose is to influence the behaviour of the viewer. An overview of the production process of commercial material is offered for the reader to understand the complexity and the features which make this genre worth of serious academic study and professional training, even though it has been traditionally either misunderstood or ignored. Voice-over, in turn, is viewed in the Film Studies sense, as sonorization, as is the case with the ads that appear in chapter one.

MATAMALA, Anna (2002)
La traducción para voice-over: Online module for the Master's Degree in Audiovisual Translation. Barcelona: Universitat Autònoma de Barcelona.

In this module, Matamala creates a unit on voice-over addressed to students in which the main characteristics and main challenges of this transfer mode are analysed, and different exercises are proposed. A special emphasis is placed on practical aspects since training future translators is the aim of the course.

MATAMALA, Anna (2004)
"Teaching voice-over translation", in *Languages and the media: New markets, new tools. Conference Proceedings* (3–5 November 2004), Berlin: ICWE, 24–26.

In this paper Matamala describes a course designed to teach voice-over translation within the master's programme in Audiovisual Translation at the *Universitat Autònoma de Barcelona*. Different modalities of voice-over are presented and their main challenges are identified. Matamala highlights erroneous transcripts, comprehension problems, the presence of proper nouns and terminological units as well as the need to reword the language of the original as the main hindrances of this type of audiovisual translation.

MATAMALA, Anna (2005)
"Translating for Catalan television: Interview with free-lance translator Anna Matamala (25 September 2004)", *Jostrans* 4, 45–48. <http://www.jostrans.org/issue04/articles/matamala.html>.

In this interview, Matamala describes the working conditions of audiovisual translators today, taking into account her own experience as well as the specific features of voice-over and answers questions concerning specific problems when translating into Catalan. Matamala also deals with the process of revision and, finally, she explains her experience as a voice-over lecturer.

MATAMALA, Anna (2008)
"Teaching voice-over translation: A practical approach", in Jorge Díaz Cintas (ed.) *The didactics of audiovisual translation*, Amsterdam: John Benjamins, 231–262.

In this article Matamala describes the curricular design of a course on voice-over within the Master in Audiovisual Translation (see Matamala 2002), an innovative and unique module offered at the *Universitat Autònoma de Barcelona* since 2001. After identifying different modalities of voice-over and their main problems – a task which also serves to systematize this audiovisual transfer mode –, sample exercises analysed by students in face-to-face seminars are presented.

MATAMALA, Anna (forthcoming)
"Main challenges of documentary translation", in Jorge Díaz Cintas & Gunilla Anderman (eds) *In so many words: Translating for the screen*. Clevedon: Multilingual Matters.

After presenting a general overview of documentary translation, the article tackles the main challenges that a translator faces when translating this genre. On the one hand, Matamala highlights problems which are not unique to these products, such as working conditions (deadlines, erroneous transcriptions, content errors in the original). On the other hand, specific problems related to documentary translation are described, such as terminology, types of speakers and translation modes. Within these translation modes voice-over occupies a prominent position and its main characteristics are defined. At the end, the different techniques used on Catalan television are analysed, taking into account a corpus of documentaries broadcast during a one-week period in 2003. The analysis leads to the conclusion that talking heads and interviewees are usually revoiced using voice-over whereas in the case of narrators the original soundtrack disappears and only the target language narrator is heard. Thus, besides pointing to a specific cultural practice (Catalan TV), findings also point to the difference between voice-over and off-screen dubbing.

MAYORAL, Roberto (2001)
"El espectador y la traducción audiovisual", in Rosa Agost & Frederic Chaume (eds) *La traducción en los medios audiovisuales*. Castelló de la Plana: Universitat Jaume I, 33–46.

This article takes into account the audience with regard to audiovisual translation, which is considered to be a specific type of translation due to four elements: the multiplicity of channels, the fact that the translator works with other professionals, the coexistence of different languages simultaneously in certain transfer modes and the existence of conventions. Regarding voice-over, Mayoral introduces the issue of adjusting the translation to the reading speed of the voice talent and also points at the "vulnerability" of this translation type, since two oral messages are delivered at the same time. Finally, the use of voice-over as the typical transfer mode for documentaries in Spain is questioned, arguing that the supposed authenticity effect has no logic since most of the spectators do not understand the original language. Therefore, the voice-over simply hinders the reception of the original product. This is why Mayoral asks for a debate concerning the transfer mode that should be used for documentaries.

MAYORAL, Roberto (2003)
"Procedimientos que persiguen la reducción o expansión en la traducción audiovisual", *Sendebar* 14, 107–26.

The presence of different elements in audiovisual translation that have to be synchronized or adapted implies the use of reduction (synthesis and omission) or expansion processes (longer words, paraphrases, phatic language, redundancy, etc.) depending on the relationship between the original text and the translation. Elements such as the language structures involved, the diction speed or the translation mode are decisive and dictate the use of either process in a task which cannot break language norms. Although this article does not deal specifically with the voice-over synchronization processes, some remarks are made, such as the fact that the voice-over translator usually synchronizes by ear and opts for shorter versions in the English-Spanish combination. Finally, Mayoral states that, in this dynamic world, translators should be prepared to work with different audiovisual translation systems and apply synchronization techniques.

MOREAU, Hubert (1998)
"L'interprétation sur la chaîne Arte", in Yves Gambier (ed.) *Translating for the Media*. Papers from the International Conference (Berlin, 22–23 November 1996), Turku: Centre for Translation and Interpreting, 225–229.

The article analyses the language transfer modes used in the bilingual (French/German) *Arte* project. Dubbing, subtitling and voice-over co-exist as language transfer modes, and the article presents the norms or in-house style for its broadcasting production: one man one voice, same gender, voice fidelity to original voice (age, diction, pitch, etc.), interpretation for live broadcasting, and voice-over for recorded programmes. Although Moreau treats voice-over as a transfer mode, his discussion does not go beyond observations about translation delivery or recording. The approach is not from the translation perspective but from the delivery perspective, or the requirements for translation recording (age, gender, voice, etc.).

ORERO, Pilar (2001)
"La traducción de entrevistas para voice-over". *Programa y versión escrita Pre-congreso de las comunicaciones.* I Congreso SETAM Estado Actual del Estudio de la Traducción Audiovisual en España" (Barcelona, Universitat Pompeu Fabra, 27–28 April 2001), 44–47.

The article works towards a classification of the many elements present in a translation for TV interviews which will be broadcast in voice-over. From the translator's perspective, the article looks at issues that range from the support in which material to be translated is received by the translator to the many features of speech, at physical and linguistic levels. This is an article with basic and realistic information which can be used to understand the voice-over translation of TV interviews.

ORERO, Pilar (2004)
"The pretended easiness of voice-over translation of TV", *The Journal of Specialised Translation* 2, 76–96 <http://www.jostrans.org/issue02/issue 02toc.htm>.

Through a description of the translation process, voice-over is classified as production and postproduction, and it is the former type which is analysed from a professional perspective. Voice-over translation for production, that is, the voice-over of unedited/unfinished material – is a complex process of translation, widely misunderstood at academic level in both fields of Film Studies and Translation Studies. It has been traditionally described as the easiest of translations in the audiovisual world, with faithfulness and synchrony as two of its main defining features. The present article analyses the many features which characterize the voice-over translation for production and, in particular, the translation of interviews.

ORERO, Pilar (2006)
"Synchronization in Voice-over", in José María Bravo (ed.) *A new spectrum of Translation Studies*. Valladolid: Publicaciones de la Universidad de Valladolid, 255–264.

The audiovisual translation mode of voice-over has been traditionally classified as a form of revoicing. This early classification has given rise to systematic subordination of voice-over to a pseudo-higher translation mode: dubbing. Voice-over was then analysed and studied following dubbing parameters. This article looks at voice-over as an independent audiovisual translation mode and analyses and classifies the different forms of synchrony which are characteristic of this translation mode. Departing from Chaume's seminal *Synchronization in Dubbing* (2004), the article analyses the features which describe synchrony in voice-over and which are grouped in three categories: (1) kinetic synchrony, which is the need to match the contents of the translation with the body movements which appear on the screen; (2) action synchrony, when the voice which delivers the translation matches the actions taking place on the screen; and (3) voice-over isochrony, which is that proposed by Luyken *et al.* (1991: 80), when the original sound is either reduced entirely or to a low level of audibility so that the translated speech takes over after a few seconds and finishes also a few seconds before the original speech. Alternatively, if the translation is recorded as part of the original production, it may follow the original speech exactly.

ORERO, Pilar (2007)
"Voice-over: A case of hyper-reality". MUTRA Proceedings. <http://www.
euroconferences.info/proceedings/2006_Proceedings/2006_Orero_
Pilar.pdf>.

The paper opens with the traditional association of voice-over with non-fiction genres (Kilborn 1993: 648, Díaz Cintas & Orero 2006: 477). This association has been established by taking into account two issues: the fact that voice-over is the preferred translation modality for audiovisual genres, such as documentaries and news (Franco 2000: 235, David 2004, Espasa 2004), and the fact that translation plays a role in the construction of reality (Franco 2001). Both issues are analysed in this article. The article starts by studying the concepts of simulacrum and hyper-reality proposed by Braudillard in the field of sociology. This article proposes to import the term into Audiovisual Translation in an attempt to analyse the formal features of voice-over in translation regarding the non-fictional association, and how hyper-reality is achieved to create the overwhelming feeling of a non-fictional product.

ORERO, Pilar (forthcoming)
"Voice-over in Audiovisual Translation", in Jorge Díaz Cintas & Gunilla Anderman (eds) *Audiovisual translation: Language transfer on screen*. London: Palgrave Macmillan.

This paper starts by providing some of the many definitions and descriptions given to voice-over in the field of Translation Studies. It then factually describes the technique of translation for voice-over, taking into consideration a distinction which, suggested by Luyken *et al.* (1991), has never been properly developed: the difference between the translation process that takes place in the production stage and the translation process that takes place in the postproduction stage.

PAQUIN, Robert (1998)
"Translator, adapter, screenwriter", in *Translation Journal* 3 <http://accu rapid.com/journal/05dubb.htm>.

In this article Paquin focuses on his experience as an audiovisual translator in Montreal and discusses the notion of adaptation in audiovisual translation. Although he devotes most of the article to dubbing, he makes a few comments on his first documentary translations in which both narrations and voice-overs were used, and he points out most of the features identified in this book as the main characteristics of these transfer modes: time and tempo, relationship with the image, adaptation of the length of the text, absence of emotions in the studio actor's interpretation, and adaptation of an improvised text into a well thought out discourse. The important point is that Paquin does acknowledge voice-over as a translation mode:

> When a voice-over technique is used, the length of your text has to correspond to the length of the speaker's text, and even be shorter. That's when you see the speaker on the screen and a translation is supplied so that you hear the person speaking a foreign language in the background and an actor's voice is "voiced over" that, drowning it and taking its place, though the audience always hears the foreign language in the back,

but he also does so with narration, as opposed to the authors of this book, who have referred to the translation process of commentaries using the term *off-screen dubbing*.

PEREGO, Elisa (2005)
La traduzione audiovisiva. Roma: Carocci editore.

In a book on AVT focusing mainly on subtitling, there is a list of transfer modes where the main characteristics of voice-over are summarized on two pages. Considering voice-over as a synonym of "versione semidoppiata" *(half-dubbing)*, Perego states that this transfer mode is used mainly in documentaries and interviews. She then makes reference to technical issues, to the relationship between voice-over and other transfer modes – highlighting the features shared with dubbing, subtitling and simultaneous interpreting – and to its preferential use in TV except in some eastern European countries, where it is used probably as a result of its lower cost. Finally, Perego devotes two short sections to narration and commentary respectively, and refers to them as differentiated transfer modes.

PÖNNIÖ, Kaarina (1995)
"Voice over, narration et commentaire", in Yves Gambier (ed.) *Communication audiovisuelle et transferts linguistiques/Audiovisual communication and language transfers* (International Forum, Strasbourg, 22–24 June 1995). Special issue of *Translatio* (FIT Newsletter / Nouvelles de la FIT), pp. 303–307.

The article deals mainly with other language transfer modes used for audio-visual material, different from the two traditional modes of subtitling and dubbing: voice-over, narration, and commentary. Voice-over is described as *interpretation du discourse*, suggesting a level of manipulation/adaptation. The genres that make use of the modes studied are mainly TV news and documentaries, and the article puts forward the use of voice-over given its reduced cost for fiction in some eastern European countries. Some broad description is given of the translation and production process, concluding that the three modes analysed are neither technically sophisticated nor expensive. Consequently, they are important alternatives.

REID, Hélène (1996)
"Un domaine bien organisé: L'écrit sur les écrans aux Pays-Bas", in Yves Gambier (ed.) *Les transferts linguistiques dans les médias audiovisuels*, Villeneuve d'Ascq: Presses Universitaires du Septentrion, 87–98.

Reid, a professional translator, presents the reader with an overview of subtitling, the national preference (70% over dubbing) of the Low Countries focusing on the media in which it is applied, its types, the most important subtitling companies, the viewers' subtitling preferences, its translators, their training, working conditions and some words on the national association of audiovisual translators. With 14% of the viewers' preference, voice-over is applied in the television medium, in cartoons and documentaries. According to Reid, the only genre that makes broadcasters hesitate between subtitling and voice-over is the documentary with commentaries in voice-off. In this case, the first argument against voicing-over a documentary is the production cost, which, according to the author, is much higher than subtitling because it involves renting a studio and hiring a voice-talent. The second reason in favour of subtitling put forward by Reid is that Dutch subtitles tend to be as faithful as possible to their originals whereas voice-over adapts them whenever possible or necessary, leaving only the visuals intact. Whether true or not, voice-over is still treated here in the Film Studies sense, not as the translation recorded on top of its slightly audible original. Since the adaptation of documentary commentaries leaves intact only its accompanying image, we can say this is a case of what the authors of this book called *off-screen dubbing*.

REMAEL, Aline (1995–1996)
"From the BBC's *Voices from the Island* to the BRTN's *De President van Robbeneiland*: A case study in TV translation", *Linguistica Antverpiensia*, no. XXIX–XXX, 107–128.

In this article Remael analyses the translation of a BBC documentary for the Flemish TV channel BRTN. Her main interest is on the way the translated version combined two types of verbal translation, namely subtitling and voice-over commentary. She assumes then that commentaries are a type of verbal translation with voice-over as the way it is presented to the viewer (a voice over images) and in parallel with its use in Film Studies. Later on, when Remael describes the original documentary, terminology gets a bit complicated when she says that the documentary alternates interviews with voice-over commentaries. Here, the latter also appears as a discourse type. Voice-over seems to be only a detail in the translation discussion.

REMAEL, Aline (2007)
"Whose language, whose voice, whose message?: Different AVT modes for documentaries on VRT-Canvas television, Flanders". In Eliana P.C. Franco & Vera L.S. Araújo (eds) *TradTerm*. São Paulo: Humanitas, University of São Paulo, 31–50.

This text presents a study similar to the previous one, where the author examines how editing and three types of audiovisual translation are combined to produce the Flemish versions of three English language documentaries. This time Remael tries to explain her categorization of audiovisual translation (introductory statement, subtitling and narration) in the light of Franco's discussion of documentary translation terminology (2001). Remael rightly points out that terminology varies according to the circles (professional and academic) as well as to the cultures in which it is used (Flemish and Catalan). The argument is quite convincing, but the question that remains is: will we be able to talk about documentary/voice-over translation by making use of local terminology?

RUSSO, Mariachiara (1995)
"Media interpreting: Variables and strategies", in Yves Gambier (ed.) *Communication audiovisuelle et transferts linguistiques/Audiovisual communication and language transfers* (International Forum, Strasbourg, 22–24 June 1995). Special issue of *Translatio* (FIT Newsletter / Nouvelles de la FIT), 343–349.

The article focuses on television interpreting. Before doing so, Russo examines what she calls "the language conversion methods used in the media" following Luyken's categorization into revoicing and subtitling. Under revoicing we find lip synchronization, narration and voice-overs. The latter is then defined as recorded commentary and simultaneous translation, which again reproduces the misleading idea that voice-over means a technique of text delivery or presentation only.

SETTON, Robin (1996)
"Taïwan: Un paysage audiovisual contrasté en expansion". In Yves Gambier (ed.) *Les transferts linguistiques dans les médias audiovisuels*. Villeneuve d'Ascq: Presses Universitaires du Septentrion, 73–86.

Setton talks about the audiovisual landscape in Taiwan after the political and commercial opening of the Republic of China in 1990. After a brief introduction of audiovisual media in Taiwan, the author defines the two types of linguistic transfer that are most commonly used: (1) the translation of information (news, interviews, etc.) into Chinese (Mandarin) by bilingual journalists, or from Chinese into other languages and dialects (in the case of official propaganda, promotional clips, etc); (2) the translation of "spectacles", or the subtitling or dubbing of films, series, documentaries, variety shows, etc, performed by free-lance translators. In the case of television, foreign information such as cultural short films and the news are translated into "commentaries in voice-over", that is, they are off-screen dubbed, in the terminology used by the authors of this book. The most important information though is the fact that, on the official channel China Television (CTV), texts to be read in voice-over (i.e., as voice-off speakers) are translated mainly by journalists (50%), who also choose the interview clips to be dubbed (35%) or subtitled (10%). Related information is that CPTV, the public television channel, was preparing to become independent, and to be able to produce 70% of voiced-over news, interviews and reportages with the help of translators/journalists, 20% of subtitled documentaries, and 10% of written translation for internal services. The importance of journalists as translators attributed by the audiovisual medium in Taiwan may explain why they are better paid than translators for subtitling.

SPONHOLZ, Christine (2002–2003)
Teaching audiovisual translation: Theoretical aspects, market requirements, university training and curriculum development [unpublished monograph]. Mainz: Johannes Gutenberg-Universität.

Despite the general title, Sponholz focuses on the teaching of subtitling in Europe. In the first chapter of her work, however, she describes the main methods of audiovisual language transfer following Gambier's 1996 classification, namely dubbing, subtitling, voice-over, narration and free commentary. Definitions of voice-over as "the faithful translation of original speech, which is delivered in an approximately synchronous way" and narration as "an extended voice-over" follow Luyken *et al.*'s 1991 work, also reviewed in this bibliography. Additional information on voice-over is taken from Díaz Cintas (2001), who compares this mode with elements of dubbing and subtitling: "voice-over is transmitted orally but the contents of the original are condensed [...] no effort is being made to achieve lip-synchronicity" (in Sponholz 2002–2003: 9). So, not completely innovative as far as voice-over translation is concerned.

'VOICE-OVER'. 2007
Wikipedia. 30 May 2007 <http://en.wikipedia.org/wiki/Voice-over>.

Using the definition provided by the Merriam-Webster's Online Dictionary, voice-over is defined in the Wikipedia in the Film Studies sense and is referred to as "off camera commentary", which is called by the authors of the book "off-screen dubbing". Different types and uses of voice-over are described, such as voice-over as a character device, as a creative device, as an educational or descriptive device and as a commercial device. The entry also includes a list of prominent voice-over artists as well as different links to related sites.

WHITMAN, Candice (1992)
Through the dubbing glass. Frankfurt: Peter Lang.

Pioneer book-format PhD on dubbing from both professional and academic perspectives. Though the book concentrates in dubbing, it offers a definition of voice-over which will be much quoted in later academic works. Voice-over is described from the viewer's reception as "a technique in which a target language speaker reads the translation of the simultaneously spoken source, with the original still vaguely audible in the acoustic background" (p. 94). Though no further analysis is made, the examples given for voice-over are from TV interviews or programmes where "the original voice is to be heard".

ZINIK, Zinovy (2006)
"Freelance", *Times Literary Supplement* 5360, 14.

This is an article from a literary journal. Zinik is a writer who, from time to time, works as a voice-artist for the BBC. The article looks further into the issue of accents on voice-over proposed by Fawcett (1983). Zinik comments by saying the following: "you create an image of ethnic origin by simulating in English the idiosyncrasies of the other's original tongue." While this could have a negative reading and be interpreted as expressing a evaluative relationship with British English being rated as having more status and the other language (in this case Russian) as playing a secondary role, in fact it is read by Zinik as a demonstration of acceptance by the BBC audience of other possible English accents. The idea is that the BBC has a worldwide audience where English is the *lingua franca* with its many idiosyncrasies, accents and locutions.

References

Aaltonen, Rosa (2002) "An overview of documentary-typical translation concerns and strategies: The translation performance in focus", *Studies at the Interface of Translation and Culture* <http://www.eng.helsinki.fi/images/kuvituskuvat/sitcu_rosa.rtf>.

Agost, Rosa (1999) *Traducción y doblaje: Palabras, voces e imágenes*, Barcelona: Ariel.

Agost, Rosa & Chaume, Frederic (1996) "L'ensenyament de la traducció audiovisual", in Amparo Hurtado Albir (ed.) *La enseñanza de la traducción*. Castelló: Publicacions de la Universitat Jaume I, 207–212.

Aitken, Robin (2008) *Can we trust the BBC?* London: Continuum International.

Aleksonyte, Zivilè (1999) *Comparative analysis of subtitles and voice-over in Danish and Lithuanian respectively as compared to English (based on the Danish film* Breaking the Waves*)* [term paper]. Vilnius: Faculty of Philology, University of Vilnius.

Allouba, Esmat (1992) "Translator investigator: A discussion of the problems of translating voiceovers". *Professional Translator & Interpreter* 1, 9–10.

Amador, Miquel, Dorado, Carles & Orero, Pilar (2004) "e-AVT: A perfect match. Strategies, functions and interactions in an on-line environment for learning audiovisual translation", in Pilar Orero (ed.) *Topics in Audiovisual Translation*. Amsterdam: John Benjamins, 141–154.

Amador, Miquel, Dorado, Carles & Orero, Pilar (forthcoming) "Teaching AVT on-line: A reality", in *Proceedings of the international conference on translation and information technology in professional practice in university programmes in distance learning applications*, September 2004, Université de Rennes 2.

Antia, Bassey (1996) "Situation audiovisuelle dans un pays multilingue: le Nigéria", in Yves Gambier (ed.) *Les transferts linguistiques dans les médias audiovisuels*, Villeneuve d'Ascq: Presses Universitaires du Septentrion, 61–72.

Arango-Keeth, Fanny & Koby, Geoffrey S. (2003) "Assessing assessment: Translator training evaluation and the needs of industry quality assessment", in Brian James Baer & Geoffrey S. Koby (eds) *Beyond the Ivory Tower*. Amsterdam: John Benjamins, 112–134.

Ávila, Alejandro (1997) *El doblaje*. Madrid: Cátedra.

Baker, Mona (1992) *In other words: A coursebook on translation*. London: Routledge.

Baker, Mona (ed.) (assisted by Kirsten Malmkjær) (1998) *The Routledge Encyclopedia of Translation Studies*. London: Routledge.

Baranitch, Vladimir (1995) "General situation with electronic media in Belarus", in Yves Gambier (ed.) *Communication audiovisuelle et transferts linguistiques. Audiovisual communication and language transfers* (International Forum, Strasbourg, 22–24 June 1995). Special issue of *Translatio* (FIT Newsletter / Nouvelles de la FIT), 308–311.

Bartoll, Eduard & Orero, Pilar (2008) "Teaching subtitling on-line", in Jorge Díaz Cintas (ed.) *The didactics of audiovisual translation*. Amsterdam: John Benjamins, 105–114.

Bartrina, Francesca (2001) "La prevision del procés d'ajust com a estratègia de traducció per a l'ensenyament del doblatge", in Rosa Agost & Frederic Chaume (eds) *La traducción en los medios audiovisuales*, Castelló: Publicacions de la Universitat Jaume I, 65–71.

Bartrina, Francesca & Espasa, Eva (2001) "Doblar y subtitular en el aula: El reto hacia la profesionalización mediante la didáctica", in Eterio Pajares, Raquel Merino & José Miguel Santamaría (eds) *La traducción en los medios audiovisuales*, Vitoria: Universidad del País Vasco, 429–436.

Bartrina, Francesca & Espasa, Eva (2003) "Traducción de textos audiovisuales", in Maria González Davies (coordinator.) *Secuencias: Tareas para el aprendizaje interactivo de la traducción especializada*, Barcelona: Octaedro, 19–38.

Bartrina, Francesca & Espasa, Eva (2005) "Audiovisual translation", in Martha Tennent (ed.) *Training for the new millennium*. Amsterdam: John Benjamins, 83–100.

BBC Broadcasting Research (1985) *Spoken translations and subtitles in documentaries*. Special report provided by the BBC Written Archives Centre.

Belton, John (1985) "Technology and Aesthetics of Film Sound", in Elisabeth Weis & John Belton (eds) *Film Sound: Theory and Practice*, New York: Columbia University Press, 63–72.

BITRA – Bibliografia de Traducció i d'Interpretació, University of Alicante (created by Javier Aixelà) <http://cv1.cpd.ua.es/tra_int/usu/buscar.asp?idioma=va>.

Bogucki, Łukasz (2004) *A relevance framework for constraints on cinema subtitling*, Łódź: Wydawnictwo Uniwersytetu Łódzkiego.

Braun, Sabine and Pilar Orero (forthcoming) "Audiodescription with audiosubtitling: An emergent modality of audiovisual localization". Book of Abstracts of the International Conference *Languages & the Media* (Berlin, October 2008).

Brondeel, Herman (1994) "Teaching subtitling routines", *Meta* 39 (1), 26–33.

Brown, Lesley (1993) *The New Shorter Oxford English Dictionary*. Oxford: Oxford University Press.

Carroll, Mary (1998) "Subtitler training: Continuing training for translators", in Yves Gambier (ed.) *Translating for the Media*, Turku: University of Turku, 265–266.

Carroll, Mary (2004) "Translation: A changing profession", *Translating Today* 1, 4–7.

Chaume, Frederic (1999) "La traducción audiovisual: Investigación y docencia", *Perspectives* 7(2), 209–219.

Chaume, Frederic (2003a) "Nuevas tecnologías y documentación en la enseñanza de la traducción audiovisual", *Actes de les VII Jornades de Traducció de Vic. Interfícies. Apropant la pedagogia de la traducció i de les llengües estrangeres*. Vic: Universitat de Vic <http://www.uvic.cat/fchtd/_fitxers/jornades_2003/fitxers/chaume.doc>.

Chaume, Frederic (2003b) *Doblatge i subtitulació per a la TV*. Vic: EUMO.

Chaume, Frederic (2004) *Cine y traducción*. Madrid: Cátedra.

Chaves, M. José (1999) *La traducción cinematográfica: El doblaje*. Huelva: Universidad de Huelva.

Chesterman, Andrew (2005) "Causality in Translation Training", in Martha Tennent (ed.) *Training for the new millennium*. Amsterdam: John Benjamins, 191–208.

Collins, Richard (1986) "Seeing is believing: The ideology of naturalism", in John Corner (ed.) *Documentary and the Mass Media*. London: Edward Arnold, 29–44.

Corner, John (1983) "Textuality, communication and media power", in Howard Davies and Paul Walton (eds) *Language, image, media*. Oxford: Basil Blackwell, 266–281.

Crone, John (1998) "The role and nature of translation in international broadcasting: An Asian-Pacific viewpoint", in Yves Gambier (ed.) *Translating for the Media*. Papers from the International Conference (Berlin, 22–23 November 1996), Turku: Centre for Translation and Interpreting, 87–96.

Daly, Albert F. (1985) "Interpreting for international satellite television", in Hildegund Bühler (ed.) *Translators and their position in society / Der Übersetzer und seine Stellung in der Öffentlichkeit*. Xth World Congress of FIT/ Kongressakte X. Weltkongress der FIT. Vienna: Wilhelm Braumüller, 203–209.

Darwish, Ali (2006) "Attributing terror: Evidence on authorship – a forensic Translation analysis of culturally divergent clandestine coded messages", *Translation Watch Quarterly* 2(4), 41–66.

Darwish, Ali & Orero, Pilar (forthcoming) "Rhetorical dissonance of unsynchronized voices: Issues of voiceover in News Broadcasts", *Translation Watch Quarterly*. Melbourne: TSI.

David, Valentina (2004) *Il voice-over: Una proposta di traduzione del documentario* F. Scott Fitzgerald: Winter dreams [unpublished thesis]. Università degli Studi di Trieste.

Delabastita, Dirk & Lambert, José (1996) "La traduction de textes audiovisuels: Modes et enjeux culturels", in Yves Gambier (ed.) *Les transferts linguistiques dans les médias audiovisuels*. Paris: Presses, 33–58.

Del Águila, María E. & Rodero Antón, Emma (2005) *El proceso de doblaje take a take*. Salamanca: Universidad Pontificia.

Díaz Cintas, Jorge (1995) "El subtitulado como técnica docente", *Vida Hispánica* 12: 10–12.

Díaz Cintas, Jorge (1997) "Un ejemplo de explotación de los medios audiovisuales en la didáctica de las lenguas extranjeras", in María del Carmen Cuéllar (ed.) *Las nuevas tecnologías integradas en la programación didáctica de lenguas extranjeras*. València: Universitat de València, 181–191.

Díaz Cintas, Jorge (2001a) "Teaching subtitling at university", in Sonia Cunico (ed.) *Training translators and interpreters in the new millennium*. Portsmouth: University of Portsmouth, 29–44.

Díaz Cintas, Jorge (2001b). *La traducción audiovisual: El subtitulado*. Salamanca: Almar.

Díaz Cintas, Jorge (2003a) *Teoría y práctica de la subtitulación. Inglés-Español*. Barcelona: Ariel.

Díaz Cintas, Jorge (2003b) "Audiovisual translation in the third millennium", in Gunilla Anderman & Margaret Rogers (eds) *Translation today: Trends and perspectives*. Clevedon: Multilingual Matters, 192–204.

Díaz Cintas, Jorge & Orero, Pilar (2003) "Postgraduate course in audiovisual translation", *The Translator* (9) 2, 371–388.

Díaz Cintas, Jorge & Orero, Pilar (2005) "Screen translation, voice-over", in Keith Brown (ed.) *Encyclopedia of languages*. London: Elsevier, 473.

Díaz Cintas, Jorge, Mas López, Jordi & Orero, Pilar (2006) "La traducción audiovisual en España: Propuestas de futuro", in Pardu Nobel Honeyman, Francisco García Marcos,

Emilio Ortega Arjonilla & M. Ángel García Peinado (eds) *Inmigración, cultura y traducción: Reflexiones interdisciplinares*, Almería: Universidad de Almería, 605–611.

Doane, Mary A. (1985) "The Voice in the cinema: The articulation of body and space", in Elisabeth Weis & John Belton (eds) *Film sound: Theory and practice*, New York: Columbia University Press, 163–176.

Dries, Josephine (1994) "Slightly out of synch", *Television Business International*, 62–63.

Dries, Josephine (1995). *Dubbing and subtitling: Guidelines for production and distribution*. Düsseldorf: The European Institute for the Media.

Dries, Josephine (1996) "Circulation des programmes télévisés et des films en Europe", in Yves Gambier (ed.) *Les transferts linguistiques dans les médias audiovisuels*. Villeneuve d'Ascq: Presses Universitaires du Septentrion, 15–32.

Dym, Jeffery A. (2003). *Benshi, Japanese silent film narrators, and their forgotten narrative art of setsumei: A history of Japanese silent film narration*. Lampeter: Edward Mellen.

Elias, Caroline (2006) "Live voice-overing for film festivals", Book of Abstracts of the International Conference *Languages & the Media* (Berlin, 25–27 October 2006), 39.

Espasa, Eva (2001) "La traducció per al teatre i per al doblatge a l'aula: Un laboratori de proves", in Rosa Agost & Frederic Chaume (eds) *La traducción en los medios audiovisuales*. Castelló de la Plana: Publicacions de la Universitat Jaume I, 57–64.

Espasa, Eva (2002) "Traducir documentales: Paisajes híbridos", in John D. Anderson (ed.) *Traductores para todo: Actas de las III Jornadas de doblaje y subtitulación*. Alicante: Universidad de Alicante, 29–39.

Espasa, Eva (2004) "Myths about documentary translation", in Pilar Orero (ed.) *Topics in audiovisual translation*. Amsterdam: John Benjamins, 183–197.

Fairclough, Norman (1995) *Media discourse*. London: Edward Arnold.

Fawcett, Peter (1983) "Translation modes and constraints", *The Incorporated Linguist* 22(4), 186–190.

Fawcett, Peter (1996) "Translating film", in Geoffrey T. Harris (ed.) *On translating French literature and film*. Amsterdam: Rodopi, 65–88.

Franco, Eliana P. C. (2000a) "Documentary film translation: A specific practice?", in Andrew Chesterman, Natividad Gallardo & Yves Gambier (eds) *Translation in context: Selected contributions from the EST congress, Granada 1998* (Granada, 23–26 September 1998). Amsterdam: John Benjamins, 233–242.

Franco, Eliana P.C. (2000b) *Revoicing the alien in documentaries: Cultural agency, norms and the translation of audiovisual reality* [doctoral thesis]. Leuven: Katholieke Universiteit Leuven. Available as PDF file at <http://tede.ibict.br/tde_arquivos/1/TDE-2005-02-23T06:09:47Z-94/Publico/ElianaPCFranco.pdf.>

Franco, Eliana P.C. (2001a) "Inevitable exoticism: The translation of culture-specific items in documentaries". In Frederic Chaume & Rosa Agost (eds) *La traducción en los medios audiovisuales* (Collecció "Estudis sobre la traducció", no. 7), Castelló de la Plana: Publicacions de la Universitat Jaume I, 177–181.

Franco, Eliana P.C. (2001b) "Voiced-over television documentaries: Terminological and conceptual issues for their research", *Target* 13(2), 289–304.

Gabr, Moustafa (2001) "Program evaluation: A missing critical link in translator training", *Translation Journal* 5, 1 <http://www.accurapid.com/journal/15training.htm>.

Gambier, Yves & Suomela-Salme, Eija (1994) "Subtitling: A type of transfer", in Federico Eguíluz *et al.* (eds) *Transvases culturales: Literatura, cine, traducción*. Proceedings of the symposium. Vitoria-Gasteiz: Universidad del País Vasco, 243–252.

Gambier, Yves (ed.) (1996) "La traduction audiovisuelle un genre nouveau?", in Yves Gambier (ed.) *Les transferts linguistiques dans les médias audiovisuels*. Villeneuve d'Ascq: Presses Universitaires du Septentrion, 7–12.

Gambier, Yves (ed.) (1997) *Language transfer and audiovisual communication bibliography* (2nd ed.). Turku: Unipaps.

Gambier, Yves (2000) "Comunicación audiovisual y traducción: Perspectivas y contribuciones", in Lourdes Lorenzo & Ana M. Pereira (eds) *Traducción subordinada (I): El doblaje (inglés-español/galego)*. Vigo: Servicio de Publicaciones, Universidade de Vigo, 91–101.

Gambier, Yves (director) (2004) "La traduction audiovisuelle: Un genre en expansion", *Meta*, 49(1), 1–11.

Garcarz, Michał (2006) "Polskie tłumaczenia filmowe", *The Journal of Specialised Translation* 5, 110–119 <http://www.jostrans.org/issue05/art_garcarz.pdf>.

'Gavrilov translation' (2007) *Wikipedia*. [Retrieved on 7 May 2007] <http://en.wikipedia.org/wiki/Gavrilov_translation>.

Gile, Daniel (2004) "Training students for quality: Ideas and methods". *Actas de IV Jornadas sobre la formación y profesión del traductor e intérprete. Calidad y traducción. Perspectivas académicas y Profesionales*. Madrid: Universidad Europea de Madrid <http://www.uem.es/web/fil/invest/publicaciones/web/EN/autores/gile_art.htm>

Goldstein, Irwin L. (1980) "Training in work organizations", *Annual Review of Psychology* 31, 229–272.

Gottlieb, Henrik (1993) "Subtitling: People translating people", in Cay Dollerup & Annette Lindegaard (eds) *Teaching translation and interpreting 2: Insights, aims, visions*. Amsterdam: John Benjamins, 261–274.

Gottlieb, Henrik (1996) "Theory into practice: Designing a symbiotic course in subtitling", in Christine Heiss & Rosa Maria Bolletieri Bosinelli (eds) *Traduzione multimediale per il cinema, la televisione e la scena*. Bologna: Clueb, 281–295.

Grigaravičiūtė, Ieva & Gottlieb, Henrik (1999) "Danish voices, Lithuanian voice-over: The mechanics of non-synchronous translation", *Perspectives: Studies in Translatology* 7(1), 41–80.

Grigaravičiūtė, Ieva & Gottlieb, Henrik (2000) "Danish voices, Lithuanian voice-over: The mechanics of non-synchronous translation", in Henrik Gottlieb (ed.) *Screen Translation 2000: Six studies in subtitling, dubbing and voice-over*. Copenhagen: Centre for Translation Studies, Department of English, University of Copenhagen, 75–114.

Handzo, Stephen (1985) "Appendix: A narrative glossary of film sound technology", in Elisabeth Weis & John Belton (eds) *Film sound: Theory and practice*. New York: Columbia University Press, 383–426.

Harrington, John (1973) *The rhetoric of film*, New York: Holt, Rinehart and Winston.

Harris, David (1994) "'Effective teaching' and 'study skills': The return of the technical fix", in Terry Evans & David Murphy (eds) *Research in distance education 3*. Geelong: Deakin University Press, 201–214.

Hayward, Susan (1996) *Key concepts in cinema studies*. London: Routledge.

Hatim, Basil & Mason, Ian (1997) *The translator as communicator*. London: Routledge.

House, Juliane (2001) "Translation quality assessment: Linguistic description vs social evaluation", *Meta* 46(2), 243–257.

Izard, Natàlia (2001) "L'ensenyament de la traducció d'audiovisuals en el marc de la formació de traductors", in Rosa Agost & Frederic Chaume (eds) *La traducción en los medios audiovisuales*. Castelló de la Plana: Publicacions de la Universitat Jaume I, 73–76.

James, Heulwen (1998) "Screen translation training and European cooperation", in Yves Gambier (ed.) *Translating for the Media*. Turku: University of Turku, 243–258.

John Benjamins's Translation Studies Bibliography <http://www.benjamins.com/online/tsb>.

Jong, Frans de (2006) "Access services for digital television", in Ricardo Pérez-Amat & Álvaro Pérez-Ugena (eds) *Sociedad, integración y televisión en España*. Madrid: Laberinto, 331–343.

Karamitroglou, Fotius (2000) *Towards a methodology for the investigation of norms in audiovisual translation*. Amsterdam: Rodopi.

Kaufmann, Francine (1995) "Formation à la traduction et à l'interprétation pour les médias audiovisuels", in Yves Gambier (ed.) *Communication audiovisuelle et transferts linguistiques. Audiovisual communication and language transfers* (International Forum, Strasbourg, 22–24 June 1995). Special issue of *Translatio* (FIT Newsletter / Nouvelles de la FIT), 431–442.

Kaufmann, Francine (2004) "Un exemple d'effet pervers de l'uniformisation linguistique dans la traduction d'un documentaire: De l'hebreu des immigrants de "Saint'Jean" au français normatif d'ARTE", in Yves Gambier (director) *Meta*, 49(1), 148–160.

Kilborn, Richard (1993) "'Speak my language': Current attitudes to television subtitling and dubbing", *Media, Culture and Society* 15, 641–660.

Klerkx, Jan (1998) "The place of subtitling in a translator training course", in Yves Gambier (ed.) *Translating for the Media*, Turku: University of Turku, 259–264.

Koumi, Jack (1995) "Building good quality in, rather than inspecting bad quality out", in Fred Lockwood (ed.) *Open and distance learning today*. London: Routledge, 335–342.

Kovačič, Irena (1998) "Language in the media: A new challenge for translator trainers", in Yves Gambier (ed.) *Translating for the Media*. Papers from the International Conference (Berlin, 22–23 November 1996), Turku: Centre for Translation and Interpreting, 123–129.

Kozloff, Sarah (1988) *Invisible storytellers: Voice-over narration in American fiction film*. Los Angeles: University of California Press.

Krasovska, Daina (2004) "Simultaneous use of voice-over and subtitles for bilingual audiences", *Translating Today* (1), 25–27.

Kurz, Ingrid and Bros-Brann, Eliane (1996) "L'interprétation en direct pour la télévision", in Yves Gambier (ed.) *Les transferts linguistiques dans les médias audiovisuels*. Villeneuve d'Ascq: Presses Universitaires du Septentrion, 207–216.

Kussmaul, Paul (1995) *Training the Translator*. Amsterdam: John Benjamins.

Laine, Marsa (1996) "Le comentaire comme mode de traduction", in Yves Gambier (ed.) *Les transferts linguistiques dans les médias audiovisuels*. Villeneuve d'Ascq: Presses Universitaires du Septentrion, 197–205.

Lee-Jahnke, Hannelore (2002) "Aspectes pédagogiques de l'evaluation en traduction", *Meta* 46(2), 258–271 <http://www.erudit.org/revue/meta/>.

León, Bienvenido (1999) *El documental de divulgación científica*. Barcelona: Paidós.

Locke, Walter (1998) "Translating MTV-speak. From PO through VO: A video translation post-production timeline", *Language International* 10(4), 40–42.

Luyken, Georg-Michael, Herbst, Thomas, Langham-Brown, Jo, Reid, Helen & Spinhof Herman (1991) *Overcoming language barriers in television: Dubbing and subtitling for the European audience* [Media Monographs no. 13]. Manchester: The European Institute for the Media.

Mackenzie, Rosemary (2004) "The competencies required by the translator's roles as a professional", in Kirsten Malmkjær (ed.) *Translation in undergraduate degree programmes*. Amsterdam: John Benjamins, 31–38.

Mailhac, Jean-Pierre (1998) "Optimising the linguistic transfer in the case of commercial videos", in Yves Gambier (ed.) *Translating for the Media*. Papers from the International Conference (Berlin, 22–23 November 1996), Turku: Centre for Translation and Interpreting, 207–223.

Mailhac, Jean-Pierre (2000) "Translating commercial video material", in Michel Ballard (ed.) *Oralité et traduction*. Arras: Presses de l'Université d'Artois, 401–423.

Malmkjær, Kirsten (ed.) (2004) *Translation in undergraduate degree programmes*. Amsterdam: John Benjamins.

Mas López, Jordi & Orero, Pilar (2003) "Diplôme de spécialiste en Traduction Audiovisuelle (TAV)", *Traduire* (October-December 2003), 73–74.

Mas López, Jordi & Pilar Orero (2004a) "Competencias extracurriculares necesarias en la formación de especialistas en traducción audiovisual: El caso del PTAV de la UAB". Proceeding of the III Congrés Internacional de Docència Universitària (CIDUI). Girona: Universitat de Girona. [Available on CD-ROM].

Mas López, Jordi & Pilar Orero (2004b) "La escritura de guiones: Una asignatura a tener en cuenta para la enseñanza de la traducción audiovisual". *Actas de IV Jornadas sobre la formación y profesión del traductor e intérprete. Calidad y traducción. Perspectivas académicas y profesionales*. Madrid: Universidad Europea de Madrid <http://www.uem.es/web/fil/invest/publicaciones/web/EN/AUTORES/MAS_ART. HTM>.

Matamala, Anna (2002) *La traducción para voice-over: Online module for the Master's Degree in Audiovisual Translation*. Barcelona: Universitat Autònoma de Barcelona.

Matamala, Anna (2004) "Teaching voice-over translation", in *Languages and the media: New markets, new tools. Conference Proceedings* (3–5 November 2004), Berlin: ICWE, 24–26.

Matamala, Anna (2005a) "Live audio description in Catalonia", *Translating Today* 4, 9–11.

Matamala, Anna (2005b) "Translating for Catalan television: Interview with free-lance translator Anna Matamala (25 September 2004)", *Jostrans* 4, 45–48. <http://www.jostrans.org/issue04/articles/matamala.html>.

Matamala, Anna (2005c) "La estación de trabajo del traductor de productos audiovisuales: Herramientas y recursos", *Cadernos de Tradução* XVI, 251–268.

Matamala, Anna (2006) "Les noves tecnologies en l'ensenyament de la traducció audio-visual". Paper delivered at the *X Jornades de Traducció i Interpretació*, Vic: Tecnologies a l'Abast, March 2006. <http://www.upf.edu/bolonya/obolonya/titulac/upf/trad/docs/noves.pdf>.

Matamala, Anna (2008) "Teaching voice-over translation: A practical approach", in Jorge Díaz Cintas (ed.) *The didactics of audiovisual translation*. Amsterdam: John Benjamins, 231–262.

Matamala, Anna (forthcoming) "Main challenges of documentary translation", in Jorge Díaz Cintas & Gunilla Anderman (eds) *In so many words: Translating for the screen*. Clevedon: Multilingual Matters.

Matamala, Anna & Orero, Pilar. 2007. "Accessible Opera in Catalonia". In Jorge Díaz Cintas, Pilar Orero and Aline Remael (eds) *Media for All: Subtitling for the Deaf, Audio Description and Sign Language*, Amsterdam: Rodopi, 201–214.

Mayoral, Roberto (2001) "El espectador y la traducción audiovisual", in Rosa Agost & Frederic Chaume (eds) *La traducción en los medios audiovisuales*. Castelló de la Plana: Publicacions de la Universitat Jaume I, 33–46.

Mayoral, Roberto (2003) "Procedimientos que persiguen la reducción o expansión en la traducción audiovisual", *Sendebar* 14, 107–26.

Meier, Carol (2000) Evaluation and Translation. Special Issue of *The Translator* (vol. 6: 2). Manchester: St. Jerome.

Moreau, Hubert (1998) "L'interprétation sur la chaîne Arte", in Yves Gambier (ed.) *Translating for the Media*. Papers from the International Conference (Berlin, 22–23 November 1996), Turku: Centre for Translation and Interpreting, 225–229.

Moreno, Lina (2003) "La traducción audiovisual en España: Estado de la cuestión" [unpublished dissertation]. Granada: Universidad de Granada.

Moreno, Lina (2005) "El estado actual de la traducción audiovisual en España: La formación", *Puentes* 6, 95–107.

Morgan, Alistair R. (1995) "Student learning and students' experiences: Research, theory and practice", in Fred Lockwood (ed.) *Open and distance learning today*, London: Routledge, 55–66.

Neto, Lourival N. (2002) *O intérprete de tribunal: Um mero intérprete?* [unpublished dissertation]. Fortaleza: Universidade Estadual do Ceará.

Neves, Joselia (2004) "Subtitling: An opportunity for language learning and teaching", in Pilar Orero (ed.) *Topics in Audiovisual Translation*. Amsterdam: John Benjamins, 127–140.

Nichols, Bill (1991) *Representing reality: Issues and concepts in documentary*. Bloomington, IN: Indiana University Press.

Nord, Christiane (2005) "Training functional translators", in Martha Tennent (ed.) *Training for the new millennium*. Amsterdam: John Benjamins, 209–223.

Orero, Pilar (2001) "La traducción de entrevistas para voice-over". *Programa y versión escrita Pre-congreso de las comunicaciones*. I Congreso SETAM Estado Actual del Estudio de la Traducción Audiovisual en España" (Barcelona, Universitat Pompeu Fabra, 27–28 April 2001), 44–47.

Orero, Pilar (2004a) "The pretended easiness of voice-over translation of TV", *The Journal of Specialised Translation* 2, 76–96 <http://www.jostrans.org/issue02/issue02toc.htm>.

Orero, Pilar (2004b) "Audiovisual translation: A new dynamic umbrella", in Pilar Orero (ed.) *Topics in audiovisual translation*, Amsterdam: John Benjamins, vii–xiii.

Orero, Pilar (2006a) "Synchronization in voice-over", in José María Bravo (ed.) *A new spectrum of Translation Studies*. Valladolid: Publicaciones de la Universidad de Valladolid, 255–264.

Orero, Pilar (2006b) 'The Ugly Duckling of Audiovisual Translation: Voice-over'. Paper delivered at the MuTra Conference (Copenhagen, 2–5 May 2006). Unpublished paper.

Orero, Pilar (2007a) "Audiosubtitling: A possible solution for opera accessibility in Catalonia", in Franco, Eliana P. C. & Santiago Araújo, Vera (organizers) TradTerm *(Revista do Centro Interdepartamental de Tradução e Terminologia)* 13, São Paulo: Humanitas (FFLCH-USP), 135–149.

Orero, Pilar (2007b) "Voice-over: A case of hyper-reality". MUTRA Proceedings. <http://www.euroconferences.info/proceedings/2006_Proceedings/2006_Orero_Pilar.pdf>.

Orero, Pilar (forthcoming) "The process of translation for the production of TV programmes broadcast by voice-over", in Gunilla Anderman & Jorge Díaz Cintas (eds) *Audiovisual translation: Language transfer on screen*. London: Palgrave Macmillan, 130–139.

Orero, Pilar & Santamaria, Laura (2002) "Adapting new software to the (virtual) translation class", in *Languages and the media: Viewers, languages and marketing. Conference Proceedings* (4–6 December 2002), ICWE GmbH, Berlin.

Paquin, Robert (1998) "Translator, adapter, screenwriter", *Translation Journal* 3, <http://accurapid.com/journal/05dubb.htm>.

Perego, Elisa (2005) *La traduzione audiovisiva*. Roma: Carocci.

Pönniö, Kaarina (1995) "Voice over, narration et commentaire", in Yves Gambier (ed.) *Communication audiovisuelle et transferts linguistiques/Audiovisual communication and language transfers* (International Forum, Strasbourg, 22–24 June 1995). Special issue of *Translatio* (FIT Newsletter / Nouvelles de la FIT), 303–307.

Pujol, Joaquim & Orero, Pilar (2007) "Audio description precursors: Ekphrasis, film narrators and radio journalists", *Translation Watch Quarterly* 3(2), 49–60.

Rabiger, Michael (1998) *Directing the documentary* (3rd ed.). Boston: Focal Press.

Reid, Hélène (1996) "Un domaine bien organisé: L'écrit sur les écrans aux Pays-Bas", in Yves Gambier (ed.) *Les transferts linguistiques dans les médias audiovisuels*, Villeneuve d'Ascq: Presses Universitaires du Septentrion, 87–98.

Remael, Aline (1995–1996) "From the BBC's *Voices from the Island* to the BRTN's *De President van Robbeneiland*: A case study in TV translation", *Linguistica Antverpiensia*, no. XXIX–XXX, 107–128.

Remael, Aline (2004) "A place for film dialogue in subtitling courses", in Pilar Orero (ed.) *Topics in Audiovisual Translation*. Amsterdam: John Benjamins, 103–123.

Remael, Aline (2007) "Whose language, whose voice, whose message?: Different AVT modes for documentaries on VRT-Canvas television, Flanders", in Eliana P. C. Franco & Vera L. Santiago Araújo (eds) *TradTerm*. São Paulo: Humanitas, University of São Paulo, 31–50.

Rosen, Philip (1993) "Document and documentary: On the persistence of historical concepts", in Michael Renov (ed.) *Theorizing documentary*. London: Routledge, 58–89.

Russo, Mariachiara (1995) "Media interpreting: Variables and strategies", in Yves Gambier (ed.) *Communication audiovisuelle et transferts linguistiques/Audiovisual communication and language transfers* (International Forum, Strasbourg, 22–24 June 1995). Special issue of *Translatio* (FIT Newsletter / Nouvelles de la FIT), 343–349.

Santamaria, Laura (2003) "Les TIC i la didàctica de la traducció audiovisual". *Actes de les VII Jornades de Traducció de Vic. Interfícies. Apropant la pedagogia de la traducció i de les llengües estrangeres*, Vic: Universitat de Vic <http://www.uvic.cat/fchtd/_fitxers/jornades_2003/fitxers/santamaria.doc>.

Scannell, Paddy (1996) *Radio, television & modern life*. Oxford: Blackwell.

Setton, Robin (1996) "Taïwan: Un paysage audiovisual contrasté en expansion", in Yves Gambier (ed.) *Les transferts linguistiques dans les médias audiovisuels*. Villeneuve d'Ascq: Presses Universitaires du Septentrion, 73–86.

Silverstone, Roger (1986) "The agonistic narratives of television science", in John Corner (ed.) *Documentary and the mass media*. London: Edward Arnold, 81–106.

Singleton, Ralph (1990) *Filmmaker's dictionary*. Beverly Hills: Lone Eagle.

Sponholz, Christine (2002–2003) Teaching audiovisual translation: Theoretical aspects, market requirements, university training and curriculum development [unpublished monograph]. Mainz: Johannes Gutenberg-Universität.

Standish, Isolde (2005) *A new history of Japanese cinema: A century of narrative film*. New York: Continuum.

St. Jerome's Translation Studies Abstracts cum Bibliography of Translation Studies <http://www.stjerome.co.uk/tsaonline/index.php>.

Straub, Jean-Marie & Huillet, Danièle (1985) "Direct sound: An interview with Jean-Marie Straub and Danièle Huillet", in Elisabeth Weis & John Belton (eds) *Film sound: Theory and practice*. New York: Columbia University Press, 150–153.

Taylor, Christopher (1996) "The relevance of film dubbing and subtitling to language teaching", in Christina Heiss & Rosa Maria Bolletieri Bosinelli (eds) *Traduzione multimediale per il cinema, la televisione e la scena*, Bologna: Clueb, 271–277.

Tennent, Martha (ed.) (2005) *Training for the new millennium*. Amsterdam: John Benjamins.

Theunisz, Mildred (2002) "Audiosubtitling: A new service in the Netherlands making subtitling programmes accessible" <http://www.sb-belang.nl>.

Thorpe, Mary (1995) "The challenge facing course design", in Fred Lockwood (ed.) *Open and distance learning today*. London: Routledge, 175–184.

'Voice-over'. 2007. *Wikipedia*. <http://en.wikipedia.org/wiki/Voice-over>.

Webster's On-line Dictionary <http://www.merriam-webster.com/>.

Weis, Elisabeth & John Belton (eds) (1985) *Film sound: Theory and practice*. New York: Columbia University Press.

Whitman, Candice (1992) *Through the dubbing glass*. Frankfurt: Peter Lang.

Wilss, Wolfram (2004) "Translation Studies: A didactic approach", in Kirsten Malmkjær (ed.) *Translation in undergraduate degree programmes*. Amsterdam: John Benjamins, 9–15.

Winston, Brian (1995) *Claiming the Real: The documentary film revisited*. London: British Film Institute.

Yagolkowski, Daniel (2006) "El traductor de cine: Elementos para su formación", in Pardu Nobel Honeyman, Francisco García Marcos, Emilio Ortega Arjonilla & M. Angel García Peinado (eds) *Inmigración, cultura y traducción: Reflexiones interdisciplinares.* Almería: Universidad de Almería, 548–551.

Zinik, Zinovy (2006) "Freelance", *Times Literary Supplement* 5360, 14.

Appendix 1. Questionnaire

General Questions

Before answering the questionnaire, we would like you to answer a couple of general questions. You may tick one or more answers and add additional comments if you feel that this is necessary.

A. GENERAL QUESTIONS				
1. Personal profile (tick one or more options)				
b) Job	Academic	☐	Institution	_____
	Professional	☐	Company	_____
	Other	☐		_____
c) Country			_____	
d) Working languages	source language(s)		_____	
	target language(s)		_____	
2. How long have you been working as an academic/professional in audiovisual translation?				
	a) _____ month(s)			
	b) _____ year(s)			
	c) other _____			
3. What are the audiovisual transfer modes that you teach / do research on / work with? Please use the numbers below to indicate frequency.				
(5) for *very often*, (4) for *often*, (3) for *sometimes*, (2) for *rarely*, (1) for *never*.				
	a) _____ audio-description			
	b) _____ closed subtitling			
	c) _____ dubbing			
	d) _____ live interpreting			
	e) _____ open subtitling			
	f) _____ surtitling			
	g) _____ voice-over			
4. (For television professionals only) Which channels do you work for?				

B.   SPECIFIC QUESTIONS

We would like to ask you a few questions on voice-over translation, understanding the term *voice-over translation* as an audiovisual mode of transfer consisting of two consecutive steps: firstly, the translation of the original version, and secondly, the recording of the target language version (no lip-synch) on top of the original speech, which – in turn – remains audible.

1. On the terminology used ...

a) In your professional/academic life, do you refer to the transfer mode described above as voice-over?

☐ yes

☐ no

b) If not, what do you call it?

c) Do you use the term *voice-over* to refer to other processes in audiovisual translation?

☐ yes

☐ no

d) If yes, to which processes?

2. On voice-over usage ...

a) In your country, when is voice-over translation used for audiovisual products?

☐ fiction films

☐ documentaries (narrator off-screen)

☐ documentaries (narrator on-screen)

☐ documentaries (talking heads, interviewees)

☐ television news (interviews)

☐ commercials

☐ radio news (interviews)

☐ other (please specify)

b) Are there any particularities you want to highlight?

c) Why would you say voice-over is used in these cases?

☐ tradition

☐ money-saving measure

☐ sense of authenticity

☐ other reason (please specify)

3. On voice-over features ...

3.1. Original sound

a) Is the original soundtrack volume eliminated or reduced?	☐ eliminated ☐ reduced ☐ It depends, both cases are possible ☐ I don't know
b) If both cases are possible, what are the factors on which the choice in (a) above depends on?	

3.2. Seconds left at the beginning and at the end

a) Before the target language version is heard, do voice talents leave a few seconds so that the original soundtrack can be heard?	☐ yes ☐ no ☐ sometimes ☐ I don't know
b) If sometimes, when exactly?	
c) Do you think a few seconds should be left at the beginning?	☐ yes ☐ no ☐ sometimes ☐ I don't know
d) At the end of each intervention, do voice talents leave a few seconds so that the original soundtrack can be heard again?	☐ yes ☐ no ☐ sometimes ☐ I don't know
e) If sometimes, when exactly?	
f) Do you think a few seconds should be left at the end?	☐ yes ☐ no ☐ sometimes ☐ I don't know

3.3. Literality

a) Do you think translators tend to be as literal as possible at the beginning of the intervention, when the original soundtrack is heard?

☐ yes
☐ no
☐ sometimes
☐ I don't know

b) If sometimes, when exactly?

3.4. Singular accents and gender

a) (In your country) Does the voice talent have a slight accent to copy the people who are talking in the original product? That is to say, if a Spanish person is talking, does the English-speaking voice talent imitate the accent of a Spanish-speaking person?

☐ yes
☐ no
☐ sometimes
☐ I don't know

b) If sometimes, when exactly?

c) Is gender maintained? That is to say, if a man is talking in the original product, is the voice talent always a man?

☐ yes
☐ no
☐ sometimes
☐ I don't know

d) If sometimes, when exactly?

3.5. Pre-recorded / live

a) Is voice-over always pre-recorded in your country?

☐ yes
☐ no
☐ generally yes
☐ I don't know

b) Although there is no universal consent, do you think live interpreting of interviews on television should be included within the voice-over mode?

☐ yes
☐ no
☐ I don't know

c) Why? _____

4. On voice-over perception ...

a) Do you know any studies on voice-over reception?	☐ yes ☐ no ☐ I don't know
b) If yes, can you give us the referene(s)?	

5. On voice-over teaching ...

a) Is voice-over taught in your country?	☐ yes ☐ no ☐ I don't know
b) If yes, where and at what level (undergraduate, postgraduate, specialization, training at a company, etc.)?	
c) Do you teach voice-over translation?	☐ yes ☐ no
d) Write down the main elements that you would like students/trainees to master.	

6. (Only for professionals) On voice-over translation from a professional perspective ...
6.1. The client and the products to be translated

a) What type of client asks you for voice-over translation?
b) What kind of products do you translate by using the voice-over mode?
c) Do you translate finished products (post-production) or products which will be edited after your translation is delivered (production)?

6.2. The main difficulties

a) What materials do you get to do the translation?

☐ only VHS (If you have ticked this answer, move on to question 6.2.1. below.)

☐ VHS + script (If you have ticked this answer, move on to question 6.2.2. below)

☐ Only a script without image (If you have ticked this answer, move on to question 6.2.3. below)

☐ other (please specify)

6.2.1.   When doing voice-over translation from screen (no script provided), what are the main difficulties that you encounter? Please use the numbers below to indicate frequency.

(5) for *very often*, (4) for *often*, (3) for *sometimes*, (2) for *rarely*, (1) for *never*.

a) _____ adapting the length of the interventions

b) _____ documentation process

c) _____ language rewording

d) _____ literality at the beginning

e) _____ slang

f) _____ speaker's accents

g) _____ speaker's deliver speech

h) _____ speaker's errors

i) _____ speaker's speech impediment/particularity

j) _____ speaker's style

k) _____ terminology

l) _____ text-image synchronization

m)_____ tight deadlines

n) _____ translation of proper nouns

o) _____ other (please specify)

Which of the difficulties above do you consider to
be unique to voice-over?

6.2.2. **When doing voice-over translation with a VHS and a script, what are the main difficulties that you encounter? Please use the numbers below to indicate frequency.**

(5) for *very often*, (4) for *often*, (3) for *sometimes*, (2) for *rarely*, (1) for *never*.

a) _____ adapting the length of the interventions

b) _____ content errors in the original

c) _____ documentation process

d) _____ language rewording

e) _____ literality at the beginning

f) _____ narrator's style

g) _____ script errors

h) _____ slang

i) _____ terminology

j) _____ text-image synchronization

k) _____ tight deadlines

l) _____ translation of proper nouns

m)_____ other (please specify)

Which of the difficulties above do you consider to
be unique to voice-over?

6.2.3. When doing voice-over translation with a script but without image, what are the main difficulties you encounter? Please use the numbers below to indicate frequency.

(5) for *very often*, (4) for *often*, (3) for *sometimes*, (2) for *rarely*, (1) for *never*.

a) _____ absence of a visual reference which implies ambiguity

b) _____ adapting the length of the interventions

c) _____ documentation process

d) _____ language rewording

e) _____ literality at the beginning

f) _____ narrator's style

g) _____ script errors

h) _____ slang

i) _____ terminology

j) _____ text-image synchronization

k) _____ tight deadlines

l) _____ translation of proper nouns

m)_____ other (please specify)

Which of the difficulties above do you consider to be unique to voice-over?

6.3. Isochrony	

a) Do you check the lengths of your translations so that they fit into the space available?	☐ yes ☐ no
b) If yes, how do you do it?	☐ specific software (please specify) ☐ by reading the translations aloud ☐ I can fit the translations into the space instinctively ☐ by eliminating oral features ☐ other system (please specify)
c) If not, why?	☐ I haven't been asked to do so ☐ Someone else is in charge of this task ☐ other reason (please specify)

6.4. Time codes	

a) Do you have to insert time codes in your translation?	☐ yes ☐ no
b) If yes, how do you do this?	☐ manually ☐ specific software (please specify)
c) If not, is someone else in charge of this task?	☐ yes (Who? _____) ☐ no

6.5. Revision	

a) Does your translation go directly to the voice talent with no previous control?	☐ yes ☐ no
b) Does someone adapt your translation?	☐ yes ☐ no
c) If yes, who and what does he/she do?	
d) Can you check the final version?	☐ yes ☐ no

6.6. Other (specific) details		
a) Have you ever been asked to create a free version, totally adapted to the target audience, from an original product?	☐	yes
	☐	no
b) If yes, what did you have to do?		
c) What sort of text did you adapt? (an interview? a commentary? a talking head?)		

Please, add any comments concerning voice-over translation that you find interesting, and that may help us get a complete view of this mode of audiovisual transfer worldwide. Comments regarding voice-over difficulties, job contexts and specific tasks you are asked to do are especially welcome.

Do you know of any other academic/professional in any country who works with voice-over translation and who could fill in this questionnaire? Would you mind giving us his/her name and e-mail address?

Thank you very much for your cooperation.